SOPHOCLES, the Greek tragic dramatist, was born at Colonus near Athens about 496 B.C. Although hopelessness and misfortune plague the characters in his great plays, Sophocles' own life was a long, prosperous one. He was from a good family, well educated, handsome, wealthy, healthy, and highly respected by his fellow Athenians. As an adolescent, his beauty of physique, athletic ability, and skill in music won him the lead in the chorus celebrating the Greek sea victory over the Persians at Salamis. His first dramatic production, in 468, won the prize over Aeschylus'. He wrote two dozen more plays before 450, by which date he had made important changes in the form of tragedy by adding a third speaking actor to the traditional two, by reducing the importance of the chorus, and by improving the stage scenery. Sophocles wrote over 120 plays; seven complete plays survive (plus half a light satyr play, some fragments, and ninety titles). Aristotle, in his *Poetics,* praised Sophocles above other tragedians and regarded his masterpiece, *Oedipus the King,* as a model for Greek tragedy. Sophocles' plays won more victories (perhaps as many as twenty-four) than the plays of either his older contemporary Aeschylus or the younger Euripides. He was nicknamed "The Attic Bee," for it was said he could extract pure honey from words. The circumstances of his life, as well as his plays, suggest that Sophocles was conservative, and opposed to innovation in religion and politics. At eighty-three he was still active in the Athenian government. One of his greatest plays, *Oedipus at Colonus,* was written the year before his death. He died in 406 B.C. in Athens at the age of ninety.

THE
COMPLETE PLAYS
OF SOPHOCLES

Translated by Sir Richard Claverhouse Jebb

Edited and with an Introduction by Moses Hadas

BANTAM CLASSIC

THE COMPLETE PLAYS OF SOPHOCLES
A Bantam Book

PUBLISHING HISTORY
First Bantam edition published September 1967
Bantam Classic edition published May 1982
Bantam Classic reissue / April 2006

Published by Bantam Dell
A Division of Random House, Inc.
New York, New York

Library of Congress Catalog Card Number: 57-25660

ISBN-10: 0-553-21354-7
ISBN-13: 978-0-553-21354-6

Printed in the United States of America
Published simultaneously in Canada

www.bantamdell.com
OPM 40 39 38 37

CONTENTS

INTRODUCTION

by Moses Hadas

A LIFE MORE satisfactory than Sophocles' is difficult to
imagine. Its timing, first of all, could not be more propi-
tious, for his lifespan coincided precisely with the Golden Age
of Athenian intellectual, artistic, and political glory. He was
born in 496 B.C., and so was reaching maturity at the time of
the great victory over the Persians at Salamis (480 B.C.) which
initiated the era of Athenian preeminence, and he died in 406,
two years before Athens fell to the Spartans. On his youth we
are informed by a single but revealing passage in Athenaeus
(1.20 e f):

> Sophocles, besides being handsome in his youth, became
> proficient in dancing and music, while still a lad, under
> the instruction of Lampus. After the battle of Salamis, at
> any rate, he danced to accompaniment of his lyre around
> the trophy, naked and anointed with oil. Others say he
> danced with his cloak on. And when he brought out the
> *Thamyris* he played the lyre himself. He also played ball
> with great skill when he produced the *Nausicaa*.

To perform in the chorus celebrating the victory he must have
been wealthy and of good family as well as handsome and a
good singer. In his maturity his circle included the greatest
galaxy of thinkers and artists the world has known. He appears
to have been an intimate of Herodotus, to whom he addressed
a poem and from whom he borrowed motifs in *Antigone* and
Oedipus at Colonus. He was a popular favorite; in Aristophanes' *Frogs* (completed after Sophocles' death) it is said of

him, that "he was amiable on earth and he is amiable here." The respect and affection which he enjoyed brought him election to high office, which he bore with modesty. Plutarch (*Life of Nicias* 15) has this story:

> Once when his fellow commanders were deliberating on some matter of general moment, Nicias bade Sophocles the poet state his opinion first, as being the senior general on the board. Hereupon Sophocles said: "I am the oldest man but you are the senior general."

He wrote more plays than his rivals and won far more prizes. He retained his intellectual and physical vigor to the end of his very long life; the superb *Philoctetes* and no less superb *Oedipus at Colonus* were written when he was approaching or had reached ninety. The story is told (in Cicero's treatise *On Old Age* and elsewhere) that when his family instituted a friendly suit to declare him senile in order to relieve him of business cares, he was asked by the judge to show what he was occupying himself with, and read the famous ode in praise of White Colonus; the family naturally lost the suit. Not long before this he is said to have fallen in love with a woman called Theoris, though at the beginning of Plato's *Republic* he is quoted as expressing great relief at being freed at last from the tyranny of love.

And a final satisfaction, especially for a Greek, was that he left behind a son who followed his own profession with success. We can only agree with the lines of the comic poet Phrynichus: "Blessed Sophocles who died after a long life, a man fortunate and successful, who made many fine tragedies. And finely did he die, having had no evil to endure." The concluding phrase seems to allude to a recurrent thought in Sophocles, expressed as follows at the end of the *Oedipus*: "While our eyes wait to see the destined final day, we must call no one happy who is of mortal race, until he has crossed life's border, free from pain." His own good fortune did not blind Sophocles to the precariousness of human existence and the tragedy implicit in human life. He saw life steadily (in Matthew Arnold's phrase) and he saw it whole.

Sophocles composed more than 120 plays, thus outdoing his older contemporary Aeschylus and his younger Euripides. His tetralogies won twenty-four "firsts," which means that ninety-six of his plays were victorious. Of the whole number only the seven in this volume have survived intact—because they were selected for school use in later antiquity. Of the others we have some snippets, either in quotations by later Greek authors or on scraps of papyrus recovered in Egypt. The most extensive papyrus fragment contains some 400 lines of the *Ichneutae* or *Trackers,* a satyr play dealing with the prodigious infancy of Hermes; but these lines are too broken to yield a readable translation. We can only hope that the ancient scholars who chose the plays that survived have given us a fair representation of Sophocles' work.

Ancient criticism agreed with the judges of Sophocles' own day in regarding him as the greatest master of tragedy. The *Poetics* of Aristotle, our indispensable (though not flawless) guide to Greek tragedy, shows a preference for Sophocles over his rivals. But the Academy as well as the Lyceum preferred Sophocles. Polemo (314–276), who was head of the Academy, says that Homer is the Sophocles of epic and Sophocles the Homer of tragedy. Ancient criticism generally agrees with this view. It agrees too with Aristotle's preference for *Oedipus the King* as the best play. "Would anyone in his senses," writes the author of *On the Sublime,* "give the single tragedy of Oedipus for all the works of Ion in a row?" Traditional criticism has tended to follow the ancient view of Sophocles as the model, with Aeschylus marking the preparation and Euripides the decline; we now recognize that categorization of this kind is meaningless, for each poet had his own objectives and his own methods for reaching them.

Superficially the plays of all three surviving Greek tragedians are similar: they quarry the same cycles of myths, and often use the same story and the same dramatis personae, they show the same structure of "spoken" portions interlarded with choral lyrics, and they are all concerned with questions of man's fate. The lives of the three overlapped and they learned from one another, Aeschylus from Sophocles, Sophocles from Aeschylus and Euripides, Euripides from Aeschylus and Sophocles. Even slight variations in outlook and technique are therefore conscious and meaningful. The easiest approach to the special qualities of each as playwright and thinker, and especially of Sophocles who is our present concern, is to compare his techniques with those of the other two.

According to Aristotle, innovations introduced by Sophocles include enlargement of the chorus from twelve to fifteen members, introduction of painted scenery, and the addition of a third actor. This last was far the most important, and was adopted in the later plays of Aeschylus. The availability of a third actor multiplied opportunities for dramatic intrigue, with consequent enrichment of plot, and made fuller and more subtle characterization possible. Even if the third actor has little to add to a dialogue his very presence on the stage sharpens the significance of others' speeches and reactions. All of these contributions are in keeping with Sophocles' highly developed and sophisticated sense of theater, in which he surpasses both Aeschylus and Euripides. A character may go on some errand, like Chrysothemis in *Electra,* or be summoned for some information, like the shepherd in *Oedipus the King,* be virtually forgotten, and then dramatically arrive on the scene to a situation drastically changed. Or, just before the catastrophe, the chorus will sing an exultant song of joyous anticipation to give the disaster that comes upon its heels greater impact.

The two actors in Aeschylus' early plays tend to illustrate clashes of large principles, in which Aeschylus was more interested than in individuals, and serve almost as impersonal symbols. Sophocles is content to accept the principles as fixed data, as if they were laws of gravity or electricity, part of the world order, and instead concerns himself with the individual's reaction to them. This explains another peculiarity of Sophocles (in which he was followed by Euripides) as contrasted with Aeschylus. Aeschylus composed trilogies on interconnected subjects, so that they are in effect triptychs, almost three acts of one large play. For working out the history of crime and countercrime and their eventual solution, as in the *Oresteia* (which is the only complete trilogy we have), such spaciousness is required. But if it is the reaction of the individual as a person, not as an abstract figure in the history of a principle, that is paramount, then a single play is sufficient. Sophocles, too, composed trilogies, as the usage of the Greek theater required, but the three plays were not connected in subject and might derive from different cycles of myth.

Sophocles' concern with individual character and the maturity of his dramatic structure suggest a move in the direction of the theater as we know it; but Sophocles did not travel so far in this direction as did Euripides. Euripides, too, used the familiar myths, but in Euripides the figures who bear the great names of the heroic past are essentially contemporary types oppressed by contemporary problems. His descent from the heroic is a perceptible move in the direction of Menander and the comedy of manners. Sophocles maintains the high dignity of the heroic level; his major figures are indeed as grandiose as Homer's. Not that he was ignorant of what men are actually like: he himself said that Euripides showed men as they are while he portrayed men as they should be. It is even possible that plays like Sophocles' *Electra* or his *Trachinian Women* are in part intended as "corrections" of Euripides' vulgarity in handling similar themes. Euripides' Electra is slatternly, self-pitying, sex-ridden; and because she and the other characters in his *Electra,* victims as well as slayers, are recognizable as commonplace types, the murders of Aegisthus and Clytemnestra are as unjustifiable as they are shocking. Euripides does not keep within the heroic code but is criticizing it from without. We do not apply contemporary criteria to Sophocles' *Electra* because the traditional level of heroic remoteness is maintained and raises the problem above the contemporary. Euripides' Medea is a wildly passionate woman who knowingly uses a poisoned garment to destroy her rival; in Sophocles' *Trachinian Women* Deianeira also uses a poisoned garment, but with the thought that the drug is beneficent, not lethal. She is a mature and gentle creature who wanted only to ensure domestic felicity. And while her mistake causes her suicide and

Heracles' painful death, that death was the fated instrument of his transfiguration.

The Heracles of the *Trachinian Women* may serve as the type of the Sophoclean hero, the large and intense and tormented character who is by no means faultless but who nevertheless achieves the status of hero. A hero, in the Greek sense, is a man who by his extraordinary career has pushed back the horizons of what is possible for humanity and is therefore deemed worthy of commemoration after his death. He is not a flawless man, above the nature of ordinary humanity, but his flaws are inherent in and inseparable from the virtues which enable him to become a hero. Achilles himself was self-centered and ruthless, but without these traits he would not have been Achilles, and his status as hero is unquestioned. Some of Sophocles' heroes may be questionable, and his plays then amount to a weighing of merits and demerits and an eventual demonstration that the hero is in fact worthy of heroization.

The clearest example is in the oldest Sophoclean play, *Ajax*. Ajax is an unqualified brute, arrogant, obsessed with self, savage, unfeeling to his wife and his crew who are dependent upon him. His flaws are serious indeed, but he is the only Greek who could stem the rush of the Trojan army to burn the Greek fleet—not a service a nambypamby could render. Did such a man deserve heroization? The *Ajax* is a demonstration that he did. More popular plays like *Oedipus the King* and the *Antigone* receive fuller illumination from this viewpoint. It is always tempting to readers to look upon the *Oedipus* as a tableau of horrible crimes and their just requital: Oedipus had done lawless things and in the end received deserved punishment. So conceived, the requital seems monstrously unfair, for Oedipus had done his best to avoid the crimes and had committed them unwittingly. Actually the play is rather a glorification than a condemnation of Oedipus. Only an uncommonly good man would persist in his investigation so unflaggingly even after it had become manifest that it might be disastrous. He did indeed have flaws: he was self-righteous and hasty and suspicious of his well-wishers; but if he had not been these things he could never have gone on with his inquiry. Though he is destroyed in the end, in a true sense he is the victor, and the conclusion is satisfying rather than disturbing to the perceptive reader. According to human standards (what Greek could know what divine standards might be?) Oedipus had behaved not only well, but extraordinarily well and had asserted the dignity of manhood. If there is a villain in the piece it is not Oedipus but Apollo; however, Apollo cannot be a villain for he is a god, and the moral arithmetic of the gods is different from men's and inscrutable to men. When a man behaving well as man is nevertheless tripped up by powers he cannot control or even understand, then we have tragedy. And the "big" man who has the mind and the energy to pioneer is most exposed. That is why tragedy, and the tragedy of Sophocles in particular, is concerned with the fate of "big" men.

The Sophoclean heroine whom modern readers are most tempted to consider flawless is Antigone, who suffered martyrdom for loyalty to her dead brother. But martyrdom is not necessarily a virtue among the Greeks; and to look upon her as a saint and her persecutor Creon as a villain is to make of the play a black-and-white melodrama, which Greek tragedy never is. To the original audience Creon's position must have seemed sounder than Antigone's. Could a conscientious ruler honor a traitor who had come to destroy the city equally with the patriot who had saved it? And should not Antigone have accepted the authoritative decree, as Ismene says it was proper for a woman and a subject to do? In the end Creon suffers more than Antigone, who got the martyrdom she seems to crave, and we might almost expect the play to be called *Creon* instead of *Antigone*. But the title is right, for Antigone is the one who enlarges ordinary human limitations by being willing to sacrifice love and life for a principle. She too may be obsessed and twisted, but unless she were these things she could never have carried her enlargement of humanity through. As always in Sophocles the chorus and lesser characters counsel the moderation appropriate to ordinary humanity, but it is an enrichment for ordinary humanity to see one self-willed woman, flawed though she be, step out of ordinary limitations. Just as Oedipus though blinded is the victor in his play, so Antigone though dead is victor in hers.

Involved in both *Ajax* and *Antigone* is the question of the proper balance between the claims of the individual and the claims of the society of which he is a part. How far must a man suppress his own will in the interests of his society? What if society's demands are unreasonable or wrong? How far may an individual disregard society in order to do what he himself is convinced is right? To some degree the theme is touched upon in all the plays; it is central in the *Philoctetes*. Philoctetes was a respected member of the original Greek expedition against Troy and possessor of the wonderful bow which Heracles had used in his labors. En route to Troy he had offered to guide his fellow-chieftains to a particular shrine, and had there been bitten by a serpent. Because of the stench of his wound and his loud cries of pain his shipmates marooned him on a desert island. (The island in question was in fact inhabited, as everyone in the audience would know and as Aeschylus and Euripides represented it in their plays on Philoctetes; the fact that Sophocles makes it deserted demonstrates that his theme is isolation vs. participation.) On this island the helpless cripple, thanks to his bow, eked out a living for ten years, when the Greeks, admonished that Troy could not be taken without Philoctetes and his bow, sent Odysseus and Achilles' son Neoptolemus to fetch Philoctetes back to the army. Philoctetes refuses to go, though he is promised recovery and fame, and would actually use the bow, which Neoptolemus voluntarily restores to him after robbing him of it, to kill Odysseus. His desire is to live in isolation with Neoptolemus who, in his view, is being corrupted by Odysseus and the Greek host. Heracles, who had used the bow for the benefit of mankind, appears as *deus ex machina* and persuades Philoctetes to rejoin the society he has abjured.

The problem of Neoptolemus echoes and underscores the problem of Philoctetes. He too was a member of society in good standing, was utterly disillusioned by society's apparent immorality, and then made to realize that duty and interest alike dictated rational subservience to the claims of society.

Neoptolemus had come to Troy after the death of his father Achilles in the tenth year of the war. But instead of the noble warrior's career he had envisioned he finds his first assignment is to trick a helpless man of his only means of subsistence. He is sickened; but in the end he rejoins society as a mature and responsible member. Odysseus is not the villainous corrupter of youth he is sometimes represented to be but the conscientious and realistic agent of the state. At another time, as Odysseus himself says, he could enjoy being honest as much as any man, but it was a luxury he could not afford when the interests of all demanded chicanery.

Sophocles was reputed to be a pious man, and indeed his plays are filled with the power of the gods and the unfailing fulfillment of their oracles. But what are we to think of gods who are the ultimate cause of the heroes' catastrophes? How could a god cause a serpent to ruin Philoctetes when he was on a religious mission, or why should a god trap Oedipus in a hopeless snare? Aeschylus had labored to justify the ways of the gods to men according to human notions of justice, and Euripides went so far as to say that gods who do evil are no gods. Sophocles acknowledges the power of the gods but does not assume that their standards of justice are the same as man's. Protagoras, a philosopher contemporary with Sophocles, said "Man is the measure of all things," and also said, "Of the gods I cannot speak because I do not know." The sphere of the gods and the sphere of men are disparate. The gods behave as it becomes gods to behave, and men must behave as it becomes men to behave, not necessarily as the gods behave. Actually man has a greater responsibility for moral choice than if he were bidden to follow a prescribed code. When he does transgress, even unwittingly as Oedipus did, he is tainted; and in *Oedipus the King* Oedipus acknowledges that he is "vile." In *Oedipus at Colonus,* however, we detect a new note. Oedipus does not deny that he is tainted, for he had in fact killed his father and married his mother, but he insists that he is not in a moral sense a guilty man: "In *nature* how was I evil?" This is not rebelliousness but a clarification and an enhancement of the notion of moral responsibility. And the justice of the argument is approved, for at his death Oedipus receives divine recognition and his tomb becomes a seat of beneficent power.

In its conception of tragedy as in its art, *Oedipus at Colonus* is the culmination of Sophocles' career. The play is something of a valedictory, like Shakespeare's *Tempest,* and something of an apocalypse. The scene is the parish of Sophocles' boyhood and the description of the landscape and religious ritual suggest cherished memories of long ago. The dramatis personae, Oedipus, Antigone, and the rest, are those associated with his greatest successes. And as Athens is sinking to its fall, Sophocles recalls, in the person of its ideal king of legend, its nobility, integrity, and hospitality and its mission of championship of the weak, and ends with a note of hope and benediction. Oedipus enters as a blind old man who has walked a long way, but has retained his pride and his integrity, and when the moment of his departure comes, he walks on and out, this time with clearer vision than his guides, to the destined secret spot where, amidst peals of thunder, he is translated to a new and eternal existence.

Such observations on Sophocles' dramaturgy as the foregoing, whether of similar or widely different tenor, are accessible to the Greekless reader who looks at the plays attentively. But the refinements of Sophocles' literary techniques most of us must take on faith. For a helpful analogy we might turn to architecture, which uses stones instead of foreign words, and specifically to the Parthenon, which was built while Sophocles was writing. What makes the Parthenon so rhythmically satisfying is not its apparent regularity but its subtly calculated irregularities. The columns are not straight-sided, perpendicular, and evenly spaced, as they appear, and the base line is not level but curved. The result is a seemingly natural and powerful whole, so rhythmical and harmonious that its power is never obtrusive. The analogous art of Sophocles serves similarly to regularize extremes of passionate intensity into serene and natural entities of classical detachment and permanence.

What is wanted and possible in a translation of Sophocles is not a reproduction of his art but the sense that the art is there. Admirable as certain poetic versions of Sophocles are, their excellence is not (and should not be) identical with the excellence of their originals. A reader who attends to Sophocles as a monument in the history of the human spirit may find transparent prose a truer reflection than verse. But the prose must not be commonplace, as it may be for Euripides; it must communicate the stately remoteness of the original. The most carefully wrought prose version of Sophocles in English is that of Sir Richard Claverhouse Jebb (1841–1905), which has the merit not only of extreme accuracy but also of maintaining a high formalism and dignity appropriate to Sophocles. Jebb's device for lending dignity to a prose version of stately poetry was to use archaism in vocabulary, wordforms, word order—in a word, to emulate the English of the King James Bible. But to readers not brought up on the King James Bible the extremes of the "forsoothly" mode are sometimes unintelligible and may sometimes seem ludicrous. The object of the present edition has been to substitute moderate for extreme archaism in vocabulary, syntax, and word order in cases where the modern reader might be puzzled, but without distorting the emphasis or vitiating the sense of stately remoteness which is Jebb's special merit. The choral portions have been left untouched or very slightly edited; their differences from the "spoken" portions should be perceptible, and the use of italic type as well as the retention of archaisms is intended to make them so.

THE
COMPLETE PLAYS
OF SOPHOCLES

AJAX

THE CHARACTER OF AJAX, AS FIXED IN THE *ILIAD*
and therefore familiar to the audience, was of an extraordinarily powerful man, next to Achilles the best of the Greek warriors at Troy, but also of a man extraordinarily headstrong and self-centered. After Achilles' death, according to legend, the divine armor made for him by Hephaestus was to be given to the worthiest of his survivors, and Ajax naturally expected the prize. Instead the chieftains voted to award it to Odysseus. Ajax' consequent hatred of Odysseus is mentioned in the *Odyssey*: when the two meet in Hades, Ajax refuses to speak to Odysseus but turns his back on him.

The opening of the play informs us that in chagrin at his disappointment Ajax was on the point of murdering the Greek generals; to save them Athena darkened Ajax' senses so that he mistook the army's livestock for the generals and slaughtered them instead. When Ajax recovers and realizes, not that his intention was wrong, but that its miscarriage would make him ridiculous, he determines on suicide. He ignores the pleas of Tecmessa and the chorus, bids his child farewell, and departs. Soon he returns, ostensibly reconciled to life; he says he will go and bury his unlucky sword by the seaside and then have peace forevermore. After Ajax has gone and the chorus has sung its premature joy, a messenger from Teucer brings Calchas' warning that Ajax must be kept indoors that day. The chorus and Tecmessa leave to find him. The scene changes to seaside sedge (the only change of scene in the extant plays of Sophocles) and there Ajax makes a farewell speech, with a curse for the Atreidae, buries his sword point up, and falls upon it. The searchers enter and the body of Ajax is found, fittingly by Tecmessa. Teucer comes to bury the body but is forbidden to do so, first by Menelaus, whom he outfaces, and then by Agamemnon, who presents a reasonable argument for denying burial. Odysseus, despite Ajax' animosity toward him, persuades Agamemnon to allow the burial.

Modern readers sometimes find the dispute about the burial anticlimactic and irrelevant; but the last third of the *Ajax* is not a *Hamlet* without Hamlet. It is not an episode in Ajax' life which is the theme but the totality of his career. To assess his career justly the arguments for and against burial are relevant, and the final decision puts the seal on Ajax' claim to heroization.

PERSONS

ATHENA
ODYSSEUS
AJAX
CHORUS OF SALAMINIAN
   SAILORS
EURYSACES, ATTENDANTS,
   HERALDS (*mute characters*)

TECMESSA
TEUCER
MENELAUS
AGAMEMNON

SCENE: *Before the tent of Ajax at Troy.*

(ODYSSEUS *is seen scanning footprints,* ATHENA *aloft.*)

ATHENA. Always I have seen you, son of Laertes, seeking to snatch some occasion against your enemies; and now at the tent of Ajax by the ships, where he is posted at the very edge of the camp, I see you pausing long on his trail and scanning his fresh tracks, to find whether he is within or abroad. Your course keen-scenting as a Laconian hound's leads you well to your goal. Even now the man is gone within, sweat streaming from his face and from hands that have slain with the sword. There is no further need for you to peer within these doors. But what is your aim in this eager quest? Speak, so that you may learn from her who can give you light.

ODYSSEUS. Voice of Athena, dearest to me of the Immortals, how clearly, though you are unseen, do I hear your call and seize it in my soul, as when a Tyrrhenian clarion speaks from mouth of bronze! You have rightly discerned that I am hunting to and fro on the trail of a foeman, Ajax of the mighty shield. It is he and no other that I have been tracking so long. This night he has done to us a thing unthinkable—if he is indeed the doer. We know nothing certain but drift in doubt, and I took upon me the burden of this search. We have lately found the cattle, our spoil, dead, slaughtered by human hand, and dead beside them the guardians of the flock.

All men lay this crime to him. A scout who had descried him bounding alone over the plain with reeking sword brought me tidings and declared the matter. Then straightway I rushed upon his track; sometimes I recognize the footprints as his, but sometimes I am bewildered and cannot read whose they are. Your help is timely; yours is the hand that always guides my course, as in the past so for the days to come.

ATHENA. I know it, Odysseus, and came early on the path, a watcher friendly to your chase.

ODYSSEUS. Dear mistress, is my toil to some purpose?

ATHENA. Know that yonder man is the doer of these deeds.

ODYSSEUS. Why was his insensate hand so fierce?

ATHENA. In bitter wrath touching the arms of Achilles.

ODYSSEUS. Why then this furious onslaught upon the flocks?

ATHENA. It was in your blood, as he thought, that he was dyeing his hand.

ODYSSEUS. What? Was this design aimed against the Greeks?

ATHENA. He would have accomplished it too if I had been careless.

ODYSSEUS. How had he laid these bold plans? What could inspire such hardihood?

ATHENA. He went forth against you in the night, by stealth and alone.

ODYSSEUS. And did he come near us? Did he reach his goal?

ATHENA. He was already at the doors of the two chiefs.

ODYSSEUS. What cause stayed his eager hand from murder?

ATHENA. I, even I, withheld him, for I cast upon his eyes the tyrannous fancies of his baneful joy. I turned his fury aside on the flocks of sheep and the confused droves guarded by herdsmen, the spoil which you had not yet divided. He fell upon the horned throng dealing death and hewing them to the earth around him. Now he thought that the two Atreidae were the prisoners whom he slew with his hand, now it was this chief and now that, at each new onset. And while the man raved in the throes of frenzy I still urged him and hurled him into the toils of doom. Presently, when he rested from this work, he bound together the living oxen and the sheep and brought them home, as though his captives were men and not good cattle. And now he is tormenting them, bound together, in the house.

But I will show you this madness openly, so that when you have seen it you may proclaim it to all the Greeks. Be steadfast and of good courage, nor look for evil from the man, for I will turn the vision of his eyes away and keep them from seeing your face.

Ho, you who are binding the back-bent arms of your captives with cords, you I call; come here! Ajax, what ho! come forth from the house!

ODYSSEUS. What are you doing, Athena? Never call him out.

ATHENA. Hold your peace! Do not earn the name of coward!

ODYSSEUS. Forbear, I pray you; be content that he stay inside.

ATHENA. What is the danger? Was he not a man before?

ODYSSEUS. Yes, an enemy to your servant, and still is.

ATHENA. And to mock at enemies—is that not the sweetest mockery?

ODYSSEUS. Enough for me that he remain within his doors.

ATHENA. You are afraid of seeing a madman in full view?

ODYSSEUS. No fear could make me shun him if he were sane.

ATHENA. But even now he shall not see you, though you are near.

ODYSSEUS. How so, if he still sees with the same eyes?

ATHENA. I will darken them though they are open.

ODYSSEUS. Well, all is possible when a god contrives.

ATHENA. Stand silent, then, and stay where you are.

ODYSSEUS. I must stay. I wish that I were far from here!

ATHENA. What ho, Ajax, once again I call you! Is this your scanty regard for your ally?

AJAX (*enters, holding a bloodstained scourge*). Hail, Athena! Hail, Zeus-born maid! How well you have stood by me! Yes, I will crown your shrine with trophies of pure gold for this prize!

ATHENA. Fairly spoken. But tell me this—have you dyed your sword well in the Greek camp?

AJAX. That is my boast; I do not disclaim it.

ATHENA. And perhaps turned your armed hand on the Atreidae?

AJAX. So that they will never again dishonor Ajax.

ATHENA. The men are dead, as I take your meaning?

AJAX. Dead. Now let them rob me of my arms!

ATHENA. Good. And then the son of Laertes—in what plight have you left him? Has he escaped you?

AJAX. What, you ask me about that accursed fox?

ATHENA. Yes, about Odysseus, your adversary.

AJAX. No guest so welcome, lady. He is sitting in the house—in bonds. I do not mean him to die just yet.

ATHENA. What would you do first? What larger advantage would you win?

AJAX. First he shall be bound to a pillar beneath my roof—

ATHENA. The unlucky man; what will you do to him?

AJAX. —and have his back crimsoned with the scourge before he dies.

ATHENA. Do not torture the wretch so cruelly.

AJAX. In all else, Athena, have your will, I say; but *his* doom shall be no other than this.

ATHENA. Since it pleases you to do this, then, do not hold your hand, do not abate one jot of your intention.

AJAX. I go to my work. Always stand at my side, I charge you, as you have stood today! (*Exit.*)

ATHENA. Do you see, Odysseus, how great is the strength of the gods? Whom could you have found more prudent than this man or more valiant for the service of the time?

ODYSSEUS. I know none. I pity him in his misery for all that he is my foe, because he is bound fast to a dread doom. I think of my own lot no less than his. For I see that we are but phantoms, all we who live, or fleeting shadows.

ATHENA. Marking such things, therefore, see that your own lips never speak a haughty word against the gods, and assume no proud posture if you prevail above another in prowess or by store of ample wealth. For a day can humble all human things and a day can lift them up, but the wise of heart are loved of the gods, and the evil are abhorred.

CHORUS (*enters*). *Son of Telamon, you whose wave-girt Salamis is firmly throned upon the sea, when your fortunes are fair I rejoice, but when the stroke of Zeus comes upon you, or the angry rumor of the Danai with noise of evil tongues, then I tremble and am in great fear, like a winged dove with troubled eye.*

And so, telling of the night now spent, loud murmurs beset us for our shame; telling how you visited the meadow wild with steeds and destroyed the cattle of the Greeks, their spoil, prizes of the spear which had not yet been shared, slaying them with flashing sword.

Such are the whispered slanders that Odysseus breathes into all ears, and he wins large belief. For now the tale that he tells of you is specious; and each hearer rejoices more than he who told, despitefully exulting in your woes.

Yes, point your arrow at a noble spirit and you shall not miss; but should a man speak such things against me he would win no faith. 'Tis on the powerful that envy creeps. Yet the small without the great can ill be trusted to guard the walls; lowly leagued with great will prosper best, great served by less.

But foolish men cannot be led to learn these truths. Even such are the men who rail against you, and we are helpless to repel these charges without you, O King. Verily, when they have escaped your eye they chatter like flocking birds; but terrified by the mighty vulture, suddenly, if you should perchance appear, they will cower still and dumb.

Was it the Tauric Artemis, child of Zeus, that drove you— O dread rumor, parent of my shame!—against the herds of all our host, in revenge, I suppose, for a victory that had paid no tribute, whether it was that she had been disappointed of glorious spoil, or because a stag had been slain without a thank-offering? Or can it have been the mail-clad Lord of War that was wroth for dishonor to his aiding spear and took vengeance by nightly wiles?

Never of your own heart, son of Telamon, would you have gone so far astray as to fall upon the flocks. Verily, when the gods send madness it must come; but may Zeus and Phoebus avert the evil rumor of the Greeks!

And if the great chiefs charge you falsely in the rumors which they spread, or sons of the wicked line of Sisyphus, forbear, O my king, forbear to win me an evil name by still keeping your face thus hidden in the tent by the sea.

Nay, up from your seat, wheresoever you are brooding in this pause of many days from battle, making the flame of mischief blaze up to heaven! But the insolence of your foes goes abroad without fear in the breezy glens, while all men mock with taunts most grievous; and my sorrow passes not away.

TECMESSA (*enters*). *Mariners of Ajax, of the race that springs from the Erechtheidae, sons of the soil—mourning is the portion of us who care for the house of Telamon far away. Ajax, our dread lord of rugged might, now lies stricken with a storm that darkens the soul.*

CHORUS. *What is the heavy change from yesterday's fortune which this night has produced? Daughter of the Phrygian Teleutas, speak; for to you, his spear-won bride, bold Ajax has borne a constant love. You may therefore hint the answer with knowledge.*

TECMESSA. *Oh, how shall I tell a tale too dire for words? Terrible as death is the fate which you must hear. Seized with madness in the night, our glorious Ajax has been utterly undone. For evidence you may see within his dwelling the butchered victims weltering in their blood, sacrifices of no hand but his.*

CHORUS. *What tidings of the fiery warrior have you told, not to be borne nor yet escaped, tidings which the mighty Danai noise abroad, which their strong rumor spreads! Woe is me, I dread the doom to come. Shamed before all eyes, the man will die, if his frenzied hand has slain with dark sword the herds and the horse-guiding herdsmen.*

TECMESSA. *Alas! It was from those pastures that he came to me with his captive flock! Of part he cut the throats on the floor within; some he rent asunder, hewing their sides. Then he*

caught up two white-footed rams. Of one he sheared off the
head and the tongue-tip and flung them away; the other he
bound upright to a pillar, and seized a heavy thong of har-
ness, and flogged with shrill, doubled lash, while he uttered
revilings which a god, and no mortal had taught.

CHORUS. *The time has come for each of us to veil his head and*
betake him to stealthy speed of foot, or to sit on the bench at
the quick oar and give her way to the seafaring ship. Such
angry threats are hurled against us by the brother-kings, the
sons of Atreus, that I fear to share a death by stoning, smit-
ten at the side of this man who is swayed by a fate to which
none may draw near.

TECMESSA. *It sways him no longer. The lightnings flash no*
more. Like a southern gale, fierce in its first onset, his rage
is abating; and now, in his right mind, he has new pain. To
look on self-wrought woes, when no other has had a hand in
them—this lays sharp pangs to the soul.

CHORUS. But if his frenzy has ceased I have good hope that all
may yet be well. The trouble is of less account when once it
is past.

TECMESSA. Which would you choose, if the choice were given
you: to pain your friends and have delights yourself, or to
share the grief of friends who grieve?

CHORUS. Twofold sorrow is the greater ill, lady.

TECMESSA. Then we are now losers, though the plague is past.

CHORUS. What is your meaning? I do not understand.

TECMESSA. While he was frenzied that man found his own joy
in the dire fantasies which held him, though his presence
was grievous to us who were sane; but now since he has had
pause and respite from the plague, *he* is utterly afflicted with
deep grief and we likewise, no less than before. Have we not
here two sorrows instead of one?

CHORUS. We have indeed; and I fear lest the stroke of a god has
fallen. How else, if his spirit is no lighter now that the malady is past than when it vexed him?

TECMESSA. That is how the matter stands, be sure.

CHORUS. How did the plague first swoop upon him? Tell us,
who share your pain, how it came about.

TECMESSA. You shall hear all that happened, for you have a share in it. At dead of night, when the evening lamps were out, he seized a two-edged sword and was eager to go forth on an aimless path. I chided him and said, "What are you about, Ajax? Why will you make this sally unsummoned? No messenger has called you, no trumpet has sounded; the whole army is asleep."

He answered me in curt phrase and trite: "Woman, silence graces women." Thus taught, I desisted, and he rushed out alone. What happened abroad I cannot tell. He came in with his captives bound together—bulls, shepherd dogs, and fleecy prisoners. Some he beheaded; of some he cut the back-bent throat or cleft the chine; others he tormented in their bonds as though they were men, with onslaughts on the cattle.

At last he darted forward through the door and began ranting to some creature of his brain, now against the Atreidae, now about Odysseus, with many a mocking boast of all the hurt he had wreaked on them in his raid. Presently he rushed back into the house once more; and then by slow, painful steps regained his reason.

As his gaze ranged over the room full of his wild work, he struck his head and uttered a great cry; he fell down, a wreck amid the wrecks of the slaughtered sheep, and there he sat, with clenched nails tightly clutching his hair. At first, and for a long while, he sat dumb; then he threatened me with those dreadful threats if I did not describe all that had happened, and he asked in what strange plight he stood. I told him all that had happened, friends, so far as I surely knew it. He straightway broke into bitter lamentations, such as I had never heard from him before, for he had always asserted that such wailing was for craven and lowhearted men. No cry of shrill complaint would pass his lips, only a deep sound, as of a moaning bull.

Prostrate now in his utter woe, tasting no food or drink, the man sits quiet where he has fallen, amidst the sword-slain cattle. Plainly he yearns to do some dreadful deed; there is some such meaning in his words and his laments.

Ah, my friends—indeed, this was my errand—come in and help if in any way you can. Men in his case can be won by the words of friends.

CHORUS. Tecmessa, daughter of Teleutas, dreadful are your tidings that our lord has been frenzied by his sorrows.

AJAX (*within*). Woe, woe is me!

TECMESSA. Soon, it seems, there will be worse. Did you not hear Ajax, did you not hear that resounding cry?

AJAX. Woe, woe is me!

CHORUS. The man seems to be distempered, or else to be grieving for the distempers which lately vexed him, when he sees their work.

AJAX. O my son, my son!

TECMESSA. Ah me! Eurysaces, it's for you he is calling! What can his purpose be? Where are you? Unhappy me!

AJAX. Ho, Teucer! Where is Teucer? Will his foray last forever? And I am perishing!

CHORUS. He seems to be sane. Come, open there, open! Perhaps even at the sight of us he may come to a more sober mood.

TECMESSA. Look, I open. You can see the man's deeds and his own plight.

(AJAX *is discovered sitting amidst the slaughtered cattle.*)

AJAX. *Alas, good sailors, alone of my friends, alone still constant to your loyalty, see what a wave has just now surged around me and hemmed me in, under stress of a deadly storm!*

CHORUS. Ah, lady, how sadly true your report shows! The fact proves that no sane mind is here.

AJAX. *Alas, mates staunch in seacraft, you who manned the ship and made the oar-blade flash upon the brine—in you alone I see a defense against misery: come, slaughter me too!*

CHORUS. Hush your wild lips. Do not cure ill by ill, do not increase the anguish of the doom.

AJAX. *Do you see the bold, the strong of heart, the dauntless in battles with the foe—do you see how I have shown my prowess on creatures that feared no harm? Alas, the mockery! How I have been shamed!*

TECMESSA. Ajax my lord, I implore you, do not speak so!

AJAX. Out with you, begone!—Woe is me! Woe is me!

CHORUS. For the gods' love, yield to counsel and learn wisdom!

AJAX. *Wretch that I am, who suffered the accursed men to slip through my hands but fell on horned cattle and fine flocks and made their dark blood flow!*

CHORUS. Why grieve when the deed is past recall? These things can never be other than they are.

AJAX. *Ah, you who watch everything, you ready tool of every crime, ah, son of Laertes, you foulest knave in all the host, I warrant you are laughing loud and long for joy!*

CHORUS. As the god gives, so every man laughs or mourns.

AJAX. *Yet would that I could see him, shattered though I am! Ah me, ah me!*

CHORUS. Speak no proud word. Do you not see to what a plight you have come?

AJAX. *O Zeus, father of my sires, would that I might slay that deep dissembler, that hateful knave, and the two brother-chiefs, and lastly die myself also!*

TECMESSA. When you make that prayer pray also that I too die. Why should I live when you are dead?

AJAX. *Alas, you darkness, my sole light! O you nether gloom, fairer for me than any sunshine! take me to dwell with you, yes take me. I am no longer worthy to look for help to the race of the gods, or for any good from men, the children of a day.*

No, the daughter of Zeus, the strong goddess, is tormenting me to the death. Where then shall a man flee? Where shall I go to find rest? If my past fame is destroyed, my friends, along with such victims as these near me—if I have set myself to win a madman's triumphs, and all the host, with sword uplifted in both hands, would strike me dead!

TECMESSA. Unhappy me, that a good man and true should utter such words—words that till now he would never have deigned to speak!

AJAX. *Alas, you paths of the sounding wave, you sea-caves and wooded pastures by the shore, long time, long time and very weary have you known me tarrying at Troy; but no more shall you know me—no more with the breath of life. Of so much let sane men be sure.*

Ah, streams of Scamander near us, kindly to the Greeks, never shall you look on Ajax more. His peer in the host—I will utter a proud word—Troy has never seen come from the land of Hellas. But now, look, he has been humbled to the dust.

CHORUS. Truly, I do not know how to restrain you or how suffer you to speak; woes so grievous have befallen you.

AJAX. Ay me! Who could ever have thought that my name would chime so meetly with my doom? Well may I now mourn—yes, twice and three times mourn—in those sad syllables that shape my name, such heavy griefs are mine. By his prowess my sire won the fairest prize of all the host and brought all glory home from this land of Ida; but I his son, who came after him with might no less to this same ground of Troy and proved the service of my hand in no lesser deeds, am thus perishing, dishonored by the Greeks. But of so much, I think, I can be sure. If Achilles were alive and had been called to decree the first place of valor to any claimant of his arms, no one would have grasped them before me. But now the Atreidae have conveyed them to a villain and thrust away the high deeds of Ajax.

And if these eyes, if this warped mind had not swerved from the purpose that was mine, never would they have procured such a judgment against another man. As it was, the daughter of Zeus, the fierce-eyed unconquerable goddess, foiled me at the instant when I was making ready my hand against them, struck me with a plague of frenzy, made me imbrue my hands in the blood of these poor cattle. And yonder men exult to have escaped me—by no good-will of

mine. But if a god send harm, verily even the base man can
elude the worthier.

Now what shall I do? Plainly I am hateful to the gods, abhorred by the Greek host, hated by all Troy and all these
plains. Shall I forsake the station of the ships, leave the
Atreidae forlorn, and go homeward across the Aegean? And
what face shall I show to my father when I come, to
Telamon? How will he find heart to look on me when I stand
before him ungraced, without that meed of valor whereby
he won a great crown of fame? It is not to be endured.

But then shall I go to the stronghold of the Trojans, at-
tack alone where all are foes, and in doing some good service die at last? No, for thus I might gladden the Atreidae. It
must not be. Some emprise must be sought whereby I may
prove to my aged sire that at heart, at least, his son is not a
dastard.

It is base for a man to crave the full term of life when he
finds no varying in his woes. What joy is there in day following day, now pushing us forward, now drawing us back,
on the verge—of death? I rate that man as nothing worth
who feels the glow of idle hopes. No, one of generous strain
should nobly live, or forthwith nobly die. You have heard all.

CHORUS. No man shall say that you have spoken a bastard
word, Ajax, or one not bred of your true soul. Yet forbear;
dismiss these thoughts and suffer friends to overrule your
purpose.

TECMESSA. Ajax my lord, the doom given by fate is the hardest
of evils among men. I was the daughter of a freeborn sire,
wealthy and mighty if any Phrygian was; and now I am a
slave, for so the gods ordained, I suppose, and chiefly your
strong hand. And so since wedlock has made me yours, I
wish you well. I entreat you, by the Zeus of our hearth, by
the marriage that has made us one, do not doom me to the
cruel rumor of your foes, do not abandon me to the hand of
a stranger! On whatever day you die and leave me alone by
your death, on that same day, be sure, I also shall be seized
forcibly by the Greeks and, with your son, shall have the
portion of a slave. Then some one of my masters shall name

me in bitter phrase with keen taunts: "See the concubine of
Ajax, who was mightiest of the host; see what menial tasks
are hers who had such bliss!" So shall men speak, and destiny will afflict me; but these words shall be shameful for
you and for your race.

Have thought for your father, whom you are forsaking
in dreary old age; for your mother, whose years are many
and who often prays to the gods that you come home alive;
and pity, O King, your son, if, bereft of fostering care, he
must spend his days forlorn of you, the ward of unloving
guardians. Think how great is this sorrow which, at your
death, you will bequeath to him and me.

I have nothing to which I can look save you. You ravaged
my country with the spear, and another doom laid my
mother and father low, to dwell with Hades in their death.
What home could I then find if I lost you? What wealth? On
you hangs all my welfare. Do have thought for me also; a
true man should cherish remembrance if anywhere he reap
a joy. It is kindness that still begets kindness. But whoever
suffers the memory of benefits to slip from him, that man
can no more rank as noble.

CHORUS. Ajax, I would that pity touched your soul as it does
mine; then you would approve her words.

AJAX. She shall indeed have approval on my part, if only she
take heart to do my bidding well.

TECMESSA. I will obey in all things, dear Ajax.

AJAX. Then bring me my son; I wish to see him.

TECMESSA. Oh, but in those fears I released him from my
keeping.

AJAX. During these troubles of mine? Or what do you mean?

TECMESSA. Yes, lest the poor child should happen to meet you
and die.

AJAX. Aye truly, that would have been worthy of my fortune.

TECMESSA. Well, at least I was watchful to avert *that* woe.

AJAX. I praise your act and the foresight you have shown.

TECMESSA. How then can I serve you as the case stands now?

AJAX. Let me speak to him and see him face to face.

TECMESSA. Oh yes; he is close by, in charge of attendants.

AJAX. Then why is his coming delayed?

TECMESSA. My child, your father is calling you. Bring him here, servant, whichever of you is guiding his steps.

AJAX. Is the man coming at your call? Or has he failed to hear your words?

TECMESSA. One of the servants is drawing near with him right now.

(*Enter* ATTENDANT *with* EURYSACES.)

AJAX. Lift him, lift him to my arms. He will feel no dread, I think, in looking on this newly shed blood if he is indeed my true-born son. But he must at once be broken into his father's rugged ways and molded to the likeness of his nature. Ah, boy, may you prove happier than your father but in all else like him, and you will not prove base. Yet even now I may well envy you for this, that you have no sense of these ills. Yes, life is sweetest before the feelings are awake, until one learns to know joy or pain. But when you shall come to that knowledge then you must prove among your father's foes of what mettle and what sire you are.

Meanwhile feed on light breezes, and nurse your tender life for this your mother's joy. No fear, I think, lest any of the Greeks assail you with cruel outrage, even when you have me no more. So trusty is the warder whom I will leave to guard you, even Teucer, who will not falter in his care for you, though he is now following a far path, busied with chase of foes.

O my warriors, seafaring comrades! On you as on him I lay this task of love; do you give my behest to Teucer, to take this child to my own home and set him before the face of Telamon and of my mother Eriboea, that so he may prove the comfort of their age evermore. Charge him that no stewards of games nor he who worked my ruin make my arms a prize for the Greeks. No, *this* you take, my son, the broad shield from which you take your name; hold and wield it by

the well-wrought thong, that sevenfold spear-proof targe!
But the rest of my armor shall be buried in my grave.

(*To* TECMESSA.) Come, do not tarry. Take the child
straightway, make fast the doors, and utter no laments before the house; truly a woman is a plaintive thing. Quick,
close the house! It is not for a skillful leech to whine charms
over a sore that craves the knife.

CHORUS. I am afraid when I mark this eager haste. I do not like
the keen edge of your speech.

TECMESSA. Ajax my lord, on what deed can your mind be set?

AJAX. Do not ask, do not inquire; it is good to be discreet.

TECMESSA. Ah, my heavy heart! Now by your child, by the
gods, I implore you, do not be guilty of forsaking us!

AJAX. You vex me over much. Do you not know that I no
longer owe any service to the gods?

TECMESSA. Hush, hush!

AJAX. Speak to those who hear.

TECMESSA. And will *you* not hearken?

AJAX. Already your words have been too many.

TECMESSA. I am afraid, O Prince!

AJAX (*to* ATTENDANTS). Close the doors, I say, this instant!

TECMESSA. For the gods' love, be softened!

AJAX. It is a foolish hope, I think, if you would begin now to
school my temper.

(AJAX *is shut into the tent; exit* TECMESSA *with* EURYSACES.)

CHORUS. *O famous Salamis, you have your happy seat among
the waves that lash your shore, the joy of all men's eyes forever; but I the unfortunate have been tarrying here long,
still making my couch through countless months in the camp
on the fields of Ida, worn by time, and darkly looking for the
day when I shall pass to Hades, the abhorred, the unseen.*

*And now I must wrestle with a new grief, woe is me, the
incurable malady of Ajax, visited by a heaven-sent frenzy. In
a bygone day you sent him forth mighty in war; but now,
a changed man who nurses lonely thoughts, he has been*

*found a heavy sorrow to his friends. The former deeds of his
hands, deeds of prowess supreme, have fallen dead and
have won no love from the loveless, the miserable Atreidae.*

*Surely his mother, full of years and white with age, will
uplift a voice of wailing when she hears that he has been
stricken with the spirit's ruin. Not in the nightingale's plaintive note will she utter her anguish: in shrill-toned strains
the dirge will rise, with sound of hands that smite the breast
and with rending of hoary hair.*

*Yes, better hid with Hades is he whom vain fancies vex.
By the lineage whence he springs he is noblest of the war-
tried Achaeans; now he is true no more to the promptings of
his inbred nature but dwells with alien thoughts.*

*Ah, unlucky father, how heavy a curse upon your son
does it rest for you to hear, a curse which never yet has
clung to any life of the Aeacidae save his!*

AJAX (*enters, sword in hand*). All things the long and countless years first draw from darkness, then bury from light;
and there is nothing for which man may not look. The dread
oath is vanquished, and the stubborn will. Even I, once so
wonderfully firm, like iron hardened in the dipping, have
felt the keen edge of my temper softened by yonder woman's words. I feel the pity of leaving her a widow with my
foes and the boy an orphan.

But I will go to the bathing place and the meadows by the
shore, that in purging of my stains I may flee the heavy
anger of the goddess. Then I will seek out some untrodden
spot and bury this sword, hatefulest of weapons, in a hole
dug where none shall see; no, let Night and Hades keep it
underground! For since my hand took this gift from Hector,
my worst foe, to this hour I have had no good from the
Greeks. Yes, men's proverb is true: "The gifts of enemies are
no gifts and bring no good."

I shall henceforth know, therefore, how to yield to the
gods and shall learn to revere the Atreidae. They are rulers,
so we must submit. How else? Dread things and things most
potent bow to office; thus it is that snow-strewn winter gives

place to fruitful summer; and thus night's weary round makes room for day with her white steeds to kindle light; and the breath of dreadful winds can allow the groaning sea to slumber; and, like the rest, almighty Sleep looses whom he has bound, nor holds with a perpetual grasp.

And we—must we not learn discretion? I, at least, will learn it; for I am newly aware that our enemy is to be hated but as one who will hereafter be a friend; and toward a friend I would wish but thus far to show aid and service, as knowing that he will not always abide. For to most men the haven of friendship is false.

But concerning these things it will be well. Woman, go you within and pray to the gods that in all fullness the desires of my heart may be fulfilled. And you, my friends, do you honor these my wishes just as she does; and bid Teucer when he comes to have care for me and also good will toward you. For I will go whither I must pass, but you do my bidding. Before long, perhaps, though I am now suffering you will hear that I have found peace. (*Exit.*)

CHORUS. *I thrill with rapture, I soar on the wings of sudden joy! O Pan, O Pan, appear to us, O Pan, roving over the sea, from the craggy ridge of snow-beaten Cyllene, king who makes dances for the gods, that with me you may move blithely in the measures that none has taught you, the measures of Nysa and of Cnossus! For now I am fain to dance. And may Apollo, lord of Delos, come over the Icarian waters to be with me, in presence manifest and spirit ever kind!*

The destroying god has lifted the cloud of dread trouble from our eyes. Joy, joy! Now once again, now, O Zeus, can the pure brightness of good days come to the swift sea-cleaving ships; since Ajax again forgets his trouble and has turned to perform the law of the gods with all due rites, in perfectness of loyal worship.

The strong years make all things fade; nor would I say anything was too strange for belief when thus beyond our hopes Ajax has been led to repent of his wrath against the Atreidae and his dread feuds.

(*Enter* MESSENGER *from the Greek camp.*)

MESSENGER. Friends, I would first tell you this. Teucer is but
now returned from the Mysian heights; he has come to the
generals' quarters in midcamp, and is being reviled by all
the Greeks at once. They knew him from afar as he drew
near, gathered around him, and then assailed him with
taunts from this side and from that every man of them, calling him "that kinsman of the maniac, of the plotter against
the host," saying that he should not save himself from being
mangled to death by stoning. And so they had come to this,
that swords plucked from sheaths were drawn in men's
hands. When the strife had well-nigh run to its furthest, it
was allayed by the soothing words of elders. But where shall
I find Ajax, to tell him this? He whom most it touches must
hear all the tale.

CHORUS. He is not within. He has just now gone forth, for he
has yoked a new purpose to his new mood.

MESSENGER. Alas! Alas! Too late, then, was he who sent me on
this errand, or I have proved a laggard.

CHORUS. And what urgent business has been scanted here?

MESSENGER. Teucer enjoined that the man should not go forth
from the house until he himself should come.

CHORUS. Well, he is gone, I tell you, intent on the purpose that
is best for him—to make his peace with the gods.

MESSENGER. These are words of wild folly, if there is wisdom
in the prophecy of Calchas.

CHORUS. What does he prophesy? What knowledge of this matter do you bring?

MESSENGER. This much I know, for I was present. Leaving the
circle of chiefs who sat in council, Calchas drew apart from
the Atreidae. He put his right hand with all kindness into the
hand of Teucer and strictly charged him that by all means in
his power he should keep Ajax within the house for this day
that is now shining on us and not suffer him to go abroad—
if he wished ever to see him alive. This day alone will the
wrath of divine Athena vex him—so ran the warning.

"Lives that have waxed too proud," said the seer, "and avail for good no more are struck down by heavy misfortunes from the gods, as often as one born to man's estate forgets it in thoughts too high for man. But even at his first going forth from home Ajax was found foolish when his father spoke well. His father said to him: 'My son, seek victory in arms, but seek it always with the help of heaven.' Then haughtily and foolishly he answered: 'Father, with the help of the gods even a man of nought might win the mastery, but I trust to bring that glory within my grasp even without their aid.' So proud was his boast. Then once again, in answer to divine Athena when she was urging him onward and bidding him turn a deadly hand upon his foes, he uttered a speech too dreadful for mortal lips: 'Queen, stand beside the other Greeks; where Ajax stands battle will never break our line.' By such words it was that he brought upon him the appalling anger of the goddess, since his thoughts were too great for man. But if he lives this day, perhaps with the god's help we may find means to save him."

Thus far the seer; and Teucer had no sooner risen from where they sat than he sent me with these mandates for your guidance. But if we have been foiled that man lives not or Calchas is no prophet.

CHORUS. Luckless Tecmessa, born to misery, come forth and see what tidings yonder man tells. This peril touches us too closely for our peace.

TECMESSA (*enters*). Why do you break my rest again, ah me, when I had but just found peace from relentless woes?

CHORUS. Hear that man and the tidings of Ajax that he has brought us, to my grief.

TECMESSA. Alas, what are you saying, man? Are we undone?

MESSENGER. I do not know your fortune, but only that if Ajax is abroad my mind is ill at ease for him.

TECMESSA. He is abroad indeed, and so I am in anguish to know your meaning.

MESSENGER. Teucer strictly commands that you keep Ajax under shelter of the roof and suffer him not to go forth alone.

TECMESSA. Where is Teucer, and why does he say this?

MESSENGER. He has just now returned, and he forebodes that this going forth is fraught with death for Ajax.

TECMESSA. Unhappy me! From whom can he have learned this?

MESSENGER. From the seer, Thestor's son, this day; the issue is one of life or death for Ajax.

TECMESSA. Ah me, my friends, protect me from the doom threatened by fate! Speed, some of you, to hasten Teucer's coming; let others go to the westward bays and others to the eastward and seek the man's ill-omened steps. I see now that I have been deceived by my lord, and cast out of the favor that I once found with him. Ah me, my child, what shall I do? We must not sit idle; I too will go as far as I have strength. Away, let us be quick, there is no time to rest if we would save a man who is in haste to die.

CHORUS. I am ready, and will show it in more than word; speed of act and foot shall follow.

(*Exeunt* TECMESSA *and* CHORUS. *The scene changes to a lonely spot by the seashore.*)

AJAX (*enters*). The slayer stands so that he shall do his work most surely—if leisure serves for so much thought—the gift of Hector, that foeman-friend who was most hateful to my soul and to my sight. It is fixed in hostile soil, the land of Troy, with a new edge from the iron-biting whet. I have planted it with heedful care, so that it should prove most kindly to me in a speedy death.

   Thus on my part all is ready; and next be thou, O Zeus— as is appropriate—the first to aid me; it is no large boon that I will crave. Send some messenger with the ill news to Teucer, I pray you, that he may be the first to raise me where I have fallen on this reeking sword, lest I be first espied by some enemy and cast forth a prey to dogs and birds. So much, O Zeus, I entreat you; and I call also on Hermes, guide to the nether world, that he lay me softly asleep, without a struggle, at one quick bound, when I have driven this sword into my side.

And I will call for help to the maidens who live forever
and ever look on all the woes of men, the dread far-striding
Furies; let them mark how my miserable life is blasted by
the Atreidae. May they overtake those evil men with doom
most evil and with utter blight. Come, ye swift and vengeful
Furies, glut your wrath on all the host and spare not!

And thou Sun-god whose chariot wheels climb the
heights of heaven, when you look on the land of my sires
draw in your rein overspread with gold and tell my disasters
and my death to my aged father and the hapless woman who
reared me. Poor mother! I think, when she hears those tidings, her loud wail will ring through all the city. But it avails
not to make idle moan: now for the last deed, as quickly as
I may.

O Death, Death, come now and look upon me! To you I
will speak in that other world also, when I am with you. But
you, present beam of the bright day, and Sun in his chariot,
I accost for the last, last time—never more hereafter. O sunlight! O sacred soil of my own Salamis, firm seat of my
father's hearth! O famous Athens, and your race kindred to
mine! And you, springs and rivers of this land—and you
plains of Troy, I greet you also—farewell, you who have
cherished my life! This is the last word that Ajax speaks to
you; henceforth he will speak in Hades with the dead.

(AJAX *falls upon his sword. Enter* CHORUS, *in two bands.*)

SEMICHORUS I. *Toil follows toil and brings but toil! Where,
where have my steps not been? And still no place is conscious of a secret that I share. Hark—a sudden noise!*

SEMICHORUS II. *'Tis we, the shipmates of your voyage.*

SEMICHORUS I. *How goes it?*

SEMICHORUS II. *All the westward side of the ships has been
paced.*

SEMICHORUS I. *Well, have you found anything?*

SEMICHORUS II. *Only much toil, and nothing more to see.*

SEMICHORUS I. *And clearly the man has not been seen either
along the path that fronts the morning ray.*

CHORUS. *O for tidings from some toiling fisher, busy about his sleepless quest, or from some nymph of the Olympian heights or of the streams that flow toward Bosporus—if anywhere any has seen the man of fierce spirit roaming! It is hard that I, the wanderer who have toiled so long, cannot come near him with prospered course but fail to descry where the sick man is.*

TECMESSA (*enters*). *Ah me, ah me!*

CHORUS. *Whose cry broke from the covert of the wood near us?*

TECMESSA. *Ah miserable!*

CHORUS. *I see the spear-won bride, luckless Tecmessa. Her soul is steeped in the anguish of that wail.*

TECMESSA. *I am lost, undone, left desolate, my friends!*

CHORUS. *What ails you?*

TECMESSA. *Here lies our Ajax, newly slain, a sword buried and sheathed in his corpse.*

CHORUS. *Alas for my hopes of return! Ah, prince, you have slain me, the comrade of your voyage! Unfortunate man, brokenhearted woman!*

TECMESSA. This is how it is with him; 'tis ours to wail.

CHORUS. By whose hand, then, can the wretched man have done the deed?

TECMESSA. By his own. You can tell; this sword which he planted in the ground and on which he fell convicts him.

CHORUS. *Alas for my blind folly! All alone, then, you have fallen in blood, unwatched of friends! And I took no heed, so dull was I, so witless! Where, where lies Ajax, that wayward one of ill-boding name?*

TECMESSA. No eye shall look upon him. No, in this enfolding robe I will shroud him wholly; for no man who loved him could bear to see him as up to nostrils and forth from red gash he spirts the darkened blood from the self-dealt wound. Ah me, what shall I do? What friend shall lift you in his arms? Where is Teucer? How timely would be his arrival, if he would only come, to compose the corpse of his brother! Ah, luckless Ajax, from what height fallen how low! How worthy, even in the sight of foes, to be mourned!

CHORUS. *You were fated, unfortunate man, you were fated,*

*then, with that unbending soul, at last to work out an evil
doom of woes untold! Such was the omen of those com-
plainings which by night and by day I heard you utter in
your fierce mood, bitter against the Atreidae with a deadly
passion. Aye, that time was a potent source of sorrows, when
the golden arms were made the prize in a contest of
prowess!*

TECMESSA. *Woe, woe is me!*

CHORUS. *The anguish pierces, I know, to your true heart.*

TECMESSA. *Woe, woe is me!*

CHORUS. *I do not marvel, lady, that you should wail and wail
again; you have lately been bereft of one greatly loved.*

TECMESSA. *It is for you to conjecture of these things; for me to
feel them all too sorely.*

CHORUS. *Yes, so it is.*

TECMESSA. *Alas, my child, to what a yoke of bondage are we
coming, seeing the taskmasters that are set over you and me!*

CHORUS. *Oh, the two Atreidae would be ruthless; the deeds
which you name, hinting at such a woe, would be unspeakable! But may the gods avert it!*

TECMESSA. *Never would things have been in this state save by
the will of the gods.*

CHORUS. *Yes, they have laid on us a burden too heavy to be
borne.*

TECMESSA. *Yet such is the woe that the daughter of Zeus, the
dread goddess, engenders for Odysseus' sake.*

CHORUS. *Doubtless the patient hero exults in his dark soul and
with keen mockery mocks at these sorrows born of frenzy.
Alas! And with him when they hear the tidings laugh the
royal brothers, the Atreidae.*

TECMESSA. Then let them mock and exult in this man's woes.
Perhaps, though they did not miss him while he lived they
will bewail him dead, in the straits of warfare. Ill-judging
men do not know the good that was in their hands till they
have lost it. To my pain has he died more than for their joy,
and to his own content. All that he yearned to win he has
made his own—the death for which he longed. Why then
should they triumph over this man? His death concerns the

gods, not them—truly not. Then let Odysseus revel in empty
taunts. Ajax is for them no more; to me he has left anguish
and mourning—and is gone.

TEUCER (*approaching*). Woe, woe is me!

CHORUS. Hush—methinks I hear the voice of Teucer, raised in
a strain that perceives this dire woe.

TEUCER (*enters*). Beloved Ajax, brother whose face was so dear
to me, have you indeed fared as rumor holds?

CHORUS. He has perished, Teucer; of that be sure.

TEUCER. Woe is me then for my heavy fate!

CHORUS. Know that this is how it is—

TEUCER. Wretched, wretched that I am!

CHORUS. You have cause to mourn.

TEUCER. O fierce and sudden blow!

CHORUS. You speak only too truly, Teucer.

TEUCER. Ay me! —But tell me of his child: where in Troyland
shall I find him?

CHORUS. Alone, by the tent.

TEUCER (*to* TECMESSA). Then bring him here with all speed,
lest some enemy snatch him up, as a whelp from a lioness
forlorn! Away, haste, bear help! It is all men's way to triumph over the dead when they lie low.

(*Exit* TECMESSA.)

CHORUS. Yes, when he was yet alive, Teucer, that man charged
you to have care for the child, as you are indeed doing.

TEUCER. O sight most grievous to me of all that ever my eyes
have seen! O bitter to my heart above all paths that I have
trod is the path that now has led me here when I learned
your fate, ah best-loved Ajax, as I was pursuing and tracking out your footsteps! For a swift rumor about you, as from
some god, passed through the Greek host, telling that you
were dead and gone. I heard it, ah me, while yet far off, and
groaned low; but now the sight breaks my heart! Come, lift
the covering, and let me see the worst.

(*The corpse of* AJAX *is uncovered.*)

O form dread to look on, in which dwelt such cruel courage, what sorrows have you sown for me in your death!

Where can I betake myself, to what people, after bringing you no help in your troubles? Telamon, I suppose, your father and mine, is likely to greet me with sunny face and gracious mien when I come without you. Yes indeed, a man not used to smile more brightly than before even when good fortune befalls him.

What will such a man keep back? What taunt will he not utter against the bastard begotten from the war-prize of his spear, against him who betrayed you, beloved Ajax, like a coward and a craven—or by guile, so that when you were dead he might enjoy your lordship and your house? So will he speak, a passionate man, peevish in old age, whose wrath makes strife even without a cause. And in the end I shall be thrust from the realm and cast off, branded by his taunts as no more a freeman but a slave.

Such is my prospect at home; while at Troy I have many enemies and few things to help me. All this I have reaped by your death! Ah me, what shall I do? How shall I draw you, luckless man, from the cruel point of this gleaming sword, the slayer, it seems, to whom you have yielded up your breath? Now do you see how Hector, though dead, was to destroy you at the last?

Consider, pray, the fortune of these two men. With the very girdle that had been given to him by Ajax, Hector was gripped to the chariot-rail and mangled till he gave up the ghost. It was from Hector that Ajax had this gift, and by this he had perished in his deadly fall. Was it not the Fury who forged this blade, was not that girdle wrought by Hades, the grim artificer? I at least would deem that these things, and all things ever, are planned by gods for men; but if there be any in whose mind this wins no favor, let him hold to his own thoughts as I hold to mine.

CHORUS. Do not speak at length but think how you shall lay the man in the tomb and what you will say presently; for I see an enemy, and perhaps he will come with mocking of our sorrows, as evil men would do.

TEUCER. What man of the host do you see?

CHORUS. Menelaus, for whom we made this voyage.

TEUCER. I see him; he is not hard to know when near.

MENELAUS (*enters*). You there, I tell you to bear no hand in raising yonder corpse but to leave it where it lies.

TEUCER. Why have you spent your breath in such proud words?

MENELAUS. It is my pleasure, and his who rules the host.

TEUCER. And might we hear what reason you proffer?

MENELAUS. This, that when we had hoped we were bringing him from home to be an ally and a friend for the Greeks we found him, on trial, a worse than Phrygian foe. He plotted death for all the host, and sallied by night against us, to slay with the spear. If some god had not quenched this attempt ours would have been the lot which he has found, to lie slain by an ignoble doom, while he would have been living. But now a god has turned his outrage aside, to fall on sheep and cattle.

There is no man so powerful, therefore, as to entomb the corpse of Ajax; no, he shall be cast forth somewhere on the yellow sand and become food for the birds by the sea. Then raise no storm of angry threats. If we were not able to control him while he lived, at least we shall rule him in death, whether you will or no, and control him with our hands. While he lived there was never a time when he would hearken to my words.

It is the sign of an unworthy nature when a subject does not deign to obey those who are set over him. Never can laws have prosperous course in a city where dread has no place; nor can a camp be ruled discreetly any more if it lack the guarding force of fear and reverence. No, though a man's frame have waxed mighty, he should look to fall, perhaps by a light blow. The man who has fear, and therewith shame, be sure that he is safe; but where there is license to insult and act willfully, doubt not that such a state, though favoring gales have sped her, will some day, at last, sink into the depths.

No, where fear is proper let me see fear too established;

let us not dream that we can act according to our desires
without paying the price in our pains. These things come by
turns. This man was once hot and insolent; now it is my hour
to be haughty. I warn you not to bury him, lest through that
deed you yourself should come to need a grave.

CHORUS. Menelaus, after laying down wise precepts do not
yourself be guilty of outrage on the dead.

TEUCER. Never, friends, shall I wonder more if a lowborn man
offends after his kind when they who are accounted of noble blood allow such scandalous words to pass their lips.

Come, tell me from the first once more—do you say that
you brought the man here to the Greeks as an ally found by
you? Did he not sail forth of his own act, as his own master?
What claim have you to be his chief? On what ground have
you a right to kingship of the lieges whom he brought from
home? As Sparta's king you came, not as master over us.
Nowhere was it laid down among your lawful powers that
you should dictate to him, any more than he to you. You
sailed here under the command of others, not as chief of all,
so that you should ever be captain over Ajax.

No, lord it over them whose lord you are, lash *them* with
your proud words; but this man I will duly lay in the grave
though you forbid it—aye, or your brother-chief—nor shall
I tremble at your word. It was not for your wife's sake that
Ajax came to the war, like yonder toil-worn drudges—no
but for the oath's sake that bound him—no whit for yours;
he was not in the habit of taking account of nobodies. So
when you come again bring more heralds, and the captain of
the host. At *your* noise I would not turn my head, while you
are the man you now are.

CHORUS. Such speech, again, in the midst of ills, I do not love;
for harsh words, however just, sting.

MENELAUS. The bowman, methinks, has no little pride.

TEUCER. Indeed; it is no sordid craft that I profess.

MENELAUS. How you would boast if you were given a shield!

TEUCER. Without a shield I am a match for you full-armed.

MENELAUS. How dreadful the courage that inspires your
tongue!

TEUCER. When right is with him man's spirit may be high.

MENELAUS. Is it right that this my murderer should have honor?

TEUCER. Murderer? A marvel truly, if though slain you are alive.

MENELAUS. A god rescued me; by his intention I am dead.

TEUCER. The gods have saved you; then do not dishonor the gods.

MENELAUS. What, would *I* disparage the laws of heaven?

TEUCER. If you are here to forbid the burying of the dead.

MENELAUS. Yes, of my country's enemies, for it is not proper.

TEUCER. Did Ajax ever confront you as a public enemy?

MENELAUS. There was hate between us; you too knew this.

TEUCER. Yes, it was found that you had suborned votes, to rob him.

MENELAUS. At the hands of the judges, not at mine, he had that fall.

TEUCER. You could put a fair face on many a furtive villainy.

MENELAUS. Your saying tends to pain—I know for whom.

TEUCER. No greater pain, I think, than we shall inflict.

MENELAUS. Hear my last word: that man must not be buried.

TEUCER. And hear my answer: he shall be buried forthwith.

MENELAUS. Once I saw a man bold of tongue who had urged sailors to a voyage in time of storm, but when the stress of the tempest was upon him you would have found no voice in him; hidden beneath his cloak he would suffer the crew to trample on him at will. And so with you and your fierce speech: perhaps a great tempest, though its breath come from a little cloud, shall quench your blustering.

TEUCER. Yes, and I have seen a man full of folly who triumphed in his neighbor's woes. And it came to pass that a man like me and of like mood saw him and spoke such words as these: "Man, do no evil to the dead, for if you do be sure that you will come to harm." So he warned the misguided man before him. Know that I see that man and think he is none else but you. Have I spoken in riddles?

MENELAUS. I will go. It would be a disgrace to have it known that I was chiding when I have the power to compel.

TEUCER. Begone then! For me it is the worse disgrace that I should listen to a fool's idle prate.

(*Exit* MENELAUS.)

CHORUS. A dread strife will be brought to the trial. But you, Teucer, with what you speed you can hasten to seek a hollow grave for yonder man, where he shall rest in the dark dank tomb which men shall ever hold in fame.

(*Enter* TECMESSA *and* CHILD.)

TEUCER. Look, just in time our lord's child and his wife draw near, to tend the burial of the hapless corpse.

My child, come here. Take your place near him and lay your hand, as a suppliant, upon your father. Kneel as one who implores help, with locks of hair in your hand—mine, hers, and thirdly yours—the suppliant's store. But if any man of the host should tear you by violence from this dead, then for evil doom on evil deed may he perish out of the land and find no grave, and with him be his race cut off, root and branch, even as I sever this lock. Take it, boy, and keep it; and let no one move you, but kneel there and cling to the dead.

And you, do not be like women at his side but behave like men for his defense, till I return, when I have prepared a grave for this man, though all the world forbid. (*Exit.*)

CHORUS. *When, ah when, will the number of the restless years be full, at what term will they cease, that bring on me the unending woe of a warrior's toils throughout the wide land of Troy, for the sorrow and the shame of Greece?*

Would that the man had passed into the depths of the sky or to all-receiving Hades who taught Greeks how to league themselves for war in hateful arms! Ah, those toils of his, from which so many toils have sprung! Yes, he it was who wrought the ruin of men.

No delight of garlands or bounteous winecups did that man give me for my portion, no sweet music of flutes, the wretch, or soothing rest in the night; and from love, alas, from love he has divorced my days.

And here I have my couch, uncared for, while heavy dews ever wet my hair, lest I should forget that I am in the cheerless land of Troy.

Heretofore bold Ajax was always my defense against nightly terror and the darts of the foe; but now he has become the sacrifice of a malignant fate. What joy, then, what joy shall crown me more?

O to be wafted where the wooded sea-cape stands upon the laving sea, O to pass beneath Sunium's level summit, that so we might greet sacred Athens!

(*Enter* TEUCER, *followed by* AGAMEMNON.)

TEUCER. Here I come in haste, for I saw the captain of the host, Agamemnon, quickly moving this way, and I know he will not bridle perverse lips.

AGAMEMNON. So it is you, they tell me, who have dared to open your mouth with such blustering against us—and have yet to smart for it? Yes, I mean you, the captive woman's son. Belike, had you been bred of well-born mother, your boast would have been lofty and your strut proud when, nought as you are you have stood up for him who is as nought and have vowed that we came out with no title on sea or land to rule the Greeks or you. No, as chief in his own right, you say, Ajax sailed forth.

Are not these presumptuous taunts for us to hear from slaves? What was the man whom you vaunt with such loud arrogance? Where did he go or where did he stand where I was not? Have the Greeks then no other men but him? Methinks we shall rue that day when we called the Greeks to contest the arms of Achilles if, whatever the issue, we are to be denounced as false by Teucer, and if you will never consent, though defeated, to accept the sentence for which most judges voted but must always assail us somewhere with revilings or stab us in the dark—you, the losers in the race.

Where such ways prevail no law could ever be firmly established, if we are to thrust the rightful winners aside and bring the rearmost to the front. No, this must be checked. It is not the burly broad-shouldered men that are surest at need; no, it is the wise who prevail in every field. A large-ribbed ox is yet kept straight on the road by a small whip. And this remedy, I think, will visit you before long if you fail to gain some measure of wisdom, you who, when the man is no longer alive but now a shade, are so boldly insolent and give such license to your tongue. Sober yourself, I say, recall your birth; bring someone else here, a freeborn man, who shall plead your cause for you before us. When you speak I can no more take your meaning; I do not understand your barbarian speech.

CHORUS. Would that you both could learn the wisdom of a temperate mind! No better counsel could I give you two.

TEUCER. Ah, gratitude to the dead—how quickly it falls away from men and is found a traitor if this man no longer has the slightest tribute of remembrance for you, Ajax—a man for whom you so often toiled, putting your own life to the peril of the spear! No, it is all forgotten, all flung aside!

Man, you who have just spoken many words and vain, have you no more memory of the time when you were shut within your lines, when you were like lost men in the turning back of your battle, and he alone came and saved you, when the flames were already wrapping the decks at your ships' sterns and Hector was bounding high over the trench toward the vessels? Who averted that? Were not these deeds his, who, you say, never set foot where you were not?

Would you allow that he did his duty there? Or when, another time, he confronted Hector in single fight all alone, not at any man's bidding but by right of ballot? For the lot he cast in was not one to skulk behind, no lump of moist earth but such as would be the first to leap lightly from the crested helmet. These deeds were his, and at his side was I—the slave, the son of the barbarian mother.

Wretch, how can you be so blind as to rail so? Do you not know that your father's father was Pelops of old—a barbarian, a Phrygian? That Atreus who begot you set before his brother a most impious feast, the flesh of that brother's children? And you yourself were born of a Cretan mother, with whom her father found a paramour and doomed her to be food for the dumb fishes? Being such, do you make his origin a reproach to such as I am? The father from whom I sprang is Telamon who, as prize for valor peerless in the host, won my mother for his bride. By birth she was a princess, daughter of Laomedon, and as the flower of the spoil she was given to Telamon by Alcmena's son.

Thus nobly born from two noble parents, could I disgrace my kinsman, whom, now that such sore ills have laid him low, you would thrust forth without burial—yes, and are not ashamed to say it? Now be sure of this—wheresoever you cast this man, with him you will cast forth our three corpses also. It befits me to die in his cause, before all men's eyes, rather than for your wife—or your brother's should I say? Be prudent, therefore, not for my sake but for yours also; for if you harm me you will soon wish that you had been a very coward before your rashness had been wreaked on me.

(*Enter* ODYSSEUS.)

CHORUS. King Odysseus, know that you have come in season, if you are here not to embroil but to mediate.

ODYSSEUS. What ails you friends? Far off I heard loud speech of the Atreidae over this brave man's corpse.

AGAMEMNON. But King Odysseus, have we not been just now hearing most shameful taunts from that man?

ODYSSEUS. How was that? I can pardon a man who is reviled if he engage in wordy war.

AGAMEMNON. I *had* reviled him, for his deeds toward me were vile.

ODYSSEUS. What did he do to you to give you an injury?

AGAMEMNON. He says that he will not leave yonder corpse ungraced by sepulture but will bury it in my despite.

ODYSSEUS. Now may a friend speak out the truth and still, as ever, ply his oar in time with yours?

AGAMEMNON. Speak, else I were less than sane; for I count you my greatest friend of all the Greeks.

ODYSSEUS. Listen, then. For the love of the gods, do not take heart to cast this man forth unburied so ruthlessly. Never let violence prevail with you to hate so utterly that you should trample justice underfoot.

　　To me this man was once the worst foe in the army, from the day that I became master of the arms of Achilles; but though he was so disposed toward me I would never requite him with indignity or refuse to admit that in all our Greek host which came to Troy I have seen none who was his peer save Achilles. It would not be just, then, that he should suffer dishonor at your hand; it is not he, it is the law of heaven that you would hurt. When a brave man is dead it is not right to do him injury—no, not even if you hate him.

AGAMEMNON. *You,* Odysseus, his champion against me?

ODYSSEUS. I am. I hated him when I could honorably hate.

AGAMEMNON. Should you not also set your heel on him in death?

ODYSSEUS. Do not delight in gains which sully honor, son of Atreus.

AGAMEMNON. It is not easy for a king to observe piety.

ODYSSEUS. But he can show respect to his friends when they counsel well.

AGAMEMNON. A loyal man should heed the rulers.

ODYSSEUS. Enough. The victory is yours when you yield to your friends.

AGAMEMNON. Remember to what a man you are showing grace.

ODYSSEUS. The man was once my foe, but noble.

AGAMEMNON. What can you mean? Such reverence for a dead foe?

ODYSSEUS. His worth weighs with me far more than his enmity.

AGAMEMNON. Such as you are the unstable among men.

ODYSSEUS. Full many are friends at one time, at another foes.

AGAMEMNON. Do you then approve of our making such friends?

ODYSSEUS. It is not my way to approve a stubborn soul.

AGAMEMNON. You will make us appear cowards this day.

ODYSSEUS. Not so, but just men in the sight of all the Greeks.

AGAMEMNON. So you would have me allow the burying of the dead?

ODYSSEUS. Yes; for I too shall come to that need.

AGAMEMNON. Truly, in all things alike each man works for himself!

ODYSSEUS. And for whom should I work rather than for myself?

AGAMEMNON. It must be called your doing, then, not mine.

ODYSSEUS. Call it whose you will, in any case you will be kind.

AGAMEMNON. Be well assured that I would grant *you* a larger boon than this. That man shall have my hatred, however, as on earth so in the shades. But you can do what you will. (*Exit.*)

CHORUS. Whoever says that you do not have inborn wisdom, Odysseus, being such as you are, that man is foolish.

ODYSSEUS. Yes, and I tell Teucer now that henceforth I am ready to be his friend, as staunch as I was once a foe. And I would join in the burying of your dead and partake of your cares, and omit no service which mortals should render to the noblest among men.

TEUCER. Noble Odysseus, I have only praise to give you for your words; you have greatly belied my fears. You were his deadliest foe of all the Greeks, yet you alone have stood by him with active aid. You have found no heart, in this presence, to heap the insults of the living on the dead—like yonder crazed chief that came, he and his brother, and would have cast forth the outraged corpse without burial. Therefore may the Father supreme in the heaven above us, and the remembering Fury, and Justice that brings the end, destroy those evil men with evil doom, even as they sought to cast forth this man with unmerited spite.

But, son of aged Laertes, I scruple to admit your helping hand in these funeral rites, lest so I do displeasure to the

dead; in all else be our fellow-worker. If you would bring
any man of the host we shall make you welcome. For the
rest, I will make all things ready. Know that to us you have
been a generous friend.

ODYSSEUS. It was my wish; but if it is not pleasing to you that
I should assist here I accept your decision and depart. (*Exit.*)

TEUCER. Enough; already the delay has been long drawn out.
Come, hasten some of you to dig the hollow grave; some
place the high-set caldron girt with fire in readiness for holy
ablution; and let another band bring the body-armor from
the tent.

And you too, child, with such strength as you have lay a
loving hand upon your father and help me to uplift this prostrate form, for still the warm channels are spouting upward
their dark tide.

Come, each one here who owns the name of friend, hasten, away, in service to this man of perfect prowess. Never
yet was service rendered to a nobler among men.

CHORUS. *Many things shall mortals learn by seeing; but before he sees no man may read the future or his fate.*

ELECTRA

AS COMPARED WITH THE MORAL EARNESTNESS OF
Aeschylus' *Choephoroi* and the social criticism of Euripides'
Electra, both of which cover the same ground, Sophocles'
Electra is better entertainment, but on a more theatrical level.
The play is rich in intrigue and in the rhetoric of passion, but
moral questions seem to be avoided. Orestes has asked the oracle not *whether* he should kill his mother but *how* he can do so.
And when he has committed the murder, instead of emerging
distraught, as he does in Aeschylus, or repentant, as in Euripides, he says, in a calm iambic line, "All in the house is well."
Electra herself is the usual oversized and passionate central figure of Sophoclean tragedy, but she has little function except to
lament, which she does, as Chrysothemis and the chorus say,
beyond measure. There is a stirring account of a chariot race,
but there was no chariot race. There is a tearful lament over the
ashes of Orestes, which cannot be taken as other than a display
piece because Orestes himself is standing by. Aegisthus gloats
over a covered body, which a moment's reflection would suggest could not be Orestes (only ashes, not a whole body, would
be carried across Greece), and finds it is Clytemnestra. The
cruel repartee before Aegisthus uncovers the body is little short
of ghoulish. A play which represents a man killing his own
mother and her husband starts with the cheerful singing of birds
and ends with congratulations on a good day's work. Because
Electra has so large a part it has been suggested that the role was
purposely designed for a particular virtuoso in emotional display. When Polus played the part, at the end of the fourth cen-
tury B.C., he carried the ashes of his own lately deceased son in
the urn to give his lamentations authenticity. The role has been

a favorite with modern actresses whose forte is emotional display. In the end Electra attains her goal without suffering catastrophe; our play is then rather like the *Philoctetes* than those plays in which heroism is sealed by personal destruction. But suffering, resentment, and eventual justification are also legitimate themes for drama. As in the case of Philoctetes, it is not what Electra does but what she is that makes her an absorbing and illuminating figure.

PERSONS

ORESTES, *son of Agamemnon*
    and Clytemnestra
TUTOR, *of Orestes*
ELECTRA
CHRYSOTHEMIS } *sisters of Orestes*

CLYTEMNESTRA
AEGISTHUS
PYLADES, *friend of Orestes*
    (*mute*)
CHORUS OF WOMEN OF
    MYCENAE

SCENE: *Before the palace at Mycenae.*

(*Enter* TUTOR *with* ORESTES *and* PYLADES.)

TUTOR. Son of Agamemnon who led our hosts at Troy long ago, now you can see with your own eyes all that your soul has so long desired. There is the ancient Argos of your yearning, that hallowed scene from which the gadfly drove the daughter of Inachus; and there, Orestes, is the Lycean Agora, named from the wolf-slaying god; there, on the left, Hera's famous temple; and in this place to which we have come know that you see Mycenae rich in gold, with the house of the Pelopidae, so often stained with bloodshed. It was from there that I carried you long ago from the slaying of your father, as your sister charged me to do; I saved you and reared you up to manhood, to be the avenger of your murdered sire.

Therefore, Orestes, and you Pylades, best of friends, our plans must be laid quickly. For already the sun's bright ray is waking the songs of the birds into clearness and the dark night of stars is spent. Before anyone comes forth from the house, then, take counsel; time does not allow of delay but is full ripe for deeds.

ORESTES. True friend and follower, how well you prove your
loyalty to our house! As a steed of generous race, though old,
does not lose courage in danger but pricks his ear, even so
you urge us forward and are foremost in our support. I will
tell you, then, what I have determined; listen closely to my
words and correct me if I miss the mark in any particular.

When I went to the Pythian oracle to learn how I might
avenge my father on his murderers, Phoebus gave me the response which you are now to hear: that alone and by stealth,
without aid of arms or numbers, I should snatch the righteous vengeance of my hand. Since, then, the god spoke to
us on this wise, you must go into yonder house when opportunity gives you entrance, and learn all that is passing
there, so that you may report to us from sure knowledge.
Your age and the lapse of time will prevent them from rec-
ognizing you; with that silvered hair they will never suspect
who you are. Let your tale be that you are a Phocian stranger
sent by Phanoteus; he is the greatest of their allies. Tell
them, and confirm it with your oath, that Orestes has perished by a fatal accident, hurled from his rapid chariot at the
Pythian games; let that be the substance of your story.

Meanwhile we will first crown my father's tomb, as the
god enjoined, with drink-offerings and the luxuriant tribute
of severed hair. Then we shall come back bearing in our
hands an urn of shapely bronze—now hidden in the brush-
wood, as I think you know—so to gladden them with the
false tidings that this my body is no more but has been consumed with fire and turned to ashes. Why should the omen
trouble me when by a feigned death I find life indeed and
win renown? No word is ill-omened, I avow, if fraught with
gain. Often before now I have seen wise men die in vain report; then when they return home they are held in more
abiding honor. So I trust that from this rumor I also shall
emerge in radiant life and yet shine like a star upon my foes.

O my fatherland and you gods of the land, receive me
with good fortune in this journey—and you also, halls of
my fathers, for I come with a divine mandate to cleanse you
righteously. Do not send me from the land dishonored but

grant that I may rule over my possessions and restore my house!

Enough; let it be your care now, old man, to go and heed your task. We two will go forth, for so bids opportunity, chief ruler of every enterprise for men.

ELECTRA (*within*). Ah me, ah me!

TUTOR. Hark, my son! From the doors, methought, came the sound of some handmaid moaning within.

ORESTES. Can it be the hapless Electra? Shall we stay here and listen to her laments?

TUTOR. No, no; before all else let us seek to obey the command of Loxias and make a fair beginning by pouring libations to your sire. That brings victory within our grasp and gives us the mastery in all that we do.

(*Exeunt severally* TUTOR, *and* ORESTES *and* PYLADES; *enter* ELECTRA.)

ELECTRA. *O pure sunlight, O air, earth's canopy, how often have you heard the strains of my lament, the wild blows dealt against this bleeding breast, when dark night fails! My wretched couch in yonder house of woe knows well and of old how I keep the watches of the night, how often I bewail my hapless sire. Him deadly Ares gave not of his gifts in a strange land, but my mother and her mate Aegisthus cleft his head with murderous ax as woodmen fell an oak. And for this no plaint bursts from any lip save mine, when you, my father, have died a death so cruel and so piteous!*

But never will I cease from dirge and sore lament while I look on the trembling rays of the bright stars or on this light of day; but like the nightingale, slayer of her offspring, I will wail without ceasing and cry aloud to all, here, at the doors of my father.

O home of Hades and Persephone! O Hermes of the shades! O potent Curse, and you, dread daughters of the gods, Erinyes, you who behold when a life is reft by violence, when a bed is dishonored by stealth—come, help me, avenge the murder of my father and send to me my brother.

No more have I the strength to bear up alone against the load of grief that weighs me down.

CHORUS *(enters). Ah Electra, child of a wretched mother, why are you ever pining thus in ceaseless lament for Agamemnon, who long ago was wickedly ensnared by your false mother's wiles and betrayed to death by a dastardly hand? Perish the author of that deed, if I may utter such a prayer!*

ELECTRA. *Ah, noblehearted maidens, you have come to soothe my woes. I know and feel it; it escapes me not; but I cannot leave this task undone or cease from mourning for my hapless sire. Ah, friends whose love responds to mine in every mood, leave me to rave thus—oh leave me, I entreat you!*

CHORUS. *But never by laments or prayers shall you recall your father from that lake of Hades to which all must pass. No, yours is a fatal course of grief, passing ever from due bounds into a cureless sorrow. Therein is there no deliverance from evils. Say, why are you enamored of misery?*

ELECTRA. *Foolish is the child who forgets a parent's piteous death. No, dearer to my soul is the mourner that laments for Itys, Itys, evermore, that bird distraught with grief, the messenger of Zeus. Ah, queen of sorrow, Niobe, you I deem divine, you who weep evermore in your rocky tomb!*

CHORUS. *Not to you alone of mortals, my daughter, has come sorrow. You bear it less calmly than those within, your kinswomen and sisters, Chrysothemis and Iphianassa, who still live. So does he too live, sorrowing in a secluded youth, yet happy in that this famous realm of Mycenae shall one day welcome him to his heritage, when the kindly guidance of Zeus shall have brought him to this land—Orestes.*

ELECTRA. *Yes, I wait for him with unwearied longing as I move on my sad path from day to day, unwed and childless, bathed in tears, bearing that endless doom of woe; but he forgets all that he has suffered and heard. What message has come to me that is not belied? He is ever yearning to be with us, but though he yearns he never resolves.*

CHORUS. *Courage, my daughter, courage. Great still in heaven is Zeus who sees and governs all; leave your bitter quarrel to him. Do not forget your woes, but refrain from excess of wrath against them, for Time is a god who makes rough ways smooth. Not heedless is the son of Agamemnon who dwells by Crisa's pastoral shore; not heedless is the god who reigns by Acheron.*

ELECTRA. *Nay, the best part of life has passed away from me in hopelessness and I have no strength left. I am pining away without children and no loving champion shields me. Like some despised alien I serve in the halls of my father, clad in this mean garb and standing at a meager board.*

CHORUS. *Piteous was the voice heard at his return, and piteous, as your father lay on the festal couch, when the straight swift blow was dealt him with the blade of bronze. Guile was the plotter, Lust the slayer, dread parents of a dreadful shape; whether it was mortal that wrought therein or god.*

ELECTRA. *O that bitter day, bitter beyond all that have come to me! O that night, O the horrors of that unutterable feast, the ruthless death-strokes that my father saw from the hands of two! They took my life captive by treachery, they doomed me to woe! May the great god of Olympus give them sufferings in requital, never may their splendor bring them joy who have done such deeds!*

CHORUS. *Be advised to say no more; can you not see what conduct it is which already plunges you so cruelly in self-made miseries? You have greatly aggravated your troubles, always breeding wars with your sullen soul. Such strife should not be pushed to a conflict with the strong.*

ELECTRA. *I have been forced to it, forced by dread causes. I know my own passion, it does not escape me; but seeing that the causes are so dire I will never curb these frenzied plaints while life is in me. Who indeed, kindly sisterhood, who that thinks aright would deem that any word of solace could avail me? Forbear, forbear, my comforters! Such ills must be numbered with those which have no cure; I can never know a respite from my sorrows or a limit to this wailing.*

CHORUS. *At least it is in love, like a true-hearted mother, that I dissuade you from adding misery to miseries.*

ELECTRA. *But what is there in my wretchedness? Say, how can*

*it be right to neglect the dead? Was that impiety ever born in
mortal? Never may I have praise of such; never, when my lot
is cast in pleasant places, may I cling to selfish ease or dishonor my sire by restraining the wings of shrill lamentation!*

*If the hapless dead is to lie in dust and nothingness while
the slayers pay not with blood for blood, all regard for man,
all fear of heaven, will vanish from the earth.*

CHORUS. I came, my child, in zeal for your welfare no less than
for my own; but if I do not speak well then be it as you will,
for we will follow you.

ELECTRA. I am ashamed, my friends, if you consider me too
impatient for my frequent complaining; but since a hard constraint forces me to this, bear with me. How indeed could
any woman of noble nature refrain if she saw the calamities
of a father's house as I see them continually by day and by
night, not fading but in the summer of their strength? First I
have found bitter enmity from the mother that bore me; next,
in my own home I dwell with my father's murderers; they
rule over me and with them it rests to give or withhold what
I need.

And then think what manner of days I pass when I see
Aegisthus sitting on my father's throne, wearing the robes
which he wore, and pouring libations at the hearth where he
slew my sire; and when I see the outrage that crowns all, the
murderer in our father's bed at our wretched mother's side,
if mother she should be called who is his wife. But so hardened is she that she lives with that accursed one fearing no
Erinys; nay, as if exulting in her deeds, having found the day
on which she treacherously slew my father of old she keeps
it with dance and song, and month by month sacrifices
sheep to the gods who have wrought her deliverance.

But when I behold it, in my wretchedness, I weep and
pine in the house and bewail the unholy feast named after
my sire, weep to myself alone, since I may not even indulge
my grief to the full measure of my yearning. For this
woman, in profession so noble, loudly upbraids me with
such taunts as these: "Impious and hateful girl, have you
alone lost a father and is there no other mourner in the

world? An evil doom be yours, and may the gods infernal give you no riddance from your present laments."

So she insults, save when anyone brings her word that Orestes is coming. Then infuriated she comes up to me and cries: "Have not *you* brought this upon me? Is not this deed yours who stole Orestes from my hands and secretly conveyed him away? Yet be sure that you shall have your due reward." So she shrieks, and in her support the renowned spouse at her side is vehement in the same strain—that abject dastard, that utter pest, who fights his battles with the help of women. But I, looking ever for Orestes to come and end these woes, languish in my misery. Always intending to strike a blow, he has worn out every hope that I could conceive. In such a case then, friends, there is no room for moderation or for reverence; truly, the stress of ills leaves no choice but to follow evil ways.

CHORUS. Say, is Aegisthus near while you are speaking thus or is he absent from home?

ELECTRA. Absent, certainly. Do not think that I should have come to the doors if he had been near. Just now he is afield.

CHORUS. Might I converse with you more freely if this is so?

ELECTRA. He is not here, so put your question. What do you wish?

CHORUS. I ask you, then, what you say of your brother? Will he come soon or is he delaying? I would like to know.

ELECTRA. He promises to come, but he never fulfills the promise.

CHORUS. Yes, a man will pause on the verge of a great work.

ELECTRA. And yet I saved *him* without pausing.

CHORUS. Courage; he is too noble to fail his friends.

ELECTRA. I believe it, or I should not have lived so long.

CHORUS. Say no more now. I see your sister coming from the house, Chrysothemis, daughter of the same father and mother, with sepulchral gifts in her hands such as are given to those in the world below.

CHRYSOTHEMIS (*enters*). Why, sister, have you come forth once more to declaim in this way at the public doors? Why will you not learn with lapse of time to desist from vain indulgence of idle wrath? Yet this I know: I myself am grieved at our plight; indeed, if I could find the strength I would show what love I bear them. But now, in these troubled waters, it is best, I think, to shorten sail; I do not care to seem active without the power to hurt. Would that your own conduct were the same! Nevertheless, right is on the side of your choice, not of that which I advise; but if I am to live in freedom our rulers must be obeyed in all things.

ELECTRA. Strange indeed that you, the daughter of such a father as yours, should forget him and think only of your mother! All your admonitions to me have been taught by her; no word is your own. Then take your choice—to be imprudent, or prudent and forgetful of your friends. You have just said that if you could find the strength you would show your hatred of them; yet when I am doing my utmost to avenge my father you give no help but seek to turn your sister from her deed.

Does this not crown our miseries with cowardice? For tell me—or let me tell you—what I should gain by ceasing from these laments? Do I not live?—miserably, I know, yet well enough for me. And I vex *them,* thus rendering honor to the dead, if pleasure can be felt in that world. But you who tell me of your hatred hate in word alone while in deed you are with the slayers of your father. I would never yield to them though I were promised the gifts which now make you proud; be yours the richly-spread table and the life of luxury. For me be it food enough that I do not wound my own conscience; I do not covet such privilege as yours—nor would you if you were wise. But now, when you might be called daughter of the noblest father among men, be called child of your mother; so shall your baseness be most widely seen, in betrayal of your dead father and of your kindred.

CHORUS. No angry word, I beg! For both of you there is good in what is urged—if you, Electra, would learn to profit by her counsel, and she, again, by yours.

CHRYSOTHEMIS. For my part, friends, I am not wholly unused to her discourse; nor should I have touched upon this theme had I not heard that she was threatened with a dread doom which shall restrain her from her long-drawn laments.

ELECTRA. Come, declare it then, this terror! If you can tell me of anything worse than my present lot I will resist no more.

CHRYSOTHEMIS. Indeed I will tell you all that I know. They propose, if you will not cease from these laments, to send you where you shall never look upon the sunlight but pass your days in a dungeon beyond the borders of this land, there to chant your dreary strain. Consider you, then, and do not blame me hereafter when the blow has fallen; now is the time to be wise.

ELECTRA. Have they indeed resolved to treat me so?

CHRYSOTHEMIS. Assuredly, whenever Aegisthus comes home.

ELECTRA. If that is all then may he arrive with speed!

CHRYSOTHEMIS. Misguided one! What dire prayer is this?

ELECTRA. That he may come, if he has any such intent.

CHRYSOTHEMIS. That you may suffer—what? Where are your wits?

ELECTRA. That I may fly as far as may be from you all.

CHRYSOTHEMIS. But have you no care for your present life?

ELECTRA. Aye, my life is marvelously fair.

CHRYSOTHEMIS. It might be if you could only learn prudence.

ELECTRA. Do not teach me to betray my friends.

CHRYSOTHEMIS. I do not—but to bend before the strong.

ELECTRA. Yours be such flattery; those are not my ways.

CHRYSOTHEMIS. It is well, however, not to fall by folly.

ELECTRA. I will fall, if need be, in the cause of my father.

CHRYSOTHEMIS. But our father, I know, pardons me for this.

ELECTRA. It is for cowards to find peace in such maxims.

CHRYSOTHEMIS. So you will not hearken and take my counsel?

ELECTRA. No, surely; may it be long before I am so foolish.

CHRYSOTHEMIS. Then I will go forth upon my errand.

ELECTRA. Where are you going? To whom do you bear these offerings?

CHRYSOTHEMIS. Our mother sends me with funeral libations for our father.

ELECTRA. How do you say? For her deadliest foe?

CHRYSOTHEMIS. Slain by her own hand—so you would say.

ELECTRA. What friend has persuaded her? Whose wish was this?

CHRYSOTHEMIS. The cause, I think, was some dread vision of the night.

ELECTRA. Gods of our house! Be with me now, at last!

CHRYSOTHEMIS. Do you find any encouragement in this terror?

ELECTRA. If you would tell me the vision then I could answer.

CHRYSOTHEMIS. I can tell but little of the story.

ELECTRA. Tell what you can; a little word has often marred or made men's fortunes.

CHRYSOTHEMIS. It is said that she beheld our sire, restored to sunlight, at her side once more. Then he took the scepter, once his own but now borne by Aegisthus, and planted it at the hearth; from it a fruitful bough sprang upward by which the whole land of Mycenae was overshadowed. Such is the tale that I heard told by one who was present when she declared her dream to the Sun-god. More than this I do not know, save that she sent me by reason of that fear. So by the gods of our house I beseech you, hearken to me, and do not be ruined by folly! For if you repel me now you will come back to seek me in your trouble.

ELECTRA. No, dear sister, let none of these things in your hands touch the tomb; neither custom nor piety allows you to dedicate gifts or bring libations to our father from a hateful wife. No, to the winds with them! Or bury them deep in the earth where none of them shall ever come near his place of rest; but when she dies let her find these treasures laid up for her below.

Were she not the most hardened of women she would never have sought to pour these offerings of enmity on the grave of him whom she slew. Think now if it is likely that the dead in the tomb should take these honors kindly at her hand who ruthlessly slew like a foeman and mangled him and for ablution wiped off the bloodstains on his head? Can you believe that these things which you bring will absolve her of the murder?

It is not possible. No, cast these things aside; give him rather a lock cut from your own tresses, and on my part, hapless that I am—scant gifts these but my best—this hair, not glossy with unguents, and this girdle, decked with no rich ornament. Then fall down and pray that he himself may come in kindness from the world below to aid us against our foes, and that Orestes may live to set his foot upon his foes in victorious might, that henceforth we may crown our father's tomb with wealthier hands than those which grace it now.

I think, indeed, I think that he also had some part in sending her these appalling dreams. Still, sister, do this service, to help yourself, and me, and him, that most beloved of all men, who rests in the realm of Hades, your father and mine.

CHORUS. The maiden counsels piously; and you, friend, will do her bidding if you are wise.

CHRYSOTHEMIS. I will. When a duty is clear reason forbids that two voices should contend and claims the hastening of the deed. Only when I attempt this task aid me with your silence, I entreat you, my friends. If my mother should hear of it I think I shall yet have cause to rue my venture. (*Exit.*)

CHORUS. *If I am not an erring seer and one who fails in wisdom, Justice that has sent the presage will come triumphant in her righteous strength, will come ere long, my child, to avenge. There is courage in my heart, through those new tidings of the dream that breathes comfort. Not forgetful is your sire, the lord of Hellas; not forgetful is the two-edged ax of bronze that struck the blow of old and slew him with foul cruelty.*

The Erinys of untiring feet who is lurking in her dread ambush will come, as with the march and with the might of a great host. For wicked ones have been fired with passion that hurried them to a forbidden bed, to accursed bridals, to a marriage stained with guilt of blood. Therefore am I sure that the portent will not fail to bring woe upon the partners in crime. Verily mortals cannot read the future in fearful dreams or oracles if this vision of the night find not due fulfillment.

O chariot-race of Pelops long ago, source of many a sorrow, what weary troubles have you brought upon this land!

For since Myrtilus sank to rest beneath the waves, when a fatal and cruel hand hurled him to destruction out of the golden car, this house was never yet free from misery and violence.

CLYTEMNESTRA (*enters*). At large once more you range, it seems, for Aegisthus is not here. He always kept you at least from passing the gates, to shame your friends. But now since he is absent you take no heed of me, though you have said of me often and to many that I am a bold and lawless tyrant who insults you and yours. I am guilty of no insolence; I only return the taunts that I often hear from you.

Your father—this is your constant pretext—was slain by me. Yes, by me—I know it well; it admits of no denial. For Justice slew him and not I alone, Justice whom it was your part to support if you had been right-minded. This father of yours whom you are ever lamenting was the one man of the Greeks who had the heart to sacrifice your sister to the gods—he the father, who had not shared the mother's pangs.

Come, tell me now, why did he sacrifice her or to please whom? To please the Argives, you will say? But they had no right to slay my daughter. Or if it was to screen his brother Menelaus, forsooth, that he slew my child, was he not to pay me the penalty for that? Did not Menelaus have two children who should in fairness have been taken before my daughter, as sprung from the father and mother who had caused that voyage? Or had Hades some strange desire to feast on my offspring rather than on hers? Or had that accursed father lost all tenderness for the children of my womb, while he was tender to the children of Menelaus? Was not that the part of a callous and perverse parent? I think so, though I differ from your judgment; and so would the dead child say if she could speak. For myself, then, I view the past without dismay; but if you deem me perverse, see that your own judgment is just before you blame your neighbor.

ELECTRA. This time you cannot say that I have done anything to provoke such words from you. But if you will give me

leave I would like to declare the truth, in the cause of both
my dead father and of my sister.

CLYTEMNESTRA. Indeed you have my leave. If you always addressed me in such a tone you would be heard without pain.

ELECTRA. Then I will speak. You say that you have slain my
father. What word could bring you deeper shame than that,
whether the deed was just or not? But I must tell you that
your deed was not just; no, you were drawn on to it by the
wooing of the base man who is now your spouse.

Ask the huntress Artemis what sin she punished when
she stayed the frequent winds at Aulis; or I will tell you, for
we may not learn from her. My father—so I have heard—
was once disporting himself in the grove of the goddess
when his footfall startled a dappled and antlered stag. He
shot it, and happened to utter a certain boast concerning its
slaughter. Angry at that, the daughter of Leto detained the
Greeks so that, in quittance for the wild creature's life, my
father should yield up the life of his own child. Thus it befell that she was sacrificed, since the fleet had no other release, homeward or to Troy. For that cause, under sore
constraint and with sore reluctance, at last he slew her—not
for the sake of Menelaus.

But grant—for I will take your own plea—grant that the
motive of his deed was to benefit his brother: was that a reason for his dying by your hand? Under what law? See that in
making such a law for men you do not make trouble and remorse for yourself. If we are to take blood for blood you
would be the first to die if you meet with your desert.

But see if your pretext is not false. Tell me, if you will,
why you are now doing the most shameless deeds of all, living as wife with that blood-guilty man who first helped you
slay my father and bearing children to him, while you have
cast out the earlier-born, the stainless offspring of a stainless marriage. How can I praise these things? Or will you
say that this too is your vengeance for your daughter? Nay,
a shameful plea if so you plead; it is not well to wed an enemy for a daughter's sake.

But indeed I may not even counsel you—who shriek that

I revile my mother. Truly I think that you are less a mother to me than a mistress, so wretched is the life I live, always beset with miseries by you and by your partner. And that other who scarcely escaped your hand, the hapless Orestes, is wearing his ill-starred days out in exile. Often you have charged me with rearing him to punish your crime. I would have done so if I could, you may be sure. For that matter denounce me to all as disloyal, if you will, or petulant, or impudent; for if I am accomplished in such ways I think I am no unworthy child of yours.

CHORUS. I see that she breathes forth anger; but whether justice be with her, for this she seems to care no longer.

CLYTEMNESTRA. And what manner of care do I need to use against her who has thus insulted a mother, and this at her ripe age? Do you not think that she would go forward to any deed without shame?

ELECTRA. Now be assured that I do feel shame for this, though you do not believe it. I know that my behavior is unseemly and becomes me ill. But then the enmity on your part and your treatment compel me to act so in my own despite. Base deeds are taught by base.

CLYTEMNESTRA. You brazen one! Truly I and my sayings and my deeds give you too much matter for words.

ELECTRA. The words are yours, not mine; for yours is the action, and the acts find utterance.

CLYTEMNESTRA. Now by our lady Artemis, you shall not fail to pay for this boldness, as soon as Aegisthus returns.

ELECTRA. Look, you are transported by anger, after granting me free speech, and have no patience to listen.

CLYTEMNESTRA. Now will you not hush your clamor or even suffer me to sacrifice when I have permitted *you* to speak unchecked?

ELECTRA. I am not hindering; pray begin your rites. Do not blame my voice, for I shall say no more.

CLYTEMNESTRA. Then raise the offerings of many fruits, my handmaid, that I may uplift my prayers to this our king for deliverance from my present fears. Lend now a gracious ear,

O Phoebus our defender, to my words though they be dark; for I am not speaking among friends. It is not meet to unfold my whole thought to the light while *she* stands near me, lest with her malice and her garrulous cry she spread some rash rumor throughout the town; hear me thus since on this wise I must speak.

That vision which I saw last night in doubtful dreams— if it has come for good grant, Lycean King, that it be fulfilled; but if for harm, then let it recoil upon my foes. And if any are plotting to hurl me by treachery from the high estate which now is mine, permit them not; rather vouchsafe that still living thus unscathed I may bear sway over the house of the Atreidae and this realm, sharing my prosperous days with the friends who share them now and with those of my children from whom no enmity or bitterness pursues me.

O Lycean Apollo, graciously hear these prayers and grant them to us all, even as we ask! For the rest, though I be silent I deem that thou a god must know it; all things surely, are seen by the sons of Zeus.

TUTOR (*enters*). Ladies, might a stranger crave to know if this be the palace of the king Aegisthus?

CHORUS. It is, sir; you yourself have guessed aright.

TUTOR. And am I right in assuming that this lady is his consort? She is of queenly aspect.

CHORUS. Assuredly; you are in the presence of the queen.

TUTOR. Hail, royal lady! I bring glad tidings to you and to Aegisthus from a friend.

CLYTEMNESTRA. I welcome the omen; but first I would like to know from you who may have sent you.

TUTOR. Phanoteus the Phocian, on a weighty matter.

CLYTEMNESTRA. What is it, sir? Tell me; coming from a friend you will bring, I know, a kindly message.

TUTOR. Orestes is dead; that is the sum.

ELECTRA. O miserable that I am! I am lost this day!

CLYTEMNESTRA. What do you say, friend, what do you say? Do not listen to her.

TUTOR. I said and say again: Orestes is dead.

ELECTRA. I am lost, hapless one, I am undone!

CLYTEMNESTRA (*to* ELECTRA). Look to your own concerns. But you, sir, tell me exactly—how did he perish?

TUTOR. I was sent for that purpose and will tell you all. Having gone to the renowned festival, the pride of Greece, for the Delphian games, when he heard the loud summons to the footrace which was first to be decided he entered the lists, a brilliant form, a wonder in the eyes of all there; and having finished his course at the point where it began he went out with the glorious meed of victory. To speak briefly where there is much to tell, I do not know the man whose deeds and triumphs have matched his. But one thing you must know: in all the contests that the judges announced he bore away the prize, and men deemed him happy as often as the herald proclaimed him an Argive, by name Orestes, son of Agamemnon who once gathered the famous armament of Greece.

Thus far it was well; but when a god sends harm not even the strong man can escape. For on another day, when chariots were to try their speed at sunrise, he entered, along with many charioteers. One was an Achaean, one from Sparta, two masters of yoked cars were Libyans; Orestes driving Thessalian mares came fifth among them; the sixth from Aetolia, with chestnut colts; a Magnesian was the seventh; the eighth, with white horses, was of Aenian stock; the ninth from Athens, built by the gods; there was a Boeotian too, making the tenth chariot.

They took their stations where the appointed umpire placed them by lot and ranged the cars; then at the sound of the brazen trumpet they started. All shouted to their horses and shook the reins in their hands; the whole course was filled with the noise of rattling chariots; the dust flew upward. All in a confused throng plied their goads unsparingly, each of them striving to pass the wheels and the snorting steeds of his rivals. Alike at their backs and at their rolling wheels the breath of the horses foamed and smote.

Orestes, driving close to the pillar at either end of the

course, almost grazed it with his wheel each time; giving rein to the trace-horse on the right, he checked the horse on the inner side. Hitherto all the chariots had escaped overthrow; but presently the Aenian's hard-mouthed colts ran away; swerving as they passed from the sixth into the seventh round, they dashed their foreheads against the team of the Barcaean. Other mishaps followed the first, shock on shock and crash on crash, till the whole raceground of Crisa was strewn with the wreck of the chariots.

Seeing this the wary charioteer from Athens drew aside and paused, allowing the billow of chariots surging in midcourse to go by. Orestes was driving last, keeping his horses behind, for his trust was in the end. But when he saw that the Athenian was alone left in, he sent a shrill cry ringing through the ears of his swift colts and gave chase. Team was brought level with team, and so they raced, first one man and then the other showing his head in front of the chariots.

Hitherto the ill-fated Orestes had passed safely through every round, steadfast in his steadfast car; at last, slackening his left rein while the horse was turning, unawares he struck the edge of the pillar. He broke the axle-box in two; he was thrown over the chariot-rail; he was caught in the shapely reins; and as he fell to the ground his colts were scattered into the middle of the course.

But when the people saw him fallen from the car a cry of pity went up for the youth who had done such deeds and was meeting such a doom—now dashed to earth, now tossed feet uppermost to the sky—till the charioteers, with difficulty checking the career of his horses, loosed him, so covered with blood that no friend who saw it would have known the hapless corpse. Straightway they burned it on a pyre; and chosen men of Phocis are bringing in a small urn of bronze the dust of that mighty form, to find due burial in his fatherland.

Such is my story, grievous to hear if words can grieve. For us who saw it was the greatest of sorrows that these eyes have seen.

CHORUS. Alas, alas! Now, it seems, the stock of our ancient masters has utterly perished, root and branch.

CLYTEMNESTRA. O Zeus, what shall I call these tidings—glad tidings? Or dire but gainful? It is a bitter lot when my own calamities make the safety of my life.

TUTOR. Why are you so downcast at this news, lady?

CLYTEMNESTRA. There is a strange power in motherhood; a mother may be wronged but she never learns to hate her child.

TUTOR. Then it seems that we have come in vain.

CLYTEMNESTRA. No, not in vain; how can you say "in vain" when you have brought me sure proofs of his death? He sprang from my own life, yet forsaking me who had suckled and reared him he became an exile and an alien. And after he went out of this land he saw me no more; but charging me with the murder of his father he uttered dread threats against me, so that neither by night nor by day could sweet sleep cover my eyes, but from moment to moment I lived in fear of death. Now, however—since this day I am rid of terror from him, and from this girl, that worse plague who shared my home while she still drained my very lifeblood—now, I think, for aught that she can threaten I shall pass my days in peace.

ELECTRA. Ah, woe is me! Now indeed, Orestes, your fortune may be lamented when it is thus with you and you are mocked by this your mother! Is it not well?

CLYTEMNESTRA. Not with you; but his state is well.

ELECTRA. Hear, Nemesis of him who has lately died!

CLYTEMNESTRA. She has heard who should be heard and has ordained well.

ELECTRA. Insult us, for this is the time of your triumph.

CLYTEMNESTRA. Then will not Orestes and you silence me?

ELECTRA. We are silenced, much less should we silence you.

CLYTEMNESTRA. Your coming, sir, would deserve large recompense if you had hushed her clamorous tongue.

TUTOR. Then I may take my leave if all is well.

CLYTEMNESTRA. Not so; your welcome would then be unworthy of me and of the ally who sent you. But come you in, and leave her outside to make loud lament for herself and her friends.

(*Exeunt* CLYTEMNESTRA *and* TUTOR.)

ELECTRA. What do you think? Was there not grief and anguish there, wonderful weeping and wailing of that miserable mother for the son who perished by such a fate? No, she left us with a laugh! Ah, woe is me! Dearest Orestes, how is my life quenched by your death! You have torn away with you from my heart the only hopes which still might be mine—that you would live to return some day, an avenger of your father, and of unhappy me. But now, where shall I turn? I am alone, bereft of you as of my father.

　　Henceforth I must be a slave again among those whom I most hate, my father's murderers. Is it not well with me? But at least never henceforward will I enter the house to dwell with them. No; at these gates I will lay me down, and here, without a friend, my days shall wither. Therefore if any in the house are angry let them slay me. It is a grace if I die, but if I live a pain. I desire life no more.

CHORUS. *Where are the thunderbolts of Zeus, or where is the bright Sun if they look not upon these things and rest without branding them?*

ELECTRA. *Woe, woe, ah me, ah me!*

CHORUS. *Daughter, why are you weeping?*

ELECTRA. *Alas!*

CHORUS. *Utter no rash cry!*

ELECTRA. *You will break my heart!*

CHORUS. *How do you mean?*

ELECTRA. *If you suggest a hope concerning those who have surely passed to the realm below you will trample my misery yet more.*

CHORUS. *I know how the prince Amphiaraus, ensnared by a woman for a chain of gold, found a grave; and now beneath the earth—*

ELECTRA. *Ah me, ah me!*

CHORUS. *—he reigns in fullness of force.*

ELECTRA. *Alas!*

CHORUS. *Alas indeed for the murderess—*

ELECTRA. *Was slain.*

CHORUS. *Yes.*

ELECTRA. *I know it, I know it; for a champion arose to avenge the mourning dead. But to me no champion remains, for he who yet was left has been snatched away.*

CHORUS. *Hapless are you and hapless is your lot!*

ELECTRA. *Well do I know that, too well, I whose life is a torrent of woes dread and dark, a torrent that surges through all the months.*

CHORUS. *We have seen the course of your sorrow.*

ELECTRA. *Cease then to divert me from it when no more—*

CHORUS. *How do you say?*

ELECTRA. *—when no more can I have the comfort of hope from a brother, the seed of the same noble sire.*

CHORUS. *For all men it is appointed to die.*

ELECTRA. *What, to die as that ill-starred one died, amid the tramp of racing steeds, entangled in the reins that dragged him?*

CHORUS. *Cruel was his doom, beyond thought!*

ELECTRA. *Yes, surely; when in foreign soil, without ministry of my hands—*

CHORUS. *Alas!*

ELECTRA. *—he is buried, ungraced by me with sepulture or with tears.*

CHRYSOTHEMIS (*enters*). Joy wings my feet, dear sister, not careful of seemliness if I come with speed; for I bring joyful news to relieve your long sufferings and sorrows.

ELECTRA. And whence could *you* find help for my woes, for which no cure can be imagined?

CHRYSOTHEMIS. Orestes is with us—know this from my lips—in living presence, as surely as you see me here.

ELECTRA. What, are you mad, poor girl? Are you laughing at my sorrows and your own?

CHRYSOTHEMIS. No, by our father's hearth, I do not speak in mockery. I tell you that he is with us indeed.

ELECTRA. Ah, woe is me! From whom have you heard this tale which you believe so lightly?

CHRYSOTHEMIS. I believe it on my own knowledge, not on hearsay. I have seen clear proofs.

ELECTRA. What have you seen, poor girl, to warrant your belief? Where, I wonder, have you turned your eyes that you are feverish with this baneful fire?

CHRYSOTHEMIS. Then for the gods' love listen, so that you may know my story before deciding whether I am sane or foolish.

ELECTRA. Speak on then, if you find pleasure in speaking.

CHRYSOTHEMIS. Well, you shall hear all that I have seen. When I came to our father's ancient tomb I saw that streams of milk had lately flowed from the top of the mound, and that his sepulcher was encircled with garlands of all flowers that blow. I was astonished at the sight and peered about, lest someone should chance to be close to my side. But when I perceived that all the place was in stillness I crept nearer to the tomb. On the mound's edge I saw a lock of hair, freshly severed.

The moment that I saw it, ah me, a familiar image rushed upon my soul, telling me that there I beheld a token of him whom most I love, Orestes. Then I took it in my hands and uttered no ill-omened word, but the tears of joy straightway filled my eyes. I know well, as I knew then, that this fair tribute has come from none but him. Whose part else was that save mine and yours? I did not do it, I know, nor did you. How should you when you cannot leave this house even to worship the gods but at your peril? Nor again does our mother's heart incline to do such deeds, nor could she have done so without our knowledge.

No, these offerings are from Orestes! Come, dear sister, courage! No mortal life is attended by a changeless fortune. Ours was once gloomy; but this day, perhaps, will seal the promise of much good.

ELECTRA. Alas for your folly! How I have been pitying you!

CHRYSOTHEMIS. What, are my tidings not welcome?

ELECTRA. You do not know where or into what dreams you are wandering.

CHRYSOTHEMIS. Should I not know what my own eyes have seen?

ELECTRA. He is dead, poor girl. Your hopes in that deliverer are gone; look not to him.

CHRYSOTHEMIS. Woe, woe is me! From whom have you heard this?

ELECTRA. From the man who was present when he perished.

CHRYSOTHEMIS. Where is he? Wonder steals over my mind.

ELECTRA. He is within, a guest not unpleasing to our mother.

CHRYSOTHEMIS. Ah, woe is me! Whose then can have been those ample offerings to our father's tomb?

ELECTRA. Most likely, I think, someone brought those gifts in memory of the dead Orestes.

CHRYSOTHEMIS. Oh, hapless that I am! And I was bringing such news in joyous haste, ignorant, it seems, how dire was our plight. But now that I have come I find fresh sorrows added to the old!

ELECTRA. So stands your case. Yet if you will hearken to me you will lighten the load of our present trouble.

CHRYSOTHEMIS. Can I ever raise the dead to life?

ELECTRA. I did not mean that; I am not so foolish.

CHRYSOTHEMIS. What do you bid, then, for which my strength avails?

ELECTRA. That you be brave in doing what I enjoin.

CHRYSOTHEMIS. If any good can be done I will not refuse.

ELECTRA. Remember, nothing succeeds without toil.

CHRYSOTHEMIS. I know it, and will share your burden with all my power.

ELECTRA. Hear, then, how I am resolved to act. As for the support of friends, you yourself must know that we have none; Hades has taken our friends away and we two are left alone. So long as I heard that my brother still lived and prospered, I had hopes that he would yet come to avenge the murder of our father. But now that he is no more I look next to you, not to flinch from aiding me your sister to slay our father's murderer, Aegisthus. I must have no secret from you any more.

How long are you to wait inactive? What hope is left standing to which your eyes can turn? You have to complain that you are robbed of your father's heritage, you have to mourn that thus far your life is fading without nuptial song or wedded love. No, do not hope that such joys will ever be yours; Aegisthus is not so ill-advised as ever to permit that children should spring from you or me for his own sure destruction. But if you will follow my counsel, first you will win praise of piety from our dead sire below, and from our brother too; next, you shall be called free henceforth, as you were born, and shall find worthy bridals, for noble natures draw the gaze of all.

Then do you not see what fair fame you will win for yourself and for me by hearkening to my word? What citizen or stranger when he sees us will not greet us with praises such as these? "Behold these two sisters, my friends, who saved their father's house; who, when their foes were firmly planted of old, took their lives in their hands and stood forth as avengers of blood! Worthy of love are these two, worthy of reverence from all. At festivals and wherever the folk are assembled let these be honored of all men for their prowess." Thus will everyone speak of us, so that in life and in death our glory shall not fail.

Come, dear sister, hearken! Work with your father, share the burden of your brother, win rest from woes for me and for yourself—mindful of this, that an ignoble life brings shame upon the noble.

CHORUS. In such case as this forethought is helpful for those who speak and those who hear.

CHRYSOTHEMIS. Yes, and before she spoke, my friends, if she were blest with a sound mind she would have remembered caution, as she does not remember it.

Now where can you have turned your eyes that you are arming yourself with such rashness and calling me to help you. Do you not see you are a woman, not a man, and no match for your adversaries in strength? Their fortune prospers day by day, while ours is ebbing and coming to nought. Who then plotting to vanquish a foe so strong shall escape

without suffering deadly scathe? See that we do not change
our evil plight to worse, if anyone hears these words. It
brings us no relief or benefit if, after winning fair fame, we
die an ignominious death. Mere death is not the bitterest,
but rather when one who craves to die cannot obtain even
that boon.

Nay, I beseech you, before we are utterly destroyed and
leave our house desolate, restrain your rage! I will take care
that your words remain secret and harmless; do you learn
the prudence, at last though late, of yielding, when so helpless, to your rulers.

CHORUS. Hearken; there is no better gain for mortals to win
than foresight and a prudent mind.

ELECTRA. You have said nothing unlooked-for; I well knew
that you would reject what I proferred. Well! I must do this
deed with my own hand and alone; for assuredly I will not
leave it undone.

CHRYSOTHEMIS. Alas! Would you had been so purposed on
the day of our father's death! What might you not have
wrought!

ELECTRA. My nature was the same then but my mind less ripe.

CHRYSOTHEMIS. Strive to keep such a mind through all your
life.

ELECTRA. These counsels mean that you will not share my
deed.

CHRYSOTHEMIS. No, for the venture is likely to bring disaster.

ELECTRA. I admire your prudence; your cowardice I hate.

CHRYSOTHEMIS. I will listen no less calmly when you
praise me.

ELECTRA. Never fear to suffer that from me.

CHRYSOTHEMIS. Time enough in the future to decide that.

ELECTRA. Begone; in you there is no power to help.

CHRYSOTHEMIS. Not so, but in you no mind to learn.

ELECTRA. Go, tell all this to your mother!

CHRYSOTHEMIS. But again, I do not hate you with such hate.

ELECTRA. Yet know at least to what dishonor you bring me.

CHRYSOTHEMIS. Dishonor, no! I am only thinking of your good.

ELECTRA. Am I bound, then, to follow your rule of right?

CHRYSOTHEMIS. When you are wise then you will be our guide.

ELECTRA. Sad that one who speaks so well should speak amiss!

CHRYSOTHEMIS. You have well described the fault to which you cleave.

ELECTRA. How? Do you not think that I speak with justice?

CHRYSOTHEMIS. Sometimes justice itself is fraught with harm.

ELECTRA. I do not care to live by such a law.

CHRYSOTHEMIS. Well, if you must do this you will praise me yet.

ELECTRA. Do it I will, no whit dismayed by you.

CHRYSOTHEMIS. Is this so indeed? Will you not change your counsels?

ELECTRA. No, for nothing is more hateful than bad counsel.

CHRYSOTHEMIS. You seem to agree with nothing that I urge.

ELECTRA. My resolve is not new but long since fixed.

CHRYSOTHEMIS. Then I will go. You cannot be brought to approve my words nor I to commend your conduct.

ELECTRA. Then go inside. Never will I follow you, however much you may desire it; it would be great folly even to attempt an idle quest.

CHRYSOTHEMIS. If you are wise in your own eyes, let such wisdom be yours; by and by, when you are standing in evil plight, you will praise my words. (*Exit.*)

CHORUS. *When we see the birds of the air with sure instinct careful to nourish those who give them life and nurture, why do we not pay these debts in like measure? Nay, by the lightning-flash of Zeus, by Themis throned in heaven, it is not long till sin brings sorrow.*

Voice that comes to the dead beneath the earth, send a piteous cry, I pray you, to the son of Atreus in that world, a joyless message of dishonor. Tell him that the fortunes of his house are now distempered, while among his children strife of sister with sister has broken the harmony of loving days. Electra, forsaken, braves the storm alone; she bewails always, hapless one, her father's fate, like the nightingale unwearied in lament; she recks not of death but is ready to leave the sunlight, could she but quell the two Furies of her house. Who shall match such noble child of noble sire?

No generous soul deigns by a base life to cloud a fair repute and leave a name inglorious. So you too, my daughter, have chosen to mourn all your days with those that mourn and have spurned dishonor, that you might win at once a twofold praise, as wise and as the best of daughters.

May I yet see your life raised in might and wealth above your foes, even as now it is humbled beneath their hand! For I have found you in no prosperous estate; and yet, for observance of nature's highest laws, winning the noblest renown, by your piety toward Zeus.

(*Enter* ORESTES, *with* PYLADES *and* ATTENDANTS.)

ORESTES. Ladies, have we been directed aright? Are we on the right path to our goal?

CHORUS. What are you seeking? With what desire have you come?

ORESTES. I have been searching for the home of Aegisthus.

CHORUS. You have found it. Your guide is blameless.

ORESTES. Which of you then will tell those within that our company, long desired, has arrived?

CHORUS. This maiden—if the nearest should announce it.

ORESTES. I pray you, mistress, make it known in the house that certain men of Phocis seek Aegisthus.

ELECTRA. Ah, woe is me! Surely you are not bringing the visible proofs of that rumor which we heard?

ORESTES. I know nothing of your "rumor"; but the aged Strophius charged me with tidings of Orestes.

ELECTRA. What are they, sir? Ah, how I thrill with fear!

ORESTES. He is dead. In a small urn, as you see, we bring the scanty relics home.

ELECTRA. Ah me unhappy! There at last before my eyes I see that woeful burden in your hands!

ORESTES. If your tears are for anything Orestes has suffered, know that this vessel holds his dust.

ELECTRA. Ah, sir, allow me then I implore you, if this urn indeed contains him, to take it in my hands—that I may weep and wail, not for these ashes alone, but for myself and for all our house also.

ORESTES (*to* ATTENDANT). Bring it and give it to her, whoever she may be. She who begs this boon must be one who wished him no evil but a friend, or perhaps a kinswoman in blood.

(*The urn is placed in* ELECTRA'*s hands.*)

ELECTRA. Ah, memorial of him whom I loved best on earth! Ah Orestes, whose life has no relic left save this—how far from the hopes with which I sent you forth is the manner in which I receive you back! Now I carry your poor dust in my hands; but you were radiant, my child, when I sped you forth from home! Would that I had yielded up my breath before, with these hands, I stole you away and sent you to a strange land and rescued you from death, that so you might have been stricken down on that selfsame day and had your portion in the tomb of your father!

But now, an exile from home and fatherland, you have perished miserably, far from your sister. Woe is me, these loving hands have not washed or decked your corpse nor taken up, as was meet, their sad burden from the flaming pyre. No, hapless one; those rites you have had at the hands of strangers, and so have come to us, a little dust in a narrow urn.

Ah, woe is me for my nursing long ago, so vain, that I often bestowed on you with loving toil! For you were never your mother's darling so much as mine, nor was anyone in the house your nurse but I; by you I was always called "sister." But now all this has vanished in a day with your death; like a whirlwind you have swept all away with you. Our father is gone, I am dead in regard to you, you yourself have perished. Our foes exult. That mother who is none is mad with joy—she of whom you often sent me secret messages, your heralds, saying that you yourself would appear as an avenger. But our evil fortune, yours and mine, has reft all that away and has sent you forth to me thus—no more the form that I loved so well but ashes and an idle shade.

Ah me, ah me! O piteous dust! Alas, you dear one, sent on a dire journey, how you have undone me, undone me indeed, O brother mine!

Then take me to this your home, me who am as nothing, to your nothingness, that I may dwell with you henceforth below. When you were on earth we shared alike, and now I wish to die so that I may not be parted from you in the grave. For I see that the dead have rest from pain.

CHORUS. Bethink you, Electra, you are the child of mortal father, and mortal was Orestes; therefore grieve not too much. This is a debt which all of us must pay.

ORESTES. Alas, what shall I say? What words can serve me at this pass? I can restrain my lips no longer!

ELECTRA. What has troubled you? Why did you say that?

ORESTES. Is this the form of the illustrious Electra that I behold?

ELECTRA. It is; and very grievous in her plight.

ORESTES. Alas, then, for this miserable fortune!

ELECTRA. Surely, sir, your lament is not for *me*?

ORESTES. O form cruelly, godlessly, misused!

ELECTRA. Those ill-omened words, sir, fit no one better than me.

ORESTES. Alas for your life, unwedded and all unblest!

ELECTRA. Why this steadfast gaze, stranger, and these laments?

ORESTES. How ignorant was I, then, of my own sorrow!

ELECTRA. Have you perceived this by what has been said?

ORESTES. By seeing your sufferings, so many and so great.

ELECTRA. And yet you see but a few of my woes.

ORESTES. Could any be more painful to behold?

ELECTRA. This, that I share the dwelling of the murderers.

ORESTES. Whose murderers? Where lies the guilt at which you hint?

ELECTRA. My father's; and then I am their slave perforce.

ORESTES. Who is it that subjects you to this constraint?

ELECTRA. A mother—in name, but no mother in her deeds.

ORESTES. How does she oppress you? With violence or with hardship?

ELECTRA. With violence and hardships and all manner of ill.

ORESTES. And is there none to succor or to hinder?

ELECTRA. None. I *had* one, and you have shown me his ashes.

ORESTES. Unhappy girl, how this sight has stirred my pity!

ELECTRA. Then know that you are the first who ever pitied me.

ORESTES. No other visitor has ever shared your pain.

ELECTRA. Surely you are not some unknown kinsman?

ORESTES. I would answer if these who hear us were friends.

ELECTRA Oh, they are friends; you can speak without mistrust.

ORESTES. Give up this urn, then, and you shall be told all.

ELECTRA. I beseech you, sir, do not be so cruel to me!

ORESTES. Do as I say, and never fear to do amiss.

ELECTRA. I conjure you, do not rob me of my chief treasure!

ORESTES. You must not keep it.

ELECTRA. Ah woe is me for you, Orestes, if I am not to give you burial!

ORESTES. Hush! No such word! You have no right to lament.

ELECTRA. No right to lament for my dead brother?

ORESTES. It is not proper for you to speak of him so.

ELECTRA. Am I so dishonored of the dead?

ORESTES. Dishonored of none; but this is not your part.

ELECTRA. Yes, if these are the ashes of Orestes that I hold.

ORESTES. They are not; a fiction clothed them with his name. (*Takes the urn.*)

ELECTRA. And where is that unhappy one's tomb?

ORESTES. There is none; the living have no tomb.

ELECTRA. What are you saying, boy?

ORESTES. Nothing that is not true.

ELECTRA. The man is alive?

ORESTES. If there is life in me.

ELECTRA. What? Are you he?

ORESTES. Look at this signet, once our father's, and judge if I speak truth.

ELECTRA. O blissful day!

ORESTES. Blissful in very deed!

ELECTRA. Is this your voice?

ORESTES. Let no other voice reply.

ELECTRA. Do I hold you in my arms?

ORESTES. As you may hold me always!

ELECTRA. Ah, dear friends and fellow-citizens, behold Orestes here, who was feigned dead, and now by that feigning has come safely home!

CHORUS. We see him, daughter; and for this happy fortune a tear of joy trickles from our eyes.

ELECTRA. *Offspring of him I loved best, you have come even now, you have come, and found and seen her whom your heart desired!*

ORESTES. *I am with you; but keep silence for a while.*

ELECTRA. *What do you mean?*

ORESTES. *It is better to be silent, lest someone inside should hear.*

ELECTRA. *By ever-virgin Artemis, I will never stoop to fear women, stay-at-homes, vain burdens of the ground!*

ORESTES. *Yet remember that in women too dwells the spirit of battle; of that you have good proof I think.*

ELECTRA. *Alas! Ah me! You have reminded me of my sorrow, one which from its nature cannot be veiled, cannot be done away with, cannot forget!*

ORESTES. *I know this also; but when occasion prompts there will be the moment to recall those deeds.*

ELECTRA. *Each moment of all time as it comes would be proper occasion for these my just complaints; scarcely now have I had my lips set free.*

ORESTES. *I grant it; therefore guard your freedom.*

ELECTRA. *What must I do?*

ORESTES. *When the season does not serve do not wish to speak too much.*

ELECTRA. *Who could fitly exchange speech for such silence when you have appeared? For now I have seen your face, beyond all thought and hope!*

ORESTES. *You saw it when the gods moved me to come.* . . .

[*Lacuna of one line.*]

ELECTRA. *You have told me of a grace above the first if a god has indeed brought you to our house; in that I acknowledge the work of heaven.*

ORESTES. *I am loth indeed to curb your gladness, but yet this excess of joy moves my fear.*

ELECTRA. *You who have deigned to gladden my eyes by your return after many a year, do not, now that you have seen me in all my woe—*

ORESTES. *What is your prayer?*

ELECTRA. *—do not rob me of the comfort of your face, do not force me to forego it!*

ORESTES. *I should be angry indeed if I saw another attempt it.*

ELECTRA. *My prayer is granted?*

ORESTES. *Can you doubt?*

ELECTRA. *Ah, friends, I heard a voice that I could never have hoped to hear; nor could I have restrained my emotion in silence and without a cry when I heard it.*

Ah me! But now I have you; you have come to me with the light of that dear face which never, even in sorrow, could I forget.

ORESTES. Spare all superfluous words; do not tell me of our mother's wickedness, or how Aegisthus drains the wealth of our father's house by lavish luxury or aimless waste, for the story would not suffer you to keep due limit. Tell me rather what will serve our present need, where we must show ourselves or wait in ambush, so that our coming may confound the triumphs of our foes.

And look that our mother shall not read your secret in your radiant face when we two have advanced into the house, but make lament as for the feigned disaster. When we have prospered then there will be leisure to rejoice and exult in freedom.

ELECTRA. Yes, brother, as it pleases you so shall be my conduct also, for all my joy is a gift from you and not my own. Nor would I consent to win a great good for myself at the cost of the least pain to you, for so I should ill serve the divine power that befriends us now.

But you know how matters stand here, I do not doubt. You must have heard that Aegisthus is away from home but our mother inside. Do not fear that she will ever see my face lit up with smiles, for my old hatred of her has sunk into my heart; and since I have seen you, for very joy I shall never cease to weep. How indeed should I cease, when I have seen you come home this day, first as dead and then in life? Strangely have you wrought on me, so that if my father should return alive I would no longer doubt my senses but believe that I saw him. Now that you have come to me so wonderfully, therefore, command me as you will; for if I had been alone I should have achieved one of two things, a noble deliverance or a noble death.

ORESTES. You had best be silent, for I hear someone within preparing to come forth.

ELECTRA (*to* ORESTES *and* PYLADES). Enter, sirs, especially as you bring what no one could repulse from these doors, though he receive it without joy.

TUTOR (*enters*). Foolish and senseless children! Are you weary of your lives, or was there no wit born in you, that you do not see how you stand, not on the brink but in the very midst of deadly perils? If I had not kept watch this long while at these doors, your plans would have been in the house before yourselves; as it is, my care shielded you from that. Now have done with this long discourse, these insatiate cries of joy, and pass within; for in such deeds delay is evil and it is well to make an end.

ORESTES. What then will be my prospects when I enter?

TUTOR. Good, for you are secured from recognition.

ORESTES. You have reported me, I presume, as dead?

TUTOR. Know that you are numbered with the shades.

ORESTES. Do they rejoice at these tidings, then, or what do they say?

TUTOR. I will tell you at the end. Meanwhile all is well for us on their part—even what is not well.

ELECTRA. Who is this, brother? I pray you, tell me.

ORESTES. Do you not perceive?

ELECTRA. I cannot guess.

ORESTES. Do you not know the man to whose hands you once
gave me?

ELECTRA. What man? How do you mean?

ORESTES. By whose hands, through your forethought, I was secretly conveyed forth to Phocian soil.

ELECTRA. Is this he in whom, alone of many, I found a true ally
of old, when our sire was slain?

ORESTES. It is he. Question me no further.

ELECTRA. O joyous day! O sole preserver of Agamemnon's
house, how have you come? Are you indeed he who saved
my brother and myself from many sorrows? O dearest
hands, O messenger whose feet were kindly servants! How
could you be with me so long and remain unknown, nor give
a ray of light, but afflict me by fables, while possessed of
truths most sweet? Hail, father—for it is a father that I seem
to behold! All hail—and know that I have hated you and
loved you in one day as never man before!

TUTOR. Enough, I think. As for the story of the past, many are
the circling nights and days as many which shall show it to
you in its fullness, Electra.

(*To* ORESTES *and* PYLADES.) But this is my counsel to you
two who stand there. Now is the time to act; Clytemnestra is
now alone, no man is within. But if you pause consider that
you will have to fight not with the inmates alone but with
other foes more numerous and better skilled.

ORESTES. Pylades, this task of ours seems no longer to crave
many words but rather that we should enter the house forthwith—first adoring the shrines of my father's gods who
keep these gates.

(ORESTES *and* PYLADES *enter the house, followed by* TUTOR;
ELECTRA *remains.*)

ELECTRA. O King Apollo, graciously hear them, and hear me
besides, who have so often come before your altar with
such gifts as my devout hand could bring! And now, O
Lycean Apollo, with such vows as I can make I pray you, I

supplicate, I implore, grant us your benignant aid in these designs, and show men how impiety is rewarded by the gods! (*Enters the house.*)

CHORUS. *Behold how Ares moves onward, breathing deadly vengeance, against which none may strive!*

Even now the pursuers of dark guilt have passed beneath yonder roof, the hounds which none may flee. Therefore the vision of my soul shall not long tarry in suspense.

The champion of the spirits infernal is ushered with stealthy feet into the house, the ancestral palace of his sire, bearing keen-edged death in his hands; and Hermes, son of Maia, who has shrouded the guile in darkness, leads him forward, even to the end, and delays no more.

ELECTRA (*enters*). *Ah, dearest friends, in a moment the men will do the deed; but wait in silence.*

CHORUS. *How is it? What are they doing now?*

ELECTRA. *She is decking the urn for burial, and those two stand close to her.*

CHORUS. *And why have you sped forth?*

ELECTRA. *To guard against Aegisthus entering before we are aware.*

CLYTEMNESTRA (*within*). *Alas! Woe for the house forsaken of friends and filled with murderers!*

ELECTRA. *A cry goes up within; do you not hear, friends?*

CHORUS. *I heard, ah me, sounds dire to hear, and shuddered!*

CLYTEMNESTRA (*within*). *O hapless that I am! Aegisthus, where, where, are you?*

ELECTRA. *Hark, once more a voice resounds!*

CLYTEMNESTRA (*within*). *My son, my son, have pity on your mother!*

ELECTRA. *You had none for him, nor for the father that begot him.*

CHORUS. *Ill-fated realm and race, now the fate that has pursued you day by day is dying, is dying!*

CLYTEMNESTRA (*within*). *Oh, I am smitten!*

ELECTRA. *Smite, if you can, once more!*

CLYTEMNESTRA (*within*). *Ah, woe is me again!*

ELECTRA. *Would that the woe were for Aegisthus too!*

CHORUS. *The curses are at work; the buried live; blood flows for blood, drained from the slayers by those who died long ago.*

(*Enter* ORESTES *and* PYLADES.)

See, they come! That red hand reeks with sacrifice to Ares; nor can I blame the deed.

ELECTRA. *Orestes, how fare you?*

ORESTES. *All is well within the house if Apollo's oracle spoke well.*

ELECTRA. *The guilty one is dead?*

ORESTES. *Fear no more that your proud mother will ever put you to dishonor.*

[*Lacuna of three verses.*]

CHORUS. *Cease, for I see Aegisthus full in view.*

ELECTRA. *Rash boys, back, back!*

ORESTES. *Where do you see the man?*

ELECTRA. *Yonder, at our mercy, he advances from the suburb, full of joy.*

CHORUS. *Make for the vestibule with all speed, so that as your first task prospered this may prosper now.*

ORESTES. *Fear not—we will perform it.*

ELECTRA. *Quick, then, wherever you will.*

ORESTES. *See, I am gone.*

ELECTRA. *I will look to matters here.*

(*Exeunt* ORESTES *and* PYLADES.)

CHORUS. *It were well to soothe his ear with some few words of seeming gentleness, that he may rush blindly upon the struggle with his doom.*

AEGISTHUS (*enters*). Which of you can tell me where those Phocian strangers are who, it is said, have brought us tidings of Orestes slain in the wreck of his chariot? You, you I ask, yes, you, in former days so bold, for I think it touches you most nearly; you must best know and best can tell.

ELECTRA. I know assuredly, else I were a stranger to the fortune of my nearest kinfolk.

AEGISTHUS. Where then may the strangers be? Tell me.

ELECTRA. Inside. They have found a way to the heart of their hostess.

AEGISTHUS. Have they in truth reported him dead?

ELECTRA. Not reported only; they have shown him.

AEGISTHUS. Can I see the corpse with my own eyes?

ELECTRA. You can indeed, and it is no enviable sight.

AEGISTHUS. Indeed, you have given me a joyful greeting, beyond your wont.

ELECTRA. Joy be yours, if in these things you find joy.

AEGISTHUS. Silence, I say, and throw wide the gates, for all Mycenaeans and Argives to behold, so that if any of them were once buoyed on empty hopes from this man, now seeing him dead they may receive my curb instead of waiting till my chastisement makes them wise perforce!

ELECTRA. No loyalty is lacking on my part; time has taught me the prudence of concord with the stronger.

(*A shrouded corpse is disclosed.* ORESTES *and* PYLADES *stand near it.*)

AEGISTHUS. O Zeus, I behold that which has not fallen save by the doom of jealous Heaven; but if Nemesis attend that word, be it unsaid!

Take all the covering from the face so that kinship, at least, may receive the tribute of lament from me also.

ORESTES. Lift the veil yourself. It is not my part but yours to look upon these relics and to greet them kindly.

AEGISTHUS. It is good counsel and I will follow it. (*To* ELECTRA.) But you, call me Clytemnestra, if she is within.

ORESTES. She is near you; do not turn your eyes elsewhere.

AEGISTHUS (*removes the face-cloth from the corpse*). O, what sight is this?

ORESTES. Why so scared? Is the face so strange?

AEGISTHUS. Who are the men into whose toils I have fallen, hapless that I am?

ORESTES. Have you not discovered before now that the dead, as you miscall them, are living?

AEGISTHUS. Alas, I read the riddle. This can be none but Orestes who speaks to me!

ORESTES. And though so good a prophet you were deceived so long?

AEGISTHUS. Oh lost, undone! Yet suffer me to say one word. . . .

ELECTRA. In heaven's name, brother, do not suffer him to speak further or to plead at length! When mortals are in the meshes of fate, how can such respite avail one who is to die? No, slay him forthwith and cast his corpse to the creatures from whom such as he should have burial, far from our sight! To me nothing but this can make amends for the woes of the past.

ORESTES (to AEGISTHUS). Go in, and quickly; the issue here is not of words but of your life.

AEGISTHUS. Why take me into the house? If this deed is fair what need of darkness? Why is your hand not prompt to strike?

ORESTES. Do not dictate but go where you slew my father, that you may die in the same place.

AEGISTHUS. Is this dwelling doomed to see all the woes of Pelops' line, now and in time to come?

ORESTES. Yours, at least; trust my prophetic skill so far.

AEGISTHUS. The skill you boast did not belong to your father.

ORESTES. You bandy words and our going is delayed. Move forward!

AEGISTHUS. You lead.

ORESTES. You must go first.

AEGISTHUS. Lest I escape you?

ORESTES. No, but so that you may not choose how to die; I must not spare you any bitterness of death. It would be well if this judgment came straightway upon all who deal in lawless deeds, even the judgment of the sword: wickedness would not then abound.

(ORESTES *and* PYLADES *drive* AEGISTHUS *into the palace.*)

CHORUS. *O house of Atreus, through how many sufferings have you come forth at last in freedom, crowned with good by this day's enterprise!*

OEDIPUS THE KING

SOLELY AS A MYSTERY WITH DISCOVERY ITS OBJECT, or solely as a psychological study, the *Oedipus* is a masterful play; but what gives it conviction and force is that plot and characterization combine in mutual support to produce the overwhelming tragic power which is the essence of the drama. The construction is flawless. Each new episode flows naturally out of what has gone before, and each is made plausible by the character of its participants. If Oedipus were not both well-meaning and assured of his own righteousness, as is established in the opening of the play, the story would have broken down with the revelation of Teiresias. But just as only the impetuosity of Oedipus could make Teiresias speak out, so only his quick temper could make him ignore Teiresias' revelation. Because he distrusts Teiresias Oedipus suspects Creon, and the quarrel between the men brings Iocasta out to calm Oedipus by telling him of the exposure of her infant, which did not after all prevent the killing of Laius.

The discovery is built up in stages: only after Oedipus fears that he has killed Laius does he come to fear that he has killed his *father* Laius. The only unprepared entry is the arrival of the messenger with news of the death of Polybus. And only his big-city glibness makes the reluctant shepherd speak out. The characters are not only subjects for psychological insights, especially in their unwitting expressions of tragic irony: they are themselves psychologists—though the complex called after Oedipus (which Freud named only for convenience, not because he thought it central to the play) receives only a line from Iocasta.

Oedipus is impetuous, arrogant, and suspicious of the motives of his true friends; but it is a mistake to explain his downfall as retribution for these flaws of character. No Greek hero was wholly perfect. Only a proud and impatient man—one who would kill in a traffic dispute—would also have the fortitude to pursue the truth as Oedipus did. His sins were committed unwittingly; by human calculations he had behaved well as a man. When a man behaving admirably as a man is nevertheless tripped up by forces beyond his control and understanding, we have tragedy. Oedipus then is a perfect example of the tragic hero.

PERSONS

OEDIPUS, *King of Thebes*
PRIEST
CREON, *brother of Iocasta*
TEIRESIAS, *blind prophet*
IOCASTA
MESSENGER FROM CORINTH
SHEPHERD, *formerly servant of Laius*

MESSENGER FROM THE PALACE
CHORUS OF THEBAN ELDERS
SUPPLIANTS, ATTENDANTS, ANTIGONE, *and* ISMENE (*mute characters*)

SCENE: *Before the palace at Thebes.*

(*Enter* OEDIPUS, *to address band of* SUPPLIANTS *facing the doors.*)

OEDIPUS. My children, latest-born to Cadmus who was of old, why are you set before me thus with wreathed branches of suppliants, while the city reeks with incense, rings with prayers for health and cries of woe? I deemed it unmeet, my children, to hear these things at the mouth of others, and have come here myself, I, Oedipus renowned of all.

Tell me then, venerable man, since it is your natural part to speak for these others, in what mood are you placed here, with what dread or what desire? Be sure that I would gladly give all aid; I should be hard of heart if I did not pity such suppliants as these.

PRIEST. Nay, Oedipus, ruler of my land, you see of what years we are who beset your altars, some nestlings still too tender for far flights, some bowed with age, priests, as I of Zeus, and these, the chosen youth. The rest of the folk sit with wreathed branches in the marketplaces and before the two shrines of Pallas, and where Ismenus gives answer by fire.

For the city, as you yourself see, is now too sorely vexed and can no more lift her head from beneath the angry waves of death. A blight is on her in the fruitful blossoms of the land, in the herds among the pastures, in the barren pangs of women. And that flaming god, the malign plague, has swooped on us and ravages the town; by him the house of Cadmus is made waste, but dark Hades rich in groans and tears.

It is not as deeming you ranked with gods that I and these children are suppliants at your hearth, but as deeming you first of men, both in life's common chances and when mortals have to do with more than man; for you came to the town of Cadmus and rid us of the tax we rendered to the hard songstress. This you did though you knew nothing from us that could help you and had not been instructed; no, by a god's aid, it is said and believed, did you uplift our life.

And now, Oedipus, king glorious in all eyes, we beseech you, all we suppliants, to find for us some succor, whether you know it by the whisper of a god, or perchance as in the power of man. When men have been proved in deeds past, the issues of their counsels too most often have effect.

On, best of mortals, again uplift our state! On, guard your fame, since now this land calls you savior for your former zeal. Never be it our memory of your reign that we were first restored and afterward cast down; nay, lift up this state in such wise that it fall no more!

With good omen did you give us that past happiness; now also show yourself the same. For if you are to rule this land, even as you are now its lord, it is better to be lord of men than of a waste; since neither walled town or ship is anything if it is void and no men dwell in it with you.

OEDIPUS. Oh my piteous children, known, well known to me are the desires wherewith you have come. I know well that you all suffer, yet sufferers as you are, there is not one of you whose suffering is as mine. Your pain comes on each one of you for himself alone and for no other; but my soul mourns at once for the city, and for myself, and for you.

You are not then rousing me as one sunk in sleep; no, be sure that I have wept full many tears, gone many ways in wanderings of thought. And the sole remedy which after much pondering I could find, this I have put into act. I have sent the son of Menoeceus, Creon, my own wife's brother, to the Pythian house of Phoebus, to learn by what deed or word I might deliver this town. Already, when the lapse of days is reckoned, I am troubled by his delay, for he tarries strangely, beyond the fitting space. But when he comes, then shall I be no true man if I do not all that the god shows.

PRIEST. You have spoken in season; at this moment these men show by their gestures that Creon is drawing near.

OEDIPUS. O King Apollo, may he come to us in the brightness of saving fortune, even as his face is bright!

PRIEST. To all seeming he brings comfort; else he would not be coming crowned so thickly with berry-laden bay.

OEDIPUS. We shall soon know; he is at range to hear. (*Enter* CREON.) What news have you brought us from the god?

CREON. Good news. I tell you that even troubles hard to bear, if they find the right issue, will end in perfect peace.

OEDIPUS. But what is the oracle? So far your words make me neither bold nor yet afraid.

CREON. If you would hear while these people are near I am ready to speak; or else to go inside.

OEDIPUS. Speak before all. The sorrow which I bear is for these more than for my own life.

CREON. With your leave I will tell what I heard from the god. Phoebus our lord bids us plainly to drive out a defiling thing which, he says, has been harbored in this land, and not to harbor it so that it cannot be healed.

OEDIPUS. By what rite shall we cleanse us? What is the manner of the misfortune?

CREON. By banishing a man, or by bloodshed in quittance of bloodshed, since it is that blood which brings the tempest on our city.

OEDIPUS. And who is the man whose fate he thus reveals?

CREON. Laius, King, was lord of our land before you became pilot of this state.

OEDIPUS. I know it well—by hearsay, for I saw him never.

CREON. He was slain; and the god now bids us plainly to wreak vengeance on his murderers, whoever they may be.

OEDIPUS. And where on earth are they? Where shall the dim track of this old crime be found?

CREON. In this land, said the god. What is sought for can be caught; only that which is not watched escapes.

OEDIPUS. Was it in the house or in the field or on strange soil that Laius met this bloody end?

CREON. It was on a visit to Delphi, as he said, that he had left our land; and he came home no more after he had once set forth.

OEDIPUS. And was there none to tell? Was there no comrade of his journey who saw the deed from whom tidings might have been gained and used?

CREON. All perished, save one who fled in fear; and he could tell for certain but one thing of all that he saw.

OEDIPUS. And what was that? One thing might show the clue to many, could we get but a small beginning for hope.

CREON. He said that robbers met and fell on them, not in one man's might but with full many hands.

OEDIPUS. How then, unless there was some trafficking in bribes from here, should the robber have proved so daring?

CREON. Such things were surmised; but Laius once slain, amid our troubles no avenger arose.

OEDIPUS. But when royalty had thus fallen, what trouble in your path can have hindered a full search?

CREON. The riddling Sphinx had made us let dark things go and was inviting us to think of what lay at our doors.

OEDIPUS. Nay, I will start afresh and once more make dark things plain. Right worthily has Phoebus, and worthily have you, bestowed this care on the cause of the dead; and so, as is meet, you shall find me too leagued with you in seeking vengeance for this land, and for the god besides. On behalf of no far-off friend, no, but in my own cause shall I dispel this taint. For whoever was the slayer of Laius might wish to take vengeance on me also with a hand as fierce. Therefore in doing right to Laius I serve myself.

Come, my children, hasten, rise from the altar-steps and lift these suppliant boughs. Let someone summon the folk of Cadmus here, warned that I mean to leave nothing untried. Our health (with the god's help) shall be made certain—or our ruin.

PRIEST. My children, let us rise; we came at first to seek what this man promises of himself. And may Phoebus who sent these oracles come to us, our savior and deliverer from the pest.

(*Exeunt* OEDIPUS *and* PRIEST; *enter* CHORUS.)

CHORUS. *O sweetly-speaking message of Zeus, in what spirit hast thou come from golden Pytho unto glorious Thebes? I am on the rack, terror shakes my soul. O thou Delian healer to whom wild cries rise, in holy fear of thee, what thing thou wilt work for me, perchance unknown before, perchance renewed with the revolving years: tell me, thou immortal voice, born of Golden Hope!*

First call I on thee, daughter of Zeus, divine Athena, and on thy sister, guardian of our land, Artemis, who sits on her throne of fame, above the circle of our Agora, and on Phoebus the far-darter: O shine forth on me, my threefold help against death! If ever aforetime, in arrest of ruin hurrying on the city, ye drove a fiery pest beyond our borders, come now also!

Woe is me, countless are the sorrows that I bear; a plague is on all our host, and thought can find no weapon for defense. The fruits of the glorious earth grow not; by no birth of children do women surmount the pangs in which they shriek; and life on life mayest thou see sped, like bird on nimble wing, aye, swifter than resistless fire, to the shore of the western god.

By such deaths, past numbering, the city perishes: unpitied, her children lie on the ground, spreading pestilence,

*with none to mourn: and meanwhile young wives, and gray-
haired mothers with them, uplift a wail at the steps of the altars, some here, some there, entreating for their weary
woes. The prayer to the Healer rings clear, and, blent therewith, the voice of lamentation: for these things, golden
daughter of Zeus, send us the bright face of comfort.*

*And grant that the fierce god of death, who now with no
brazen shields, yet amid cries as of battle, wraps me in the
flame on his onset, may turn his back in speedy flight from
our land, borne by a fair wind to the great deep of Amphi-
trite, or to those waters in which none find haven, even to
the Thracian wave; for if night leave aught undone, day follows to accomplish this. O thou who wieldest the powers of
the fire-fraught lightning, O Zeus our father, slay him beneath thy thunderbolt!*

*Lycean King, fain were I that thy shafts also, from thy bent
bow's string of woven gold, should go abroad in their might,
our champions in the face of the foe; yea, and the flashing
fires of Artemis wherewith she glances through the Lycian
hills. And I call him whose locks are bound with gold, who is
named with the name of this land, ruddy Bacchus to whom
Bacchants cry, the comrade of the Maenads, to draw near
with the blaze of his blithe torch, our ally against the god unhonored among gods.*

OEDIPUS. You pray; in answer to your prayer—if you will give
a loyal welcome to my words and minister to your own disease—you may hope to find succor and relief from woes.
These words I will speak publicly, as one who has been a
stranger to this report, a stranger to the deed; for I should
not be far on the track if I were racing it alone, without a
clue. But as it is, since it was only after the time of the deed
that I was numbered a Theban among Thebans, to you, the
Cadmeans all, I proclaim the following.

Whosoever of you knows by whom Laius son of
Labdacus was slain, I bid him to declare all to me. And if he
is afraid, I tell him to remove the danger of the charge by de-
nouncing himself; he shall suffer nothing else unlovely but
only leave the land, unhurt. Or if any one knows an alien,

from another land, as the assassin, let him not keep silence; for I will pay his reward, and my thanks shall rest with him besides.

But if you keep silence, if anyone through fear shall seek to screen friend or self from my behest, hear what I shall then do. I charge you that no one of this land, of which I hold dominion and throne, give shelter or speak word to that murderer, whoever he may be, make him partner of his prayer or sacrifice, to serve him with the lustral rite; all must ban him their homes, knowing that *this* is our defiling thing, as the oracle of the Pythian god has newly shown me. In this way I am the ally of the god and of the slain man. And I pray solemnly that the slayer, whoever he be, whether his hidden guilt is lonely or has partners, may he wear his unblest life out evilly, as he is evil. And for myself I pray that if, with my privity, he should become an inmate of my house, I may suffer the same things which I have just called down upon others. And on you I lay it to make all these words good, for my sake and for the sake of the god, and for our lands, so blasted with barrenness by angry heaven.

For even if the matter had not been urged on us by a god it was not meet that you should leave the guilt unpurged when one so noble, and he your king, had perished; you were bound to search it out. And now since it is I who hold the powers that once he held, who possess his bed and the wife who bore seed to him; and since, had his hope of issue not been frustrate, children born of one mother would have made ties between him and me—but as it was fate swooped upon his head; by reason of these things I will uphold this cause even as the cause of my own sire. I will leave nothing untried in seeking to find him whose hand shed that blood, for the honor of the son of Labdacus and of Polydorus and elder Cadmus and Agenor who was of old.

And for those who obey me not I pray that the god send them neither harvest of the earth nor fruit of the womb, but that they be wasted by their lot that now is or by one yet more dire. But for all you, the loyal folk of Cadmus to

whom these things seem good, may Justice our ally and all
the gods be with you graciously for ever.

CHORUS. As you have put me on my oath, on my oath, O King,
I will speak. I am not the slayer, nor can I point to him who
slew. As for the question, it was for Phoebus who sent it to
tell us this thing—who can have wrought the deed.

OEDIPUS. Justly said; but no man on the earth can force the
gods to what they will not.

CHORUS. I would fain say what seems to me next best after this.

OEDIPUS. If there is yet a third course spare not to show it.

CHORUS. I know that our lord Teiresias is the seer most like to
our lord Phoebus. From him, O King, a searcher of these
things might learn them most clearly.

OEDIPUS. Not even this have I left out of my cares. On the hint
of Creon I have twice sent a man to bring him; and this long
while I marvel why he is not here.

CHORUS. Indeed, his skill apart, the rumors are but faint and
old.

OEDIPUS. What rumors are they? I look to every story.

CHORUS. Certain wayfarers were said to have killed him.

OEDIPUS. I too have heard it, but none sees him who saw it.

CHORUS. Nay, if he knows what fear is he will not stay when he
hears your curses, so dire as they are.

OEDIPUS. When a man shrinks not from a deed neither is he
scared by a word.

CHORUS. But there is one to convict him. For here they bring at
last the godlike prophet, in whom alone of men the truth
lives.

(*Enter* TEIRESIAS, *led by a* BOY.)

OEDIPUS. Teiresias, whose soul grasps all things, the lore that
may be told and the unspeakable, the secrets of heaven and
the low things of earth, you feel, though you cannot see,
what a plague is haunting our state, from which, great
prophet, we find in you our protector and only savior. Now
Phoebus—if indeed you do not know from the messengers—sent answer to our question that the only riddance

from this pest which could come was if we should learn aright the slayers of Laius, and slay them or send them into exile from our land. Do you then grudge neither voice of birds nor any other way of seer-lore you have, but rescue yourself and the state, rescue me, rescue all that is defiled by the dead. We are in your hand, and man's noblest task is to help others by his best means and powers.

TEIRESIAS. Alas, how dreadful to have wisdom where it profits not the wise! Aye, I knew this well but let it slip out of mind; else would I never have come here.

OEDIPUS. What now? How sad have you come in!

TEIRESIAS. Let me go home; most easily will you bear your own burden to the end and I mine if you will consent.

OEDIPUS. Your words are strange and not kindly to this state which nurtured you when you withhold this response.

TEIRESIAS. Nay, I see that you on your part do not open your lips in season; therefore do I not speak, that I may not have your mishap.

OEDIPUS. For the love of the gods, do not turn away if you have knowledge; all we suppliants implore you on our knees.

TEIRESIAS. Aye, for you are all without knowledge. But I will never reveal my griefs—that I say not yours.

OEDIPUS. How do you say? You know the secret and will not tell it, but are minded to betray us and to destroy the state?

TEIRESIAS. I will pain neither myself nor you. Why vainly ask these things? You will not learn them from me.

OEDIPUS. What, basest of the base—you would anger a very stone—will you never speak out? Can nothing touch you? Will you never make an end?

TEIRESIAS. You blame my temper but do not see that to which you yourself are wedded. No, you find fault with me.

OEDIPUS. And who would not be angry to hear the words with which you now slight this city?

TEIRESIAS. The future will come of itself though I shroud it in silence.

OEDIPUS. Then seeing that it must come, you on your part should tell me of it.

TEIRESIAS. I will speak no further. Rage, if you will, with the
fiercest wrath your heart knows.

OEDIPUS. Aye, verily. I will not spare, so angry am I, to speak
all my thought. Know that you seem to me even to have
helped in plotting the deed, and to have done it, short of
slaying with your hands. If you had eyesight I would have
said that the doing of this thing also was yours alone.

TEIRESIAS. So? I charge you that you abide by the decree of
your own mouth, and from this day speak neither to these
nor to me. *You* are the accursed defiler of this land.

OEDIPUS. So brazen with your blustering taunt? And how do
you trust to escape your due?

TEIRESIAS. I have escaped. In my truth is my strength.

OEDIPUS. Who taught you this? It was not, at least, your art.

TEIRESIAS. You, for you spurred me into speech against my will.

OEDIPUS. What speech? Speak again that I may learn it better.

TEIRESIAS. Did you not take my sense before? Or are you
tempting me in talk?

OEDIPUS. No, I did not take it so that I can call it known; speak
again.

TEIRESIAS. I say that you are the slayer of the man whose slayer
you seek.

OEDIPUS. Now you shall rue that you have twice said words so
dire.

TEIRESIAS. Would you have me say more, to make you angrier
still?

OEDIPUS. What you will. It will be said in vain.

TEIRESIAS. I say that you have been living in unguessed shame
with your nearest kin, and do not see to what woe you have
come.

OEDIPUS. Do you indeed think that you shall always speak thus
without smarting?

TEIRESIAS. Yes, if there is any strength in truth.

OEDIPUS. Nay, there is, for all save you. For you there is not that
strength, since you are maimed in ear and in wit and in eye.

TEIRESIAS. And you are a poor wretch to utter taunts which
every man here will soon hurl at you.

OEDIPUS. Night, endless night, holds you in her keeping, so that you can never hurt me or any man who sees the sun.

TEIRESIAS. No, your doom is not to fall by *me*. Apollo is enough; his care it is to work that out.

OEDIPUS. Are these Creon's devices or yours?

TEIRESIAS. Nay, Creon is no plague to you. You are your own.

OEDIPUS. O wealth and empire and skill surpassing skill in life's keen rivalries, how great is the envy that cleaves to you if for the sake of this power which the city has put into my hands, a gift unsought, Creon the trusty, Creon my old friend, has crept on me by stealth, yearning to thrust me out of it, and has suborned such a scheming juggler as this, a tricky quack, who has eyes only for his gains but in his art is blind!

Come now, tell me, where have you proved yourself a seer? Why, when the watcher was here who wove dark song, did you say nothing that could free this folk? Yet the riddle, at least, was not for the first comer to read. There was need of a seer's skill, and none such were you found to have, either by help of birds or as known from any god. No, I came, I, Oedipus the ignorant, and made her mute when I had seized the answer by my wit, untaught of birds. And it is I whom you are trying to oust, thinking to stand close to Creon's throne. Methinks you and the plotter of these things will rue your zeal to purge the land. Nay, if you did not seem to be an old man you would have learned to your cost how bold you are.

CHORUS. To our thinking, both this man's words and yours, Oedipus, have been said in anger. Not for such words is our need, but to seek how we shall best discharge the mandates of the god.

TEIRESIAS. King though you are, the right of reply, at least, must be deemed the same for both; of that I too am lord. Not to you do I live servant but to Loxias; and so I shall not stand enrolled under Creon for my patron. And I tell you, since you have taunted me even with blindness, that you have sight but see not in what misery you are, nor where you live, nor with whom. Do you know of what stock you are? And

you have been an unwitting foe to your own kin, in the
shades and on the earth above. The double lash of your
mother's and your father's curse shall one day drive you
from this land in dreadful haste, with darkness then on the
eyes that now see true.

What place shall not be harbor to your shriek, what of all
Cithaeron shall not ring with it soon, when you have learnt
the meaning of the nuptials in which, within that house, you
found a fatal haven after a voyage so fair. And a throng of
other ills you cannot guess will make you level with your
true self and with your own brood.

Then heap your scorns on Creon and on my message; no
one among men shall ever be crushed more miserably than
you.

OEDIPUS. Are these taunts to be indeed borne from *him?*
Hence, ruin take you! Hence this instant! Back! Away, depart from these doors!

TEIRESIAS. I would never have come, not I, if you had not
called me.

OEDIPUS. I did not know that you were about to speak folly; else
it would have been long before I sent for you to my house.

TEIRESIAS. Such am I, as you think, a fool; but for the parents
who begot you, sane.

OEDIPUS. What parents? Stay . . . and who of men is my sire?

TEIRESIAS. This day shall show your birth and shall bring your
ruin.

OEDIPUS. What riddles, what dark words you always speak!

TEIRESIAS. Nay, are you not most skilled to unravel dark speech?

OEDIPUS. Make that my reproach in which you find me great.

TEIRESIAS. Yet it was just that fortune that undid you.

OEDIPUS. If I delivered this town, I care not.

TEIRESIAS. Then I will go. Boy, take me hence.

OEDIPUS. Yes, let him take you. While here you are a hindrance
and a trouble; when you have vanished you will not vex me
more.

TEIRESIAS. I will go when I have done my errand, fearless of
your frown, for you can never destroy me. And I tell you, the
man of whom you have this long while been in quest, utter-

ing threats and proclaiming a search into the murder of
Laius—that man is here, in seeming an alien sojourner, but
soon he shall be found a native Theban, and shall not be glad
of his fortune. A blind man, he who now has sight, a beggar
who now is rich, he shall make his way to a strange land,
feeling the ground before him with his staff. And he shall be
found at once brother and father of the children with whom
he consorts; son and husband of the woman who bore him;
heir to his father's bed, shedder of his father's blood.

Go in now and think on that; and if you find that I have
been at fault, say thenceforth that I have no wit in prophecy.

(*Exeunt.*)

CHORUS. *Who is he of whom the divine voice from the Delphian rock hath spoken, as having wrought with red hands
horrors that no tongue can tell?*

*It is time that he ply in flight a foot stronger than the feet
of storm-swift steeds: for the son of Zeus is springing on
him, all armed with fiery lightnings, and with him come the
dread, unerring Fates.*

*Yea, newly given from snowy Parnassus, the message
hath flashed forth to make all search for the unknown man.
Into the wild wood's covert, among caves and rocks, he is
roaming, fierce as a bull, wretched and forlorn on his joyless path, still seeking to put from him the doom spoken at
Earth's central shrine: but that doom ever lives, ever flits
around him.*

*Dreadly, in sooth, dreadly doth the wise augur move me,
who approve not, nor am able to deny. How to speak, I know
not; I am fluttered with forebodings; neither in the present
have I clear vision, nor of the future. Never in past days, nor
in these, have I heard how the house of Labdacus or the son
of Polybus had, either against other, any grief that I could
bring as proof in assailing the public fame of Oedipus, and
seeking to avenge the line of Labdacus for the undiscovered
murder.*

*Nay, Zeus indeed and Apollo are keen of thought, and
know the things of earth; but that mortal seer wins knowledge above mine, of this there can be no sure test; though
man may surpass man in lore. Yet, until I see the word made
good, never will I assent when men blame Oedipus. Before
all eyes, the winged maiden came against him of old, and he
was seen to be wise; he bore the test, in welcome service to
our state; never, therefore, by the verdict of my heart shall
he be adjudged guilty of crime.*

CREON (*enters*). Fellow-citizens, having learned that Oedipus
the king lays dire charges against me, I am here, indignant.
If in the present troubles he thinks that he has suffered from
me, by word or deed, aught that tends to harm, in truth I do
not crave my full term of years, when I must bear such
blame as this. The wrong of this rumor touches me not in
one point alone, but has the largest scope, if I am to be
called a traitor in the city, a traitor too by you and by my
friends.

CHORUS. No, but this taunt came under stress, perhaps, of
anger, rather than from the purpose of the heart.

CREON. And the saying was uttered, that *my* counsels won the
seer to utter his falsehoods?

CHORUS. Such things were said—I do not know with what
meaning.

CREON. And this charge laid against me with steady eyes and
steady mind?

CHORUS. I do not know; I see not what my masters do: but here
comes our lord forth from the house.

OEDIPUS (*enters*). You there, how could you come here? Have
you a front so bold that you have come to my house when
you are the proved assassin of its master, the palpable robber of my crown? Come, tell me in the name of the gods,
was it cowardice or folly you saw in me that you plotted to
do this thing? Did you think that I would not note this deed
of yours creeping on me by stealth or, aware of it, not ward
it off? Is your attempt not foolish, to seek, without followers or friends, a throne, a prize which followers and wealth
must win?

CREON. Mark me now; in answer to your words hear a fair reply, and then judge for yourself on knowledge.

OEDIPUS. You are apt in speech, but I have a poor wit for your lessons, since I have found you my malignant foe.

CREON. Now hear first how I will explain this very thing—

OEDIPUS. One thing do not explain—that you are not false.

CREON. If you think that stubbornness without sense is a good gift you are not wise.

OEDIPUS. If you think you can wrong a kinsman and escape the penalty you are not sane.

CREON. Justly said, I grant you; but tell me what is the wrong you say you have suffered from me.

OEDIPUS. Did you advise or did you not that I should send for that reverend seer?

CREON. I am still of the same mind.

OEDIPUS. How long is it then since Laius—

CREON. Since Laius . . . ? I do not understand your drift . . .

OEDIPUS. —was swept away from men's sight by a deadly violence?

CREON. The count of years would run far into the past.

OEDIPUS. Was the seer of the profession in those days?

CREON. Yes, skilled as now and in equal honor.

OEDIPUS. Did he make any mention of me at that time?

CREON. Never, certainly, when I was within hearing.

OEDIPUS. But did you hold no search touching the murder?

CREON. We held due search, of course, and learned nothing.

OEDIPUS. How was it that this sage did not tell his story *then*?

CREON. I do not know; where I lack light it is my wont to be silent.

OEDIPUS. So much, at least, you know and could declare with light enough.

CREON. What is that? If I know it I will not deny.

OEDIPUS. That if he had not conferred with you he would never have named *my* slaying of Laius.

CREON. If so he speaks you know best; but I claim to learn from you as much as you have now from me.

OEDIPUS. Learn your fill; I shall never be found guilty of the blood.

CREON. Say then: you are married to my sister?

OEDIPUS. The question does not allow of denial.

CREON. And you rule the land as she does, with like authority?

OEDIPUS. She obtains from me all her desire.

CREON. And do I not rank as a third peer of you two?

OEDIPUS. That is just where you are seen a false friend.

CREON. Not so, if you would reason with your own heart as I
with mine. First weigh this—whether you think that anyone
would choose to rule amid terrors rather than in unruffled
peace, granting that he is to have the same powers. Now I,
for one, have no yearning in my nature to be a king rather
than to do kingly deeds, no, nor has any man who knows
how to keep a sober mind. Now I win all boons from you
without fear; but if I were ruler myself I should be doing
much even against my own desire.

How then could royalty be sweeter for me to have than
painless rule and influence? Not yet am I so misguided as to
desire other honors than those which profit. Now, all wish
me joy; now, every man has a greeting for me; now, those
who have a suit to you crave speech with me, since that is all
their hope of success. Then why should I resign these things
and take those? No mind will become false while it is wise.
Nay, I am no lover of such policy, and if another put it into
deed I could never bear to act with him.

In proof of this first go to Pytho and ask if I brought you
true word of the oracle. Next, if you find that I have planned
anything in concert with the soothsayer take and slay me, by
the sentence not of one mouth but of two—by my own no
less than yours. But do not make me guilty in a corner, on
unproved surmise. It is no right to adjudge bad men good at
random, or good men bad. I count it a like thing for a man to
cast off a true friend as to cast away the life in his own bosom, which he most loves. You will learn these things with
sureness in time, for time alone shows a just man; but you
could discern a knave even in one day.

CHORUS. Well has he spoken, O King, for one who gives heed
not to fall; the quick in counsel are not sure.

OEDIPUS. When the stealthy plotter is moving on me in quick sort, I too must be quick with my counterplot. If I await him in repose his ends will have been gained and mine missed.

CREON. What would you do, then? Cast me out of the land?

OEDIPUS. No. I desire your death, not your banishment, that you may show forth what manner of thing is envy.

CREON. You speak as resolved not to yield or believe?

[OEDIPUS. No, for you do not persuade me that you are worthy of belief.]

CREON. No, for I do not find you sane.

OEDIPUS. Sane, at least, in my own interest.

CREON. You should be so in mine also.

OEDIPUS. Nay, you are false.

CREON. But if you understand nothing?

OEDIPUS. Yet must I rule.

CREON. Not if you rule ill.

OEDIPUS. Hear him, O Thebes!

CREON. Thebes is for me also, not for you alone.

(*Enter* IOCASTA.)

CHORUS. Cease, princes. In good time for you I see Iocasta coming yonder from the house; with her help you should compose your present feud.

IOCASTA. Misguided men, why have you raised such foolish strife of tongues? Are you not ashamed, while the land is thus sick, to stir up troubles of your own? Come, go you into the house, and you, Creon, to your house; forbear to make much of a petty grief.

CREON. Kinswoman, Oedipus your lord claims to do dread things to me, one or other of two ills—to thrust me from the land of my fathers or to take and slay me.

OEDIPUS. Yes; for I have caught him, lady, working evil, by ill arts, against my person.

CREON. Now may I see no good but perish accursed if I have done to you anything you charge me with.

IOCASTA. O, for the gods' love, believe it, Oedipus, first for the awful sake of this oath unto the gods, then for my sake and for theirs who stand before you.

CHORUS. *Consent, reflect, hearken, O my king, I pray you!*

OEDIPUS. *What grace, then, would you have me grant you?*

CHORUS. *Respect him who aforetime was not foolish and who now is strong in his oath.*

OEDIPUS. *Do you know what you are asking?*

CHORUS. *Yes.*

OEDIPUS. *Declare, then, what you mean.*

CHORUS. *That you should never use an unproved rumor to cast a dishonoring charge on the friend who has bound himself with a curse.*

OEDIPUS. *Then be very sure that, when you seek this, for me you are seeking destruction or exile from this land.*

CHORUS. *No, by him who stands in front of all the heavenly host, no, by the Sun! Unblest, unfriended, may I die by the uttermost doom if I have that thought! But my unhappy soul is worn by the withering of the land, and again by the thought that our old sorrows should be crowned by sorrows springing from you two.*

OEDIPUS. Then let him go, though I am surely doomed to death or to be thrust dishonored from the land. Your lips, not his, move my compassion by their plaint; but he, wherever he be, shall be hated.

CREON. Sullen in yielding you show yourself, even as you are vehement in excesses of wrath. Such natures are justly sorest for themselves to bear.

OEDIPUS. Then will you not leave me in peace and get you gone?

CREON. I will go my way. I have found you undiscerning, but in the sight of these I am just. (*Exit.*)

CHORUS. *Lady, why do you delay to take that man into the house?*

IOCASTA. *I will do so when I have learned what has happened.*

CHORUS. *Blind suspicion, bred of talk, arose; and on the other side wounds of injustice.*

IOCASTA. *It was on both sides?*

CHORUS. *Yes.*

IOCASTA. *What was the story?*

CHORUS. *Enough, surely enough, when our land is already vexed, that the matter should rest where it ceased.*

OEDIPUS. *Do you see to what you have come, for all your honest purpose, in seeking to slack and blunt my zeal?*

CHORUS. *King, I have said it not once alone: be sure that I should have been shown a madman, bankrupt in sane counsel, if I put you away, you who gave a true course to my beloved country when distraught by troubles, you who now also are likely to prove our prospering guide.*

IOCASTA. In the name of the gods, tell me also, O King, on what account you have conceived this steadfast wrath.

OEDIPUS. That I will; for I honor you, lady, above yonder men. The cause is Creon and the plots that he has laid against me.

IOCASTA. Speak on, if you can tell clearly how the feud began.

OEDIPUS. He says that I stand guilty of the blood of Laius.

IOCASTA. As on his own knowledge? Or on hearsay from another?

OEDIPUS. He has made a rascal seer his mouthpiece; as for himself, he keeps his lips wholly pure.

IOCASTA. Then absolve yourself of the things of which you speak. Hearken to me, and learn for your comfort that nothing of mortal birth is a sharer in the science of the seer. Of that I will give you pithy proof.

An oracle came to Laius once—I will not say from Phoebus himself, but from his ministers—that the doom should overtake him to die by the hand of his child, who should spring from him and me.

Now Laius—as, at least, rumor says—was murdered one day by foreign robbers at a place where three highways meet. And the child's birth was not three days past when Laius pinned its ankles together and had it thrown, by others' hands, on a trackless mountain.

So in that case Apollo did not bring it to pass that the babe should become the slayer of his sire, or that Laius should die—the dread thing which he feared—by his child's hand. Thus did the messages of seercraft map out the future. Do not you regard them, not at all. Whatever needful thing the god seeks he himself will easily bring to light.

OEDIPUS. What restlessness of soul, lady, what tumult of the mind has just come upon me since I heard you speak!

IOCASTA. What anxiety has startled you to make you say this?

OEDIPUS. I thought I heard this from you—that Laius was slain where three highways meet.

IOCASTA. Yes, that was the story; nor has it ceased yet.

OEDIPUS. And where is the place where this befell?

IOCASTA. The land is called Phocis. Branching roads lead to the same spot from Delphi and from Daulia.

OEDIPUS. And what is the time that has passed since these things happened?

IOCASTA. The news was published to the town shortly before you were first seen in power over this land.

OEDIPUS. O Zeus, what have you decreed to do to me?

IOCASTA. Why, Oedipus, does this thing weigh upon your soul?

OEDIPUS. Do not ask me yet. Tell me, what was the stature of Laius, and how ripe his manhood.

IOCASTA. He was tall, the silver just lightly strewn among his hair. His form was not greatly unlike yours.

OEDIPUS. Unhappy that I am! I think I have been laying myself even now under a dread curse without knowing it.

IOCASTA. What are you saying? I tremble when I look on you, my king.

OEDIPUS. I have dread misgivings that the seer can see. But you can show better if you will tell me one thing more.

IOCASTA. Indeed—though I tremble—I will answer all you ask when I hear it.

OEDIPUS. Did he go in small force, or with many armed followers, like a chieftain?

IOCASTA. There were five in all, one a herald; and there was one carriage, which bore Laius.

OEDIPUS. Alas! Now it is clear indeed.—Who was he who gave you these tidings, lady?

IOCASTA. A servant, the sole survivor who came home.

OEDIPUS. Is he perhaps in the house now?

IOCASTA. No, truly. As soon as he returned and found you reigning in the stead of Laius, he supplicated me, with hand laid on mine, that I would send him to the fields, to the pastures of the flocks, so that he might be far from the sight of this town. And I sent him; he was worthy, for a slave, to win even a larger boon than that.

OEDIPUS. Would, then, that he could return to us without delay!

IOCASTA. It is easy. But why do you enjoin this?

OEDIPUS. I fear, lady, that my own lips have been unguarded; that is why I am eager to behold him.

IOCASTA. He shall come. But I too, I think, have a claim to learn what lies heavy on your heart, my king.

OEDIPUS. Yes, and it shall not be kept from you, now that my forebodings have advanced so far. Who indeed is more to me than you, to whom I should speak in passing through such a fortune as this?

My father was Polybus of Corinth, my mother the Dorian Merope. I was held the first of all the folk in that town until a chance befell me, worthy indeed of wonder, but not worthy of my own heat concerning it. At a banquet a man full of wine cast it at me in his cups that I was not the true son of my sire. Though vexed I restrained myself for that day as best I might, but on the next I went to my mother and father and questioned them; and they were angry for the taunt with him who had let that word fly. So on their part I had comfort; but the thing was ever rankling in my heart, for it still crept abroad with strong rumor. Unknown to mother or father I went to Delphi. Phoebus sent me forth disappointed of that knowledge for which I came, but in his response set forth other things, full of sorrow and terror and woe: that I was fated to defile my mother's bed, that I should show unto men a brood which they could not endure to behold, and that I should be the slayer of the sire who begot me.

And I, when I had listened to this, turned to flight from the land of Corinth, calculating its site by the stars alone, to some spot where I should never see fulfillment of the infamies foretold in my evil doom. On my way I came to the regions in which you say that this prince perished. Now, lady, I will tell you the truth. When in my journey I was near to the three roads there met me a herald and a man seated in a carriage drawn by colts, as you have described. He who

was in front, and the old man himself, were for thrusting me
rudely from the path. Then in anger I struck him who
pushed me aside, the driver; and the old man, seeing it,
watched the moment when I was passing, and from the carriage brought his goad with two teeth full down upon my
head. But he was paid with interest; by one swift blow from
the staff in this hand he was rolled right out of the carriage
on his back. I slew every man of them.

But if this stranger had any tie of kinship with Laius, who
is now more wretched than the man before you? What mortal could prove more hated of heaven? Whom no stranger, no
citizen, is allowed to receive in his house; whom it is unlawful that anyone accost; whom all must repel from their
homes! And this, this curse, was laid on me by no mouth but
my own! I pollute the bed of the slain man with the hands by
which he perished. Say, am I vile? Am I not utterly unclean?
For I must be banished, and in banishment not see my own
people nor set foot in my own land, or else be joined in wedlock to my mother and slay my sire, even Polybus, who begot and reared me.

Would not a man speak aright of Oedipus if he judged
these things sent by some cruel power above man? Forbid,
forbid, you pure and awful gods, that I should see that day!
No, may I be swept from among men before I behold myself
visited with the brand of such a doom!

CHORUS. To us indeed, O King, these things are fraught with
    fear. Yet have hope, until at least you have gained full
    knowledge from him who saw the deed.

OEDIPUS. So far alone hope does rest with me: I can await the
    man summoned from the pastures.

IOCASTA. And when he has appeared what would you have of
    him?

OEDIPUS. I will tell you. If his story be found to tally with
    yours, I, at least, shall stand clear of disaster.

IOCASTA. And what of special note did you hear from me?

OEDIPUS. You were saying that he spoke of Laius as slain by
    robbers. If he speaks as before of several, I was not the
    slayer; a solitary man could not be held the same with that

band. But if he names one lonely wayfarer, then beyond doubt this guilt leans to me.

IOCASTA. Nay, be assured that is how the tale was first told; that he cannot revoke, for the city heard it, not I alone. But even if he should diverge somewhat from his former story, never, King, can he show that the murder of Laius, at least, is truly square to prophecy; of him Loxias plainly said that he must die by the hand of my child. Yet that poor innocent never slew him, but perished first itself. So henceforth, for what touches divination, I would not look to my right hand or my left.

OEDIPUS. You judge well. Nevertheless, send someone to fetch the peasant; do not neglect this matter.

IOCASTA. I will send without delay. But let us come into the house. I will do nothing save at your good pleasure.

(*Exeunt.*)

CHORUS. *May destiny still find me winning the praise of reverent purity in all words and deeds sanctioned by those laws of range sublime, called into life throughout the high clear heaven, whose father is Olympus alone; their parent was no race of mortal men, no, nor shall oblivion ever lay them to sleep; the god is mighty in them, and he grows not old.*

Insolence breeds the tyrant; insolence, once vainly surfeited on wealth that is not meet nor good for it, when it hath scaled the topmost ramparts, is hurled to a dire doom, wherein no service of the feet can serve. But I pray that the god never quell such rivalry as benefits the state; the god will I ever hold for our protector.

But if any man walks haughtily in deed or word, with no fear of Justice, no reverence for the images of gods, may an evil doom seize him for his ill-starred pride, if he will not win his vantage fairly, nor keep him from unholy deeds, but must lay profaning hands on sanctities.

Where such things are, what mortal shall boast any more that he can ward the arrows of the gods from his life? Nay, if such deeds are in honor, wherefore should we join in the sacred dance?

No more will I go reverently to earth's central and inviolate shrine, no more to Abae's temple or Olympia, if these oracles fit not the issue, so that all men shall point at them with the finger. Nay, King—if thou art rightly called—Zeus all-ruling, may it not escape thee and thine ever-deathless power!

The old prophecies concerning Laius are fading; already men are setting them at nought, and nowhere is Apollo glorified with honors; the worship of the gods is perishing.

IOCASTA (*enters with suppliant boughs*). Princes of the land, the thought has come to me to visit the shrines of the gods with this wreathed branch in my hands and these gifts of incense. For Oedipus excites his soul overmuch with all manner of alarms. He does not, like a man of sense, judge the new things by the old, but is at the will of the speaker, if he speaks terrors.

Since I can do no good by counsel, I have come to you, Lycean Apollo, for you are nearest. I supplicate you with these symbols of prayer, that you may find us some riddance from uncleanness. For now we are all afraid seeing *him* affrighted, even as they who see fear in the helmsman of their ship.

MESSENGER FROM CORINTH (*enters*). Might I learn from you, strangers, where is the house of King Oedipus? Or better still, tell me where he himself is, if you know.

CHORUS. This is his dwelling, and he himself, stranger, is within. This lady is the mother of his children.

MESSENGER. Then may she be ever happy in a happy home, since she is his heaven-blest queen.

IOCASTA. Happiness to you also, stranger! 'tis the due of your fair greeting. But say what you have come to seek or tell.

MESSENGER. Good tidings, lady, for your house and for your husband.

IOCASTA. What are they? From whom have you come?

MESSENGER. From Corinth. At the message which I will soon speak you will rejoice, doubtless, but perhaps grieve.

IOCASTA. What is it? How does it have this double potency?

MESSENGER. The people will make him king of the Isthmian land, as it was said there.

IOCASTA. How is that? Is the aged Polybus no more in power?

MESSENGER. No; death holds him in the tomb.

IOCASTA. What do you say? Is Polybus dead, old man?

MESSENGER. If I am not speaking the truth I am content to die.

IOCASTA. Handmaid, away with all speed and tell this to your master. O you oracles of the gods, where stand you now! This is the man whom Oedipus long feared and shunned, lest he should slay him; and now this man has died in the course of destiny, not by his hand.

OEDIPUS (*enters*). Iocasta, dearest wife, why have you summoned me forth from these doors?

IOCASTA. Hear this man, and judge, as you listen, to what the awful oracles of the gods have come.

OEDIPUS. And he—who may he be, and what news does he have for me?

IOCASTA. He is from Corinth, to say that your father Polybus lives no longer but has perished.

OEDIPUS. How stranger? Let me have it from your own mouth.

MESSENGER. If I must first make these tidings plain, know indeed that he is dead and gone.

OEDIPUS. By treachery, or by visit of disease?

MESSENGER. A light thing in the scale brings the aged to their rest.

OEDIPUS. Ah, he died, it seems, of sickness?

MESSENGER. Yes, and of the long years he had counted.

OEDIPUS. Alas, alas! Why indeed, my wife, should one look to the hearth of the Pythian seer, or to the birds that scream above our heads, on whose showing I was doomed to slay my sire? But he is dead and hid already beneath the earth; and here am I, who have not put hand to spear. Unless, perchance, he was killed by longing for me; so indeed I should be the cause of his death. But the oracles as they stand, at least, Polybus has swept with him to his rest in Hades; they are worth nothing.

IOCASTA. Nay, did I not so foretell you long since?

OEDIPUS. You did, but I was misled by my fear.

IOCASTA. No more lay any of those things to heart.

OEDIPUS. But surely I must needs fear my mother's bed?

IOCASTA. Nay, what should mortal fear for whom the decrees of fortune are supreme and who has clear foresight of nothing? 'Tis best to live at random, as one may. But do not fear touching wedlock with your mother. Many men before now have so fared in dreams also; but he to whom these things are as nothing bears his life most easily.

OEDIPUS. All these bold words of yours would have been well if my mother were not living; but as it is, since she is alive, I must needs fear. But you say well.

IOCASTA. However, your father's death is a great sign to cheer us.

OEDIPUS. Great, I know. But my fear is of her who lives.

MESSENGER. And who is the woman about whom you fear?

OEDIPUS. Merope, old man, the consort of Polybus.

MESSENGER. And what is it in her that moves your fear?

OEDIPUS. A heaven-sent oracle of dread import, stranger.

MESSENGER. Lawful for another to know or unlawful?

OEDIPUS. Lawful, surely. Loxias once said that I was doomed to espouse my own mother and to shed with my own hands my father's blood. That is why my home in Corinth was long kept by me afar—with happy outcome, indeed, yet still it is sweet to see the face of parents.

MESSENGER. Was it indeed in fear of this that you were an exile from the city?

OEDIPUS. And because I did not wish, old man, to be the slayer of my sire.

MESSENGER. Then why have I not freed you, King, from this fear, seeing that I came with friendly purpose?

OEDIPUS. Indeed you would have due reward from me.

MESSENGER. Indeed it was chiefly for this that I came—that, on your return home, I might reap some good.

OEDIPUS. No, I will never go near my parents.

MESSENGER. Ah my son, it is plain enough that you do not know what you are doing.

OEDIPUS. How, old man? For the gods' love, tell me.

MESSENGER. If for these reasons you shrink from going home.

OEDIPUS. Aye, I dread lest Phoebus prove himself true for me.

MESSENGER. You dread to be stained with guilt through your parents?

OEDIPUS. Just so, old man; this it is that always affrights me.

MESSENGER. Do you know then that your fears are wholly vain?

OEDIPUS. How so, if I was born of these parents?

MESSENGER. Because Polybus was nothing to you in blood.

OEDIPUS. What are you saying? Was Polybus not my sire?

MESSENGER. No more than he who speaks to you, but just so much.

OEDIPUS. And how can my sire be level with him who is nothing to me?

MESSENGER. He did not beget you any more than I.

OEDIPUS. Why then did he call me his son?

MESSENGER. Know that he had received you as a gift from my hands long ago.

OEDIPUS. And yet he loved me so dearly, when I came from another's hand?

MESSENGER. Yes, his former childlessness won him to do so.

OEDIPUS. And you—had you bought me or found me by chance when you gave me to him?

MESSENGER. Found you in Cithaeron's winding glens.

OEDIPUS. Why were you roaming in these regions?

MESSENGER. I was there in charge of mountain flocks.

OEDIPUS. What, you were a shepherd, a vagrant hireling?

MESSENGER. But your preserver, my son, in that hour.

OEDIPUS. And what pain was mine when you took me in your arms?

MESSENGER. The ankles of your feet might witness.

OEDIPUS. Ah me, why do you speak of that old trouble?

MESSENGER. I freed you when you had your ankles pinned together.

OEDIPUS. Aye, it was a dread brand of shame that I took from my cradle.

MESSENGER. Such, that from that fortune you were called by the name which is still yours.

OEDIPUS. Oh, for the gods' love, was the deed my mother's or father's? Speak!

MESSENGER. I do not know; he who gave you to me knows more of that than I.

OEDIPUS. What? You had me from another? You did not light on me yourself?

MESSENGER. No, another shepherd gave you up to me.

OEDIPUS. Who was he? Are you in position to tell clearly?

MESSENGER. I think he was called one of the household of Laius.

OEDIPUS. The king who ruled this country long ago?

MESSENGER. The same. It was in his service that the man was a herd.

OEDIPUS. Is he still alive for me to see?

MESSENGER. You folk of the country should know best.

OEDIPUS. Is there any of you here present that knows the herd of whom he speaks, any that has seen him in the pastures or the town? Answer! The hour has come that these things should be finally revealed.

CHORUS. He seems to mean no other than the peasant whom you were already eager to see; but our lady Iocasta might best tell that.

OEDIPUS. Lady, you remember the man we lately summoned? Is it of him that this man speaks?

IOCASTA. Why ask of whom he spoke? Do not regard it . . . Do not waste a thought on what he said . . . It is futile.

OEDIPUS. It must not be that with such clues in my grasp I should fail to bring my birth to light.

IOCASTA. For the gods' sake, if you have any care, for your own life, forbear this search! My anguish is enough.

OEDIPUS. Be of good courage; though I be found the son of servile mother, yes, a slave by three descents, *you* will not be proved base-born.

IOCASTA. Yet hear me, I implore you: do not do this.

OEDIPUS. I must not hear of not discovering the whole truth.

IOCASTA. Yet I wish you well, I counsel you for the best.

OEDIPUS. These best counsels, then, vex my patience.

IOCASTA. Ill-fated one! May you never come to know who you are!

OEDIPUS. Go, someone, fetch me the herdsman here, and leave yonder woman to glory in her princely stock.

IOCASTA. Alas, alas, miserable!—that word alone can I say to you, and no other word henceforth forever. (*Rushes into the house.*)

CHORUS. Why has the lady gone, Oedipus, in a transport of wild grief? I misdoubt a storm of sorrow will break forth from this silence.

OEDIPUS. Break forth what will. Be my race never so lowly I must crave to learn it. That woman perhaps—for she is proud with more than a woman's pride—thinks shame of my base source. But I hold myself son of Fortune that gives good and will not be dishonored. She is the mother from whom I spring; and the months, my kinsmen, have marked me sometimes lowly, sometimes great. Such being my lineage, never more can I prove false to it, or spare to search out the secret of my birth.

CHORUS. *If I am a seer or wise of heart, O Cithaeron, you shall not fail, by yonder heaven you shall not, to know at tomorrow's full moon that Oedipus honors you as native to him, as his nurse, and his mother, and that you are celebrated in our dance and song, because you are well-pleasing to our prince. O Phoebus to whom we cry, may these things find favor in your sight!*

Who was it, my son, who of the race whose years are many, that bore you in wedlock with Pan, the mountain-roaming father? Or was it a bride of Loxias that bore you? For dear to him are all the upland pastures. Or perchance it was Cyllene's lord, or the Bacchants' god, dweller on the hilltops, that received you, a newborn joy, from one of the nymphs of Helicon, with whom he most does sport.

OEDIPUS. Elders, if it is for me to guess, who have never met with him, I think I see the herdsman of whom we have long been in quest; for in his venerable age he tallies with yonder stranger's years, and furthermore I know those who bring him as servants of my own. But perhaps you may have the

advantage of me in knowledge, if you have seen the herdsman before.

CHORUS. Yes, I know him, be sure. He was in the service of
Laius, trusty as any man in his shepherd's place.

(*Enter* HERDSMAN.)

OEDIPUS. I ask you first, Corinthian stranger, is this the man
you mean?

MESSENGER. This man whom you see.

OEDIPUS. Ho you, old man: I would have you look this way and
answer all that I ask. You were once in the service of Laius?

HERDSMAN. I was, a slave not bought but reared in his house.

OEDIPUS. Employed in what labor or what way of life?

HERDSMAN. For the best part of my life I tended flocks.

OEDIPUS. And what the regions that you chiefly haunted?

HERDSMAN. Sometimes it was Cithaeron, sometimes the neighboring ground.

OEDIPUS. Do you recall having noted yonder man in these
parts—

HERDSMAN. Doing what? . . . What man do you mean? . . .

OEDIPUS. This man here—or of having ever met him before?

HERDSMAN. Not so that I could speak at once from memory.

MESSENGER. And no wonder, master. But I will bring clear rec-
ollection to his ignorance. I am sure that he well remembers
the time when we abode in the region of Cithaeron—he
with two flocks, I, his comrade, with one—three full half-
years, from spring to Arcturus; and then for the winter I
used to drive my flock to my own fold and he took his to the
fold of Laius. Did any of this happen as I tell or did it not?

HERDSMAN. You speak the truth, though it is long ago.

MESSENGER. Come, tell me now, do you recall having given
me a boy in those days, to be reared as my own foster-son?

HERDSMAN. What now? Why do you ask the question?

MESSENGER. Yonder man, my friend, is he who was then young.

HERDSMAN. Plague seize you, be silent once for all!

OEDIPUS. Ha! Chide him not, old man; your words need chiding more than his.

HERDSMAN. Wherein, most noble master, do I offend?

OEDIPUS. In not telling of the boy concerning whom he asks.

HERDSMAN. He speaks without knowledge, he is busy to no purpose.

OEDIPUS. You will not speak with a good grace, but you shall on pain.

HERDSMAN. Nay, for the gods' love, misuse not an old man!

OEDIPUS. Ho, someone, pinion him this instant!

HERDSMAN. Alas, why? What more would you learn?

OEDIPUS. Did you give this man the child of whom he asks?

HERDSMAN. I did—and would I had perished that day!

OEDIPUS. You will come to that unless you tell the honest truth.

HERDSMAN. Much more am I lost if I speak.

OEDIPUS. The follow is bent, it seems, on more delays.

HERDSMAN. No, no! I said before that I gave it to him.

OEDIPUS. Where had you got it? In your own house or from another?

HERDSMAN. My own it was not—I had received it from a man.

OEDIPUS. From whom of the citizens here? From what home?

HERDSMAN. Forbear, for the gods' love, master, forbear to ask more!

OEDIPUS. You are lost if I have to question you again.

HERDSMAN. It was a child, then, of the house of Laius.

OEDIPUS. A slave? or one born of his own race?

HERDSMAN. Ah me—I am on the dreaded brink of speech.

OEDIPUS. And I of hearing; yet must I hear.

HERDSMAN. You must know, then, that it was said to be his own child—but your lady within could best say how these things are.

OEDIPUS. How? She gave it to you?

HERDSMAN. Yes, O King.

OEDIPUS. For what end?

HERDSMAN. That I should make away with it.

OEDIPUS. Her own child, the wretch?

HERDSMAN. Yes, from fear of evil prophecies.

OEDIPUS. What were they?

HERDSMAN. The tale ran that he must slay his sire.

OEDIPUS. Why then did you give him up to this old man?

HERDSMAN. Through pity, master, thinking that he would bear him away to another land, from which he himself came; but he saved him for the direst woe. For if you are what this man says, know that you were born to misery.

OEDIPUS. Oh, oh! All brought to pass, all true! You light, may I now look my last on you, I who have been found accursed in birth, accursed in wedlock, accursed in the shedding of blood! (*Rushes into the palace.*)

CHORUS. *Alas, ye generations of men, how mere a shadow do I count your life! Where, where is the mortal who wins more of happiness than just the seeming, and, after the semblance, a falling away? Thine is a fate that warns me— thine, thine, unhappy Oedipus—to call no earthly creature blest.*

For he, O Zeus, sped his shaft with peerless skill, and won the prize of an all-prosperous fortune; he slew the maiden with crooked talons who sang darkly; he arose for our land as a tower against death. And from that time, Oedipus, thou hast been called our king, and hast been honored supremely, bearing sway in great Thebes.

But now whose story is more grievous in men's ears? Who is a more wretched captive to fierce plagues and troubles, with all his life reversed?

Alas, renowned Oedipus! The same bounteous place of rest sufficed thee, as child and as sire also, that thou shouldst make thereon thy nuptial couch. Oh, how can the soil wherein thy father sowed, unhappy one, have suffered thee in silence so long?

Time the all-seeing hath found thee out in thy despite: he judgeth the monstrous marriage wherein begetter and begotten have long been one.

Alas, thou child of Laius, would, would that I had never seen thee! I wail as one who pours a dirge from his lips; sooth to speak, 'twas thou that gavest me new life, and through thee darkness hath fallen upon mine eyes.

MESSENGER FROM THE PALACE (*enters*). You who are ever most honored in this land, what deeds you shall hear, what deeds behold, what burden of sorrow shall be yours, if true to your race, you still care for the house of Labdacus! Not Ister or Phasis, I declare, could wash this house clean, so many are the ills that it shrouds or will soon bring to light—ills wrought not unwittingly but of purpose. Those griefs smart most which are seen to be of our own choice.

CHORUS. Indeed those which we heard before do not fall short of claiming sore lamentation: besides them what do you announce?

MESSENGER. This is the shortest tale to tell and to hear: our royal lady Iocasta is dead.

CHORUS. Alas, luckless one! From what cause?

MESSENGER. By her own hand. The worst pain in what has chanced is not for you, for yours it is not to behold. Nevertheless, so far as my own memory serves, you shall learn that unhappy woman's fate.

When, frantic, she had passed within the vestibule, she rushed straight toward her nuptial couch, clutching her hair with the fingers of both hands. Once within the chamber she dashed the doors together at her back; then called on the name of Laius, long since a corpse, mindful of that son begotten long ago by whom the sire was slain, leaving the mother to breed accursed offspring with his own.

And she bewailed the wedlock whereby, wretched woman, she had borne a twofold brood, husband by husband, children by her child. How thereafter she perished is more than I know. For with a shriek Oedipus burst in, and suffered us not to watch her woe to the end; on him, as he rushed around, our eyes were set. To and fro he went, asking us to give him a sword, asking where he should find the wife who was no wife, but a mother whose womb had borne alike himself and his children. And in his frenzy a power above man was his guide, for it was none of us mortals who were nigh. With a dread shriek, as though someone beckoned him on, he sprang at the double doors, and from their sockets forced the bending bolts, and rushed into the room.

There we beheld the woman hanging by the neck in a twisted noose of swinging cords. But he, when he saw her, with a dread deep cry of misery loosed the halter by which she hung. When the hapless woman was stretched upon the ground, then was the sequel dread to see. He tore from her raiment the golden brooches with which she was decked, and lifted them, and smote full on his own eyeballs, uttering words like these: "No more shall you behold such horrors as I was suffering and working! Long enough have you looked on those whom you ought never to have seen, failed in knowledge of those whom I yearned to know: henceforth you shall be dark!"

To such dire refrain not once alone but oft he struck his eyes with lifted hand. At each blow the ensanguined eye-balls bedewed his beard; no sluggish drops of gore were sent forth, but all at once a dark shower of blood came down like hail.

From the deeds of both ills have broken forth not on one alone, but with mingled woe for man and wife. The old happiness of their ancestral fortune was aforetime happiness indeed; but today lamentation, ruin, death, shame, all earthly ills that can be named, all, all are theirs.

CHORUS. And has the sufferer now any respite from pain?
MESSENGER. He is crying for someone to unbar the gates and show to all the Cadmeans his father's slayer, his mother's— the unholy word must not pass my lips—as intending to cast himself out of the land and abide no more to make the house accursed under his own curse. But he lacks strength and one to guide his steps; for the anguish is more than man may bear. And he will show this to you also; for, look, the bars of the gates are withdrawn, and soon you shall behold a sight which even he who abhors it must pity.

(*Enter* OEDIPUS.)

CHORUS. O dread fate for men to see, O most dreadful of all that have met my eyes! Unhappy man, what madness has come on you? Who is the unearthly foe that, with a bound of more than mortal range, has made your ill-starred life his prey?

Alas, alas, you unfortunate! Nay, I cannot even look on

you, though there is much that I would like to ask, like to learn, much that draws my wistful gaze—you fill me with such shuddering!

OEDIPUS. *Woe is me! Alas, alas, wretched that I am! Whither, whither, am I borne in my misery? How is my voice swept abroad on the wings of the air? Oh my Fate, how far have you sprung!*

CHORUS. *To a dread place, dire in men's ears, dire in their sight.*

OEDIPUS. *O you horror of darkness that enfolds me, visitant unspeakable, resistless, sped by a wind too fair!*
Ay me! and once again, ay me!
How is my soul pierced by the stab of these goads, and too by the memory of sorrows!

CHORUS. *Yes, amid woes so many a twofold pain may well be yours to mourn and to bear.*

OEDIPUS. *Ah, friend, you still are steadfast in your tendance of me, you still have patience to care for the blind man! Ah me! Your presence is not hid from me; no, dark though I am yet I know your voice full well.*

CHORUS. *Man of dread deeds, how could you so quench your vision? What more than human power urged you?*

OEDIPUS. *Apollo, friends, Apollo was he that brought these woes of mine to pass, these sore, sore woes; but the hand that struck the eyes was none save mine, wretched that I am! Why was I to see when light could show me nothing sweet?*

CHORUS. *These things were just as you say.*

OEDIPUS. *Say, friends, what more can I behold, what can I love, what greeting can touch my ear with joy? Hasten, lead me from the land, friends, lead me hence, the utterly lost, the thrice accursed, yes, the mortal most abhorred of heaven!*

CHORUS. *Wretched alike for your fortune and for your sense of it, would that I had never so much as known you!*

OEDIPUS. *Perish the man, whoever he was, that freed me in the pastures from the cruel shackle on my feet, and saved me from death, and gave me back to life—a thankless deed! Had I died then I would not have been so sore a grief to my friends and to my own soul.*

CHORUS. *I too would have preferred it so.*

OEDIPUS. *I would not have come to shed my father's blood, nor been called among men the spouse of her from whom I sprang. But now I am forsaken of the gods, son of a defiled mother, successor to his bed who gave me my own wretched being; and if there is yet a woe surpassing woes, it has become the portion of Oedipus.*

CHORUS. I do not know how I can say that you have counseled well, for you had better be dead than living and blind.

OEDIPUS. Do not show me at length that these things had better not be done so; give me no more counsel. If I had sight I do not know with what eyes I could even have looked on my father when I came to the place of the dead, yes, or on my miserable mother, since I have sinned against both such sins as strangling could not punish. Do you suppose that the sight of children born as mine were born was lovely for me to look upon? No, no, not lovely to my eyes forever! No, nor was this town with its towered walls, nor the sacred statues of the gods, since I, thrice wretched that I am, I, noblest of the sons of Thebes, have doomed myself to know these no more by my own command that all should thrust away the impious one, even him whom the gods have shown to be unholy—and of the race of Laius.

After bearing such a stain upon me, was I to look with steady eyes on this folk? No, surely; no, if there were yet a way to choke the fount of hearing I would not have spared to make a fast prison of this wretched frame, that so I should have known neither sight nor sound; for it is sweet that our thought should dwell beyond the sphere of griefs.

Alas, Cithaeron, why did you have a shelter for me? When I was given to you why did you not slay me straightway, that so I might never have revealed my source to men? Ah Polybus, ah Corinth, and you that were called the ancient house of my fathers, how seeming fair was I your nurseling, and what ills were festering beneath! For now I am found evil, and of evil birth. O you three roads, and you secret glen, you coppice, and narrow way where three paths met, you who drank from my hands that father's blood which was my own—do you remember what deeds I wrought for you to see, and then, when I came here, what fresh deeds I went on to do?

O marriage-rites, you gave me birth, and when you had brought me forth you bore children to your child, you created an incestuous kinship of fathers and brothers and sons, of brides and wives and mothers, yes, all the foulest shame that is wrought among men! Nay, but it is improper to name what it is improper to do. Hurry, for the gods' love, hide me somewhere beyond the land, or slay me, or cast me into the sea, where you shall never more behold me! Approach, deign to lay your hands on a wretched man; hearken, fear not—my plague can rest on no mortal beside.

(*Enter* CREON.)

CHORUS. Nay, here is Creon, in apt season for your requests, whether they require act or counsel; for he alone is left to guard the land in your stead.

OEDIPUS. Ah me, how indeed shall I accost him? What claim to credence can be shown on my part? For in the past I have been found wholly false to him.

CREON. I have not come in mockery, Oedipus, nor to reproach you with any bygone fault. (*To* ATTENDANTS.) But you, if you respect the children of men no more, revere at least the all-nurturing flame of our lord the Sun, spare to show thus nakedly a pollution such as this, one which neither earth can welcome, nor the holy rain, nor the light. Nay, take him into the house as quickly as you may, for it best accords with piety that kinsfolk alone should see and hear a kinsman's woes.

OEDIPUS. For the gods' love, since you have done a gentle violence to my presage when you come in a spirit so noble to me a man most vile, grant me a boon; for your good I will speak, not for my own.

CREON. What wish are you so eager to have of me?

OEDIPUS. Cast me out of this land with all speed, to a place where no mortal shall be found to greet me more.

CREON. This I would have done, be sure, but that I craved first to learn all my duty from the god.

OEDIPUS. Nay, his behest has been set forth in full—to let me perish, the parricide, the unholy one that I am.

CREON. Such was the purport; yet seeing to what a pass we have come it is better to learn clearly what should be done.

OEDIPUS. Will you then seek a response on behalf of such a wretch as I am?

CREON. Yes, for you yourself will now surely put faith in the god.

OEDIPUS. Yes; and on you I lay this charge, to you I will make this entreaty: give to her who is within such burial as you would yourself give, for you will render the last rites to your own properly. But for me, never let this city of my sire be condemned to have me dwelling in it, so long as I live. No, suffer me to abide on the hills, yonder where Cithaeron is, famed as mine, which my mother and father while they lived set for my appointed tomb, that so I may die by the decree of those who sought to slay me. Yet of this much I am sure, that neither sickness nor anything else can destroy me; for I would never have been snatched from death except to be reserved for some strange doom.

Let my fate go where it will; but as touching my children, I pray you, Creon, take no care upon yourself for my sons; they are men, so that wherever they may be they can never lack the means to live. But my two girls, poor unfortunates, who never knew my table spread apart or lacked their father's presence, but always in all things shared my daily bread—I pray you, care for *them*. If you can, suffer me to touch them with my hands and to indulge my grief. Grant it, prince, grant it, you noble heart! Ah, could I but once touch them with my hands I should think that they were with me, even as when I had sight . . .

(ANTIGONE *and* ISMENE *are led in.*)

Ha? Gods, can it be my loved ones that I hear sobbing, can Creon have taken pity on me and sent me my children, my darlings? Am I right?

CREON. Yes, it is of my contriving, for I knew your joy in them of old, the joy that now is yours.

OEDIPUS. Then blessed be you, and for reward of this errand may heaven prove a kinder guardian to you than it has to me. My children, where are you? Come here, here to the hands of him whose mother was your own, the hands whose doings have wrought that your sire's once bright eyes should be such orbs as these; seeing nothing, knowing nothing, he became your father by her from whom he sprang. For you too I weep—behold you I cannot—when I think of the bitter life in days to come which men will make you live. To what company of the citizens will you go, to what festival, from which you will not return home in tears, instead of sharing in the holiday? When you have come to years ripe for marriage, who shall he be, who shall be the man, my daughters, who will hazard taking unto him such reproaches as must be baneful alike to my offspring and to yours? What misery is wanting? Your sire slew his sire, he had seed of her who bore him, and begot you at the sources of his own being! Such are the taunts that will be cast at you; and who then will wed? The man does not live, no, it cannot be, my children, but you must wither in barren maidenhood.

Ah, son of Menoeceus, hear me—since you are the only father left to them, since their parents, both of us, are lost—do not allow them to wander poor and unwed, for they are your kinswomen, and do not abase them to the level of my woes. Pity them, when you see them at this tender age so utterly forlorn, except for you. Signify your promise, generous man, by the touch of your hand! To you, my children, I would have given much counsel if your minds were mature; but now I would have this to be your prayer, that you live where occasion suffers, and that the life which is your portion may be happier than your sire's.

CREON. Your grief has had large enough scope. Nay, pass into the house.

OEDIPUS. I must obey, though it is in no wise sweet.

CREON. Yes, for it is in season that all things are good.

OEDIPUS. Do you know on what conditions I will go?

CREON. You shall name them; I shall know them when I hear.

OEDIPUS. See that you send me to dwell beyond this land.

CREON. You are asking me for what the god must give.

OEDIPUS. Nay, to the gods I have become most hateful.

CREON. Then you shall have your wish presently.

OEDIPUS. So you consent?

CREON. It is not my wont to speak idly what I do not mean.

OEDIPUS. Then it is time to lead me away.

CREON.   Come then—but let your children go.

OEDIPUS. Do not take these from me!

CREON. Do not crave to be master in all things; the mastery which you won has not followed you through life.

CHORUS. *Dwellers in our native Thebes, behold, this is Oedipus, who knew the famed riddle and was a man most mighty; what citizen did not gaze with envy on his fortunes? Behold into what a stormy sea of dread trouble he has come.*

    Therefore, while our eyes wait to see the destined final day, we must call no one happy who is of mortal race, until he has crossed life's border, free from pain.

ANTIGONE

FROM THE ENDING OF *OEDIPUS THE KING* WE know that Oedipus will be exiled from Thebes, blind and a beggar. From *Oedipus at Colonus* (written many years later) we know that Oedipus' sons Eteocles and Polyneices will war upon one another for the kingship of Thebes. In this war, the subject of Aeschylus' *Seven Against Thebes*, each of the brothers dies by the other's hand. Creon, who is again regent, decrees that Eteocles, who defended the city successfully, shall receive honorable burial, whereas Polyneices, who led the invading army of Argives against it, shall be denied burial. Sophocles' *Antigone* tells how Antigone, moved by piety, contravenes the decree and suffers death in consequence.

To praise Antigone as a flawless saint and condemn Creon as an unqualified tyrant is to mistake the tragic element in the play. Any conscientious ruler must have forbidden the burial, and any normal woman (Ismene, for example) would have obeyed the decree. We sympathize with Antigone when she gives her brother token burial by strewing dust on his corpse; but piety required no more, and her repetition of the merely ritual form shows that she is obsessed and in love with martyrdom. The great chorus which begins "Wonders are many and none is more wonderful than man" concludes by insisting that for all man's ingenuity he must not violate the laws of the state. Creon does bluster, to cover his weakness, but his afflictions are almost greater than Antigone's. He shows his devotion to duty, after Teiresias' admonition and the chorus' advice that he should free the living girl from her tomb and then bury the dead man, by *first* giving

Polyneices proper burial and *then* going to release Antigone. Creon's lot is sad, Antigone's tragic. No normal woman could have done what she did, yet the spectacle of a young girl giving up love and life for the sake of an ideal remains permanently edifying.

PERSONS

ANTIGONE } daughters of   TEIRESIAS, *blind prophet*
ISMENE   } *Oedipus*   GUARD
CREON, *King of Thebes*   MESSENGERS
EURYDICE, *his wife*   CHORUS OF THEBAN ELDERS
HAEMON, *his son*

SCENE: *Before the palace at Thebes.*

(*Enter* ANTIGONE, *who motions* ISMENE *from palace.*)

ANTIGONE. Sister Ismene, my own dear sister, do you know of any ill, of all those bequeathed by Oedipus, that Zeus does not fulfill for us two while we live? There is nothing painful, nothing fraught with ruin, no shame, no dishonor, that I have not seen in your woes and mine.

     And now what of this new edict of which men speak that our captain has just published to all Thebes? Have you any knowledge of it? Have you heard? Or is it hidden from you that our friends are threatened with the doom of our foes?

ISMENE. No word of friends, Antigone, cheerful or painful has come to me since we two sisters were bereft of our two brothers, killed in one day by a twofold blow. Since the Argive host fled, this past night, I know nothing more, whether my fortune is brighter or more grievous.

ANTIGONE. I know it well; that is why I sought to bring you beyond the gates of the court, so that you could hear alone.

ISMENE. What is it? It is plain that you are brooding on some dark tidings.

ANTIGONE. What? Has not Creon destined our brothers, the one to honored burial, the other to unburied shame? Eteocles,

they say, with due observance of right and custom he has laid
in the earth, for his honor among the dead below. But the
luckless corpse of Polyneices—according to rumor it has
been published to the town that none shall entomb him or
mourn but leave him unwept, unsepulchered, a welcome object for the birds, when they spy him, to feast on at will.

Such, it is said, is the edict that the good Creon has set
forth for you and for me—yes, for *me;* and he is coming
here to proclaim it to those who do not know it. He does not
count the matter light, but whoso disobeys in any way, his
doom is death by stoning before all the people. You know
now, and will soon show whether you are nobly bred or the
base daughter of a noble line.

ISMENE. Poor sister—and if this is how things stand, what
could I help to do or undo?

ANTIGONE. Consider whether you will share the toil and the
deed.

ISMENE. In what venture? What can your meaning be?

ANTIGONE. Will you aid this hand of mine to lift the dead?

ISMENE. You would bury him when it is forbidden to Thebes?

ANTIGONE. I will do my part—and yours, if you will not—to a
brother. False to him I will never be found.

ISMENE. Ah, overbold! when Creon has forbidden?

ANTIGONE. Nay, he has no right to keep me from my own.

ISMENE. Ah me! think, sister, how our father perished, amid
hate and scorn, when sins bared by his own search had
moved him to strike both eyes with self-blinding hand; then
the mother and wife, two names in one, with twisted noose
destroyed her own life; and last, our two brothers in one
day—each shedding, luckless man, a kinsman's blood—
wrought out with mutual hands their common doom. And
now *we* in turn—we two left all alone—think how we shall
perish, more miserably than all the rest if, in defiance of the
law, we brave a king's decree or his powers. Nay, we must remember, first, that we were born women, who should not
strive with men; next that we are ruled of the stronger, so
that we must obey in these things, and in things still harder.

Seeing that force is put upon me, therefore, I will ask the Spirits Infernal to pardon and will hearken to our ruler. It is foolish to meddle.

ANTIGONE. I will not urge you—no, even if you should yet have the mind would you be welcome as a worker with *me*. Be what you will, I will bury him; well for me to die in doing so. I shall rest, a loved one with him whom I have loved, sinless in my crime; for I owe a longer allegiance to the dead than to the living, for in that world I shall abide forever. If *you* will, be guilty of dishonoring laws which the gods have established in honor.

ISMENE. I do them no dishonor. But to defy the state—I have no strength for that.

ANTIGONE. So plead then; I will go to heap the earth above the brother whom I love.

ISMENE. Unhappy you! How I fear for you!

ANTIGONE. Do not fear for me; guide your own fate aright.

ISMENE. At least, then, disclose this plan to none but hide it closely—and so, too, will I.

ANTIGONE. Oh, denounce it! You will be far more hateful for your silence if you do not proclaim these things to all.

ISMENE. You have a hot heart for chilling deeds.

ANTIGONE. I know that I please where I am most bound to please.

ISMENE. Well enough if you can; but you would do what you cannot.

ANTIGONE. Why then when my strength fails I shall have done.

ISMENE. A hopeless quest should not be made at all.

ANTIGONE. If this is how you speak you will have hatred from me and will justly be subject to the lasting hatred of the dead. But leave me, and the folly that is mine alone, to suffer this dread thing; for I shall suffer nothing so dreadful as an ignoble death.

ISMENE. Go, then, if you must; and of this be sure: though your errand is foolish to your dear ones you are truly dear.

(*Exeunt; enter* CHORUS.)

CHORUS. *Beam of the sun, fairest light that ever dawned on Thebe of the seven gates, thou hast shone forth at last, eye of golden day, arisen above Dirce's streams! The warrior of the white shield, who came from Argos in his panoply, hath been stirred by thee to headlong flight, in swifter career; who set forth against our land by reason of the vexed claims of Polyneices; and, like shrill-screaming eagle, he flew over into our land, in snow-white pinion sheathed, with an armed throng, and with plumage of helms.*

He paused above our dwellings; he ravened around our sevenfold portals with spears athirst for blood; but he went hence, or ever his jaws were glutted with our gore, or the Fire-god's pine-fed flame had seized our crown of towers. So fierce was the noise of battle raised behind him, a thing too hard for him to conquer, as he wrestled with his dragon foe.

For Zeus utterly abhors the boasts of a proud tongue; and when he beheld them coming on in a great stream, in the haughty pride of clanging gold, he smote with brandished fire one who was now hasting to shout victory at his goal upon our ramparts.

Swung down, he fell on the earth with a crash, torch in hand, he who so lately, in the frenzy of the mad onset, was raging against us with the blasts of his tempestuous hate. But those threats fared not as he hoped; and to other foes the mighty War-god dispensed their several dooms, dealing havoc around, a mighty helper at our need.

For seven captains at seven gates matched against seven, left the tribute of their panoplies to Zeus who turns the battle; save those two of cruel fate, who, born of one sire and one mother, set against each other their twain conquering spears, and are sharers in a common death.

But since Victory of glorious name hath come to us, with joy responsive to the joy of Thebe whose chariots are many, let us enjoy forgetfulness after the late wars, and visit all the temples of the gods with night-long dance and song; and may Bacchus be our leader, whose dancing shakes the land of Thebe.

But lo, the king of the land comes yonder, Creon, son of Menoeceus, our new ruler by the new fortunes that the gods have given; what counsel is he pondering, that he hath proposed this special conference of elders, summoned by his general mandate?

CREON (*enters*). Sirs, the vessel of our state, after being tossed on wild waves, has once more been safely steadied by the gods; and you, out of all the folk, have been called apart by my summons, because I knew, first of all, how true and constant was your reverence for the royal power of Laius; how, again, when Oedipus was ruler of our land, and when he had perished, your steadfast loyalty still upheld their children. Since, then, his sons have fallen in one day by a twofold doom—each smitten by the other, each stained with a brother's blood—I now possess the throne and all its powers, by nearness of kinship to the dead.

No man can be fully known, in soul and spirit and mind, until he has been seen versed in rule and lawgiving. For if any, being supreme guide of the state, cleaves not to the best counsels, but, through some fear, keeps his lips locked, I hold, and have ever held, him most base; and if any makes a friend of more account than his fatherland, that man has no place in my regard. For I—be Zeus my witness, who sees all things always—would not be silent if I saw ruin, instead of safety, coming to the citizens; nor would I ever deem the country's foes a friend to myself; remembering this, that our country is the ship that bears us safe, and that only while she prospers in our voyage can we make true friends.

Such are the rules by which I guard this city's greatness. And in accord with them is the edict which I have now published to the folk touching the sons of Oedipus; that Eteocles, who has fallen fighting for our city, in all renown of arms shall be entombed and crowned with every rite that follows the noblest dead to their rest. But for his brother Polyneices, who came back from exile and sought to consume utterly with fire the city of his fathers and the shrines of his fathers' gods, sought to taste of kindred blood and to lead the remnant into slavery—touching this man it has been proclaimed to our people that none shall grace him with sepulture or lament, but leave him unburied, a corpse for birds and dogs to eat, a ghastly sight of shame.

Such the spirit of my dealing; and never, by deed of mine, shall the wicked stand in honor before the just; but whoso has good will to Thebes, he shall be honored of me, in his life and in his death.

CHORUS. Such is your pleasure, Creon son of Menoeceus, touching this city's foe and its friends; and you have power, I know, to enjoin what you will, both for the dead and for all us who live.

CREON. See to it, then, that you be guardians of the mandate.

CHORUS. Lay the burden of this task on some younger man.

CREON. Nay, watchers of the corpse have been found.

CHORUS. What then is this further charge that you would give?

CREON. That you do not side with the breakers of these commands.

CHORUS. No man is so foolish that he is enamored of death.

CREON. That is indeed the penalty; but lucre has often ruined men through their hopes.

GUARD (*enters*). My liege, I will not say that I come breathless from speed or that I have plied a nimble foot; for often did my thoughts make me pause and wheel round in my path to return. My mind was holding large discourse with me: "Fool, why are you going on to your certain doom?" "Wretch, tarrying again? And if Creon hears this from another, must you not smart for it?" So debating I went on my way with lagging steps, and thus a short road was made long. At last, however, it carried the day that I should come here to you; and though my tale is nothing yet I will tell it. I come with a good grip on one hope—that I can suffer nothing but what is my fate.

CREON. What is it that disquiets you so?

GUARD. I wish to tell you first about myself—I did not do the deed; I did not see the doer; it is not right that I should come to any harm.

CREON. You have a shrewd eye for your mark; you fence your-

self round against blame very well. Clearly, you have some
strange thing to tell.

GUARD. Yes, truly. Dread news makes a man pause long.

CREON. Then tell it, will you, and get gone.

GUARD. Well, this is it. The corpse—someone has just given it
burial, and gone away, after sprinkling thirsty dust on the
flesh, with such other rites as piety enjoins.

CREON. What are you saying? What man alive has dared this
deed?

GUARD. I do not know. No stroke of pickax was seen there, no
earth thrown up by mattock; the ground was hard and dry,
unbroken, without track of wheels. The doer was one who
left no trace. And when the first day-watchman showed it to
us, troubled wonder fell upon us all. The dead man was
veiled from us; not shut within a tomb, but lightly strewn
with dust, as by the hand of one who shunned a curse. And
no sign met the eye as though any beast of prey or any dog
had come nigh to him or torn him.

  Then evil words flew fast and loud among us, guard ac-
cusing guard; it would even have come to blows at last, nor
was there any to hinder. Every man was the culprit and no
one was convicted, but all disclaimed knowledge of the
deed. And we were ready to take red-hot iron in our hands,
to walk through fire, to make oath by the gods that we had
not done the deed, that we were not privy to the planning or
the doing.

  At last, when all our searching was fruitless, a man spoke
and made us all bend our faces on the earth in fear, for we
did not see how we could gainsay him, or escape mischance
if we obeyed. His counsel was that the deed must be reported to you and not hidden. This seemed best, and the lot
doomed unlucky me to win this prize. So here I stand, as unwelcome as unwilling, I know well; for no man delights in
the bearer of bad news.

CHORUS. O King, my thoughts have long been whispering:
might this deed perhaps be the work of gods?

CREON. Cease before your words fill me utterly with wrath,

lest you be found at once an old man and foolish. You say
what is not to be borne when you say that the gods have care
for this corpse. Was it for high reward of trusty service that
they sought to hide the nakedness of a man who came to
burn their pillared shrines and sacred treasures, to burn their
land and scatter its laws to the winds? Or do you behold the
gods honoring the wicked? It cannot be. No! From the first
there were certain in the town that muttered against me,
chafing at this edict, wagging their heads in secret; they did
not keep their necks duly under the yoke, like men con-
tented with my sway.

'Tis by them, well I know, that these have been beguiled
and bribed to do this deed. Nothing so evil as money ever
grew to be current among men. This lays cities low, this
drives men from their homes, this strains and warps honest
souls till they set themselves to works of shame; this still
teaches folk to practice villainies and to know every godless
deed.

But all the men who wrought this thing for hire have
made it sure that, soon or late, they shall pay the price. Now
as Zeus still has my reverence know this—I tell it to you
on my oath: If you do not find the very author of this burial and produce him before my eyes, death alone shall not
be enough for you till first, hung up alive, you have revealed this outrage, so that henceforth you may thieve with
better knowledge whence lucre should be won and learn
that it is not well to love gain from every source. You will
find that ill-gotten pelf brings more men to ruin than to
prosperity.

GUARD. May I speak? Or shall I just turn and go?
CREON. Do you not know that even now your voice offends?
GUARD. Is your smart in the ears or in the soul?
CREON. And why would you define the seat of my pain?
GUARD. The doer vexes your mind, I your ears.
CREON. Ah, you are a born babbler it's easy to see.
GUARD. May be, but never the doer of this deed.
CREON. More too, the seller of your life for silver.

GUARD. Alas, it's truly sad that he who judges should mis-judge.

CREON. Let your fancy play with "judgment" as it will; but if you do not show me the doers of these things you shall avow that dastardly gains work sorrows.

GUARD. Well, may he be found! that would be best. But whether he is caught or not—fortune must settle that—you will surely not see me here again. Saved even now beyond hope and thought, I owe the gods great thanks. (*Exit.*)

CHORUS. *Wonders are many, and none is more wonderful than man; the power that crosses the white sea, driven by the stormy south-wind, making a path under surges that threaten to engulf him; and Earth, the eldest of the gods, the immortal, the unwearied, doth he wear, turning the soil with the offspring of horses, as the ploughs go to and fro from year to year.*

And the lighthearted race of birds, and the tribes of savage beasts, and the sea-brood of the deep, he snares in the meshes of his woven toils, he leads captive, man excellent in wit. And he masters by his arts the beast whose lair is in the wilds, who roams the hills; he tames the horse of shaggy mane, he puts the yoke upon its neck, he tames the tireless mountain bull.

And speech, and wind-swift thought, and all the moods that mold a state, hath he taught himself; and how to flee the arrows of the frost, when 'tis hard lodging under the clear sky, and the arrows of the rushing rain; yea, he hath resource for all; without resource he meets nothing that must come: only against Death shall he call for aid in vain; but from baffling maladies he hath devised escapes.

Cunning beyond fancy's dream is the fertile skill which brings him, now to evil, now to good. When he honors the laws of the land, and that justice which he hath sworn by the gods to uphold, proudly stands his city: no city hath he who, for his rashness, dwells with sin. Never may he share my hearth, never think my thoughts, who doth these things!

(*Enter* GUARD *leading* ANTIGONE.)

> *What portent from the gods is this? My soul is amazed. I*
> *know her—how can I deny that yonder maiden is Antigone?*
> *O luckless, and child of luckless sire—of Oedipus! What*
> *does this mean? Thou brought a prisoner?—thou, disloyal*
> *to the king's laws, and taken in folly?*

GUARD. Here she is, the doer of the deed—we caught this girl
burying him—but where is Creon?

CHORUS. Look, he comes forth again from the house, at our
need.

CREON (*enters*). What is it? What has happened that makes my
coming timely?

GUARD. O King, against nothing should men pledge their
word; for the afterthought belies the first intent. I could have
vowed that I should not soon be here again, scared by your
threats with which I had just been lashed; but—since the joy
that surprises and transcends our hopes is like in fullness to
no other pleasure—I have come, though in breach of my
sworn oath, bringing this maid, who was taken showing
grace to the dead. This time there was no casting of lots; no,
this luck has fallen to me, and to none else. And now, sire,
take her yourself, question her, examine her, as you will; but
I have a right to free and final quittance of this trouble.

CREON. And your prisoner here—how and where have you
taken her?

GUARD. She was burying the man; you know all.

CREON. Do you mean what you are saying? Do you speak
aright?

GUARD. I saw her burying the corpse that you had forbidden to
bury. Is that plain and clear?

CREON. And how was she seen? how taken in the act?

GUARD. This is how it was. When we had come to the place,
with those dread menaces of yours upon us, we swept away
all the dust that covered the corpse, and bared the dank
body well; and then sat us down on the brow of the hill, to
windward, heedful that the smell from him should not strike

us; every man was wide awake, and kept his neighbor alert
with torrents of threats, if any one should be careless of this
task.

So it went, until the sun's bright orb stood in mid-heaven,
and the heat began to burn. Then suddenly a whirlwind
lifted from the earth a storm of dust, a trouble in the sky, and
filled the plain, marring all the leafage of its woods, and the
wide air was choked with it. We closed our eyes, and bore
the plague from the gods.

And when, after a long while, this storm had passed, the
maid was seen; and she cried aloud with the sharp cry of a
bird in its bitterness, even as when within the empty nest it
sees the bed stripped of its nestlings. So she also, when she
saw the corpse bare, lifted up a voice of wailing, and called
down curses on the doers of that deed. And straightway she
brought thirsty dust in her hands, and from a shapely ewer
of bronze, held high, with thrice-poured drink-offering she
crowned the dead.

We rushed forward when we saw it, and at once closed
upon our quarry, who was in no way dismayed. Then we
taxed her with her past and present doings; and she denied
nothing—at once to my joy and to my pain. To have escaped
from ills oneself is a great joy; but it is painful to bring
friends to ill. Nevertheless, all such things are of less account to me than my own safety.

CREON. You, you whose face is bent to earth, do you avow, or
disavow, this deed?

ANTIGONE. I avow it; I make no denial.

CREON (*to* GUARD). You can go wherever you will, free and
clear of a grave charge.

(*Exit* GUARD.)

(*To* ANTIGONE.) Now, tell me, not in many words but
briefly, did you know that an edict had forbidden this?

ANTIGONE. I knew it; could I help it? It was public.

CREON. Did you then dare transgress that law?

ANTIGONE. Yes, for it was not Zeus that had published that edict; not such are the laws set among men by the Justice who dwells with the gods below. Nor did I deem that your decrees were of such force that a mortal could override the unwritten and unfailing statutes of heaven. For their life is not of today or yesterday, but from all time; no man knows when they were first put forth.

Not through dread of any human pride could I answer to the gods for breaking *these*. Die I must; that I knew well (how should I not?) even without your edicts. But if I am to die before my time I count that a great gain. If anyone lives as I do compassed about with evils, could he find anything but gain in death?

So for me to meet this doom is trifling grief. But if I had suffered my mother's son to lie in death an unburied corpse, that would have grieved me; for this I am not grieved. And if my present deeds are foolish in your sight, it may be that a foolish judge arraigns my folly.

CHORUS. The girl shows herself passionate child of passionate sire; she does not know how to bend before troubles.

CREON. Yet I would have you know that overstubborn spirits are most often humbled. It is the stiffest iron, baked to hardness in the fire, that you will most often see snapped and shivered; and I have known horses that show temper brought to order by a little curb. There is no room for pride when you are your neighbor's slave. This girl was already versed in insolence when she transgressed the laws that had been set forth; that now done, look, a second insult, to boast of it and exult in her deed.

Now verily I am no man, she is the man, if this victory shall rest with her and bring no penalty. No! though she is my sister's child or nearer to me in blood than any that worships Zeus at the altar of our house, she and her kinsfolk shall not avoid a doom most dire; for I charge that other with a like share in the plotting of this burial.

Summon her; I saw her within just now, raving and not mistress of her wits. So often before the deed, when people plot mischief in the dark, the mind stands self-convicted in its treason. But this too is hateful, when one who has been caught in wickedness then seeks to make the crime a glory.

ANTIGONE. Would you do more than take and slay me?

CREON. No, no more; having that I have all.

ANTIGONE. Why then do you delay? In your discourse there is nothing that pleases me—may there never be—and so my words must needs be unpleasing to you. And yet for glory—how could I have won a nobler than by giving burial to my own brother? All here would own that they thought it well, if their lips were not sealed by fear. Royalty, blest in so much besides, has the power to do and say what it will.

CREON. In that view you differ from all these Thebans.

ANTIGONE. They also share it, but they curb their tongues for you.

CREON. And are you not ashamed to act apart from them?

ANTIGONE. No; there is nothing shameful in piety to a brother.

CREON. Was it not a brother too that died in the opposite cause?

ANTIGONE. Brother by the same mother and the same sire.

CREON. Why then do you render a grace that is impious in his sight?

ANTIGONE. The dead man will not say that he so deems it.

CREON. Yes, if you make him but equal in honor with the wicked.

ANTIGONE. It was his brother, not his slave, that perished.

CREON. Wasting this land; while *he* fell as its champion.

ANTIGONE. Nevertheless Hades desires these rites.

CREON. But the good does not desire a like portion with the evil.

ANTIGONE. Who knows but this seems blameless in the world below?

CREON. A foe is never a friend—not even in death.

ANTIGONE. 'Tis not my nature to join in hating, but in loving.

CREON. Pass then to the world of the dead, and if you must needs love love them. While I live no woman shall rule me.

(ISMENE *is led in.*)

CHORUS. *Look, yonder Ismene comes forth, shedding such tears as fond sisters weep; a cloud upon her brow casts its shadow over her darkly-flushing face and breaks in rain on her fair cheek.*

CREON. You there who lurked like a viper in my house and were secretly draining my lifeblood while I did not know that I was nurturing two pests to rise against my throne—come tell me now, will you also confess your part in the burial or will you forswear all knowledge of it?

ISMENE. I have done the deed, if she allows my claim, and share the burden of the charge.

ANTIGONE. Nay, justice will not suffer you to do that; you did not consent to the deed, nor did I give you part in it.

ISMENE. But now that ills beset you I am not ashamed to sail the sea of trouble at your side.

ANTIGONE. Whose the deed was, Hades and the dead are witnesses; a friend in words is not the friend that I love.

ISMENE. Nay, sister, reject me not, but let me die with you and duly honor the dead.

ANTIGONE. Do not share my death nor claim deeds to which you have not put your hand; my death will suffice.

ISMENE. What life is dear to me bereft of you?

ANTIGONE. Ask Creon; all your care is for him.

ISMENE. Why vex me so when it does you no good?

ANTIGONE. If I am mocking it is with pain that I mock you.

ISMENE. Tell me, how can I serve you even now?

ANTIGONE. Save yourself; I do not grudge your escape.

ISMENE. Ah, misery! Shall I have no share in your fate?

ANTIGONE. Your choice was to live, mine to die.

ISMENE. At least your choice was not made without my protest.

ANTIGONE. One world approved your wisdom, another mine.

ISMENE. Nevertheless the offense is the same for both of us.

ANTIGONE. Be of good cheer: you live. My life has long been given to death, that so I might serve the dead.

CREON. Look, one of these girls has newly shown herself foolish, as the other has been since her life began.

ISMENE. So it is, O King, such reason as nature may have given
does not abide with the unfortunate, but goes astray.

CREON. Yours did when you chose vile deeds with the vile.

ISMENE. How could I endure life without her presence?

CREON. Do not speak of her "presence"; she lives no more.

ISMENE. But will you slay the betrothed of your own son?

CREON. There are other fields for him to plow.

ISMENE. But there can never be such love as bound him to her.

CREON. I do not like an evil wife for my son.

ANTIGONE. Haemon, beloved! How your father wrongs you.

CREON. Enough, enough of you and of your marriage!

CHORUS. Will you indeed rob your son of this maiden?

CREON. 'Tis Death that shall stay these bridals for me.

CHORUS. 'Tis determined, it seems, that she shall die.

CREON. Determined, yes, for you and for me. (*To the* ATTEN-
DANTS.) No more delay: servants, take them inside!
Henceforth they must be women and not range at large;
even the bold seek to fly when they see Death now closing
on their life.

(*Exeunt* ATTENDANTS, *guarding* ANTIGONE *and* ISMENE.)

CHORUS. *Blest are they whose days have not tasted of evil. For
when a house hath once been shaken from heaven, there the
curse fails nevermore, passing from life to life of the race;
even as, when the surge is driven over the darkness of the
deep by the fierce breath of Thracian sea-winds, it rolls up
the black sand from the depths, and there is a sullen roar
from wind-vexed headlands that front the blows of the
storm.*

*I see that from olden time the sorrows in the house of the
Labdacidae are heaped upon the sorrows of the dead; and
generation is not freed by generation, but some god strikes
them down, and the race hath no deliverance.*

For now that hope of which the light had been spread

above the last root of the house of Oedipus—that hope, in turn, is brought low—by the bloodstained dust due to the Gods Infernal, and by folly in speech, and frenzy at the heart.

Thy power, O Zeus, what human trespass can limit? That power which neither Sleep, the all-ensnaring, nor the untiring months of the gods can master; but thou, a ruler to whom time brings not old age, dwellest in the dazzling splendor of Olympus.

And through the future, near and far, as through the past, shall this law hold good: Nothing that is vast enters into the life of mortals without a curse.

For that hope whose wanderings are so wide is to many men a comfort, but to many a false lure of giddy desires; and the disappointment comes on one who knoweth nought till he burn his foot against the hot fire.

For with wisdom hath someone given forth the famous saying, that evil seems good, soon or late, to him whose mind the god draws to mischief; and but for the briefest space doth he fare free of woe.

But lo, Haemon, the last of thy sons; comes he grieving for the doom of his promised bride, Antigone, and bitter for the baffled hope of his marriage?

(*Enter* HAEMON.)

CREON. We shall soon know, better than seers could tell us. My son, have you come in rage against your father, when you heard the fixed doom of your betrothed? Or do I have your good will however I may act?

HAEMON. Father, I am yours, and in your wisdom you trace the rules which I shall follow. No marriage shall be deemed by me a greater gain than your good guidance.

CREON. Yes, this, my son, should be your heart's fixed law—in all things to obey your father's will. 'Tis for this that men pray to see dutiful children grow up around them in their homes, to requite their father's foe with evil, and to honor

his friend as he himself does. But the man who begets un-
profitable children—what shall we say he has sown but
troubles for himself and much triumph for his foes? Then do
not you, my son, at pleasure's beck dethrone your reason for
a woman's sake, knowing that this is a joy that soon grows
cold in clasping arms—an evil woman to share your bed
and your home. What wound could strike deeper than a
false friend? Nay, with loathing, and as if she were your enemy, let this girl go to find a husband in the house of Hades.
For since I have taken her alone of all the city in open disobedience, I will not make myself a liar to my people: I will
slay her.

So let her appeal as she will to the majesty of kindred
blood. If I am to nurture my own kindred in naughtiness I
shall have to bear with it in aliens. He who does his duty in
his own household will be found righteous in the state also.
But if anyone transgresses and does violence to the laws or
thinks to dictate to his rulers, such a man can win no praise
from me. No, whomsoever the city may appoint, that man
must be obeyed, in little things and great, in just things and
unjust; and I should feel sure that a man who thus obeys
would be a good ruler no less than a good subject, and in the
storm of spears would stand his ground where he was set,
loyal and dauntless at his comrade's side.

But disobedience is the worst of evils. This it is that ru-
ins cities; this makes homes desolate; by this the ranks of allies are broken into headlong rout. But of the lives whose
course is fair the greater part owes safety to obedience.
Therefore we must support the cause of order and in no
wise suffer a woman to worst us. Better to fall from power,
if we must, by a man's hand; then we could not be called
weaker than a woman.

CHORUS. To us, unless our years have stolen our wit, what you
say you seem to say wisely.

HAEMON. Father, the gods implant reason in men, the highest
of all things that we call our own. Not mine the skill, and
may I never seek, to say wherein you speak not aright; and
yet another man too might have some useful thought. At

least it is my natural office to watch, on your behalf, all that men say or do or find to blame. For the dread of your frown forbids the citizen to speak such words as would offend your ear; but I can hear these murmurs in the dark, these moanings of the city for this maiden. "No woman," they say, "ever merited her doom less, none ever was to die so shamefully for deeds so glorious as hers. When her own brother had fallen in bloody strife she would not leave him unburied to be devoured by carrion dogs or by any bird: does *she* not deserve the meed of golden honor?"

Such is the darkling rumor that spreads in secret. For me, my father, no treasure is so precious as your welfare. What indeed is a nobler ornament for children than a prospering sire's fair fame, or for sire than son's? Do not then persist in one mood alone for yourself; do not think that your word and yours alone must be right. For if any man thinks that he alone is wise, that in speech or in mind he has no peer, such a soul, when laid open, is always found empty.

No, though a man be wise, it is no shame for him to learn many things and to bend in season. Do you see, beside the wintry torrent's course, how the trees that yield to it save every twig while the stiffnecked perish root and branch? Even so he who keeps the sheet of his sail taut and never slackens it upsets his boat and finishes his voyage with keel uppermost.

Nay, forgo your wrath, permit yourself to change. If I, a younger man, may offer my thought, it would be far best, I suppose, that men should be all-wise by nature; but otherwise (and often the scale does not so incline) it is good also to learn from those who speak aright.

CHORUS. It is meet that you should profit by his words, sire, if what he says is seasonable, and you, Haemon, by your father's. There has been wise speech on both parts.

CREON. Men of my age—are we to be schooled by men of his?

HAEMON. In nothing that is not right; if I am young you should look to my merits, not to my years.

CREON. Is it a merit to honor the unruly?

HAEMON. I could wish no one to show respect for evildoers.

CREON. Is not she tainted with that malady?

HAEMON. Our Theban folk with one voice denies it.

CREON. Shall Thebes prescribe to me how I must rule?

HAEMON. See, there you have spoken like a youth indeed.

CREON. Am I to rule this land by other judgment than my own?

HAEMON. That is no city which belongs to one man.

CREON. Is not the city held to be the ruler's?

HAEMON. You would make a good monarch of a desert.

CREON. This boy, it seems, is the woman's champion.

HAEMON. If you are a woman; my care is really for you.

CREON. Shameless, at open feud with your father!

HAEMON. No, I see you offending against justice.

CREON. Do I offend when I respect my own prerogatives?

HAEMON. You do not respect them when you trample on the gods' honors.

CREON. O dastard nature, yielding place to woman!

HAEMON. You will never find me yield to baseness.

CREON. All your words, at least, plead for that girl.

HAEMON. And for you, and for me, and for the gods below.

CREON. You can never marry her, on this side of the grave.

HAEMON. Then she must die, and in death destroy another.

CREON. How! Does your boldness run to open threats?

HAEMON. What threat is it to combat vain resolves?

CREON. You shall rue your witless teaching of wisdom.

HAEMON. If you were not my father I would have called you unwise.

CREON. You woman's slave, use no wheedling speech with me.

HAEMON. You would speak and then hear no reply?

CREON. So? Now by the heaven above us, be sure of it, you shall smart for taunting me in this opprobrious strain. Bring forth that hated thing to die forthwith in his presence, before his eyes, at her bridegroom's side!

HAEMON. No, not at my side, never think it, shall she perish; nor shall you ever set eyes more upon my face. Rave, then, with such friends as can endure you. (*Exit.*)

CHORUS. The man is gone, O King, in angry haste; a youthful mind when stung is fierce.

CREON. Let him do or dream more than man—good speed to him! But he shall not save these two girls from their doom.

CHORUS. Do you indeed purpose to slay both?

CREON. Not her whose hands are pure: you say well.

CHORUS. And by what doom do you mean to slay the other?

CREON. I will take her where the path is loneliest and hide her, living, in a rocky vault with so much food set forth as piety prescribes, that the city may avoid a public stain. And there, praying to Hades, the only god whom she worships, perhaps she will obtain release from death. Or else she will learn at last though late that it is lost labor to revere the dead. (*Exit.*)

CHORUS. *Love, unconquered in the fight, Love, who makest havoc of wealth, who keepest thy vigil on the soft cheek of a maiden; thou roamest over the sea, and among the homes of dwellers in the wilds; no immortal can escape thee, nor any among men whose life is for a day; and he to whom thou hast come is mad.*

The just themselves have their minds warped by thee to wrong, for their ruin: 'tis thou that hast stirred up this present strife of kinsmen; victorious is the love-kindling light from the eyes of the fair bride; it is a power enthroned in sway beside the eternal laws; for there the goddess Aphrodite is working her unconquerable will.

(ANTIGONE *is led out to her execution.*)

But now I also am carried beyond the bounds of loyalty, and can no more keep back the streaming tears, when I see Antigone thus passing to the bridal chamber where all are laid to rest.

ANTIGONE. *See me, citizens of my fatherland, setting forth on my last way, looking my last on the sunlight that is for me no more. Hades who gives sleep to all is leading me living to Acheron's shore. I have had no portion in the chant that brings the bride, nor has any song been mine for the crowning of bridals. Me the lord of the Dark Lake shall wed.*

CHORUS. *Glorious, therefore, and with praise you depart to that deep place of the dead. Wasting sickness has not smitten you, you have not found the wages of the sword. No, mistress of your own fate and still alive you shall pass to Hades as no other of mortal kind has passed.*

ANTIGONE. *I have heard in other days how dread a doom befell our Phrygian guest, the daughter of Tantalus, on the Sipylian heights; how, like clinging ivy, the growth of stone subdued her; and the rains fail not, as men tell, from her wasting form, nor fails the snow, while beneath her weeping lids the tears bedew her bosom. Most like to hers is the fate that brings me to my rest.*

CHORUS. *Yet she was a goddess, as you know, and born of gods; we are mortals and of mortal race. But it is great renown for a woman who has perished that she should have shared the doom of the godlike, in her life and afterward in death.*

ANTIGONE. *Ah, I am mocked! In the name of our fathers' gods, can you not wait till I am gone, must you taunt me to my face, O my city and you her wealthy sons? Ah, fount of Dirce, and thou holy ground of Thebe whose chariots are many; you, at least, will bear me witness, in what sort, unwept of friends, and by what laws I pass to the rock-closed prison of my strange tomb, ah me unhappy! who have no home on the earth or in the shades, no home with the living or with the dead.*

CHORUS. *You have rushed forward to the utmost verge of daring, and against that throne where Justice sits on high you have fallen, my daughter, with a grievous fall. But in this ordeal you are paying, perchance, for your father's sin.*

ANTIGONE. *You have touched on my bitterest thought, awaking the ever-new lament for my sire and for all the doom given to us, the famed house of Labdacus. Alas for the horrors of the mother's bed! alas for the wretched mother's slumber at the side of her own son—and my sire! From what manner of parents did I take my miserable being! And to them I go in this wise, accursed, unwed, to share their home. Alas, my brother, ill-starred in your marriage, in your death you have undone my life!*

CHORUS. *Reverent action claims a certain praise for reverence; but an offense against power cannot be brooked by him who has power in his keeping. Your self-willed temper has wrought your ruin.*

ANTIGONE. *Unwept, unfriended, without marriage-song, I am led forth in my sorrow on this journey that can be delayed no more. No longer, luckless me, may I behold yonder day-star's sacred eye; but for my fate no tear is shed, no friend makes moan.*

CREON (*enters*). Know you not that songs and wailings before death would never cease if it profited to utter them? Away with her, away! And when you have enclosed her, according to my word, in her vaulted grave leave her alone, forlorn, whether she wishes to die or live a buried life in such a home. Our hands are clean as touching this maiden. But this is certain: she shall be deprived of her sojourn in the light.

ANTIGONE. Tomb, bridal-chamber, eternal prison in the caverned rock whither I go to find my own, those many who have perished and whom Persephone has received among the dead! Last of all shall I pass thither and far most miserably of all, before the term of my life is spent. But I cherish good hope that my coming will be welcome to my father, and pleasant to you, my mother, and welcome, brother, to you. For when you died with my own hands I washed and dressed you and poured drink-offerings at your graves; and now, Polyneices, it is for tending your corpse that I win such recompense as this.

And yet I honored you, as the wise will deem, rightly. Never, had I been a mother of children or if a husband had been moldering in death, would I have taken this task upon me in the city's despite. What law, you ask, is my warrant for that word? The husband lost, another might have been found, and child from another to replace the first-born; but father and mother hidden with Hades, no brother's life could ever bloom for me again. Such was the law by which I held you first in honor; but for it Creon deemed me guilty of error and of outrage, ah brother mine! And now he is leading me in this way, a captive in his hands. No bridal bed, no bridal song has been mine, no joy of marriage, no portion in the nurture of children; forlorn of friends, unhappy me, I go living to the vaults of death.

And what law of heaven have I transgressed? Why, unhappy me, should I look to the gods any more, what ally should I invoke, when by piety I have earned the name of impious? Nay, then, if these things are pleasing to the gods, when I have suffered my doom I shall come to know my sin; but if the sin is with my judges, I could wish them no fuller measure of evil than they, on their part, mete wrongfully to me.

CHORUS. *Still the same tempest of the soul vexes this maiden with the same fierce gusts.*

CREON. *Then for this shall her guards have cause to rue their slowness.*

ANTIGONE. *Ah me! that word has come very near to death.*

CREON. *I can cheer you with no hope that this doom is not to be fulfilled.*

ANTIGONE. *O city of my fathers in the land of Thebe! O ye gods, eldest of our race! They are leading me hence, now, now, they tarry not! Behold me, princes of Thebes, the last daughter of the house of your kings, see what I suffer, and from whom, because I feared to cast away the fear of Heaven!*

(ANTIGONE *is led away.*)

CHORUS. *Even thus endured Danae in her beauty to change the light of day for brassbound walls; and in that chamber, secret as the grave, she was held close prisoner; yet was she of a proud lineage, O my daughter, and charged with the keeping of the seed of Zeus, that fell in the golden rain.*

But dreadful is the mysterious power of fate, there is no deliverance from it by wealth or by war, by fenced city, or dark, sea-beaten ships.

And bonds tamed the son of Dryas, swift to wrath, that king of the Edonians; so paid he for his frenzied taunts,

*when, by the will of Dionysus, he was pent in a rocky prison.
There the fierce exuberance of his madness slowly passed
away. That man learned to know the god, whom in his frenzy
he had provoked with mockeries; for he had sought to quell
the god-possessed women, and the Bacchanalian fire; and
he angered the Muses that love the flute.*

*And by the waters of the Dark Rocks, the waters of the
twofold sea, are the shores of Bosporus, and Thracian
Salmydessus; where Ares, neighbor to the city, saw the accurst, blinding wound dealt to the two sons of Phineus by
his fierce wife—the wound that brought darkness to those
vengeance-craving orbs, smitten with her bloody hands,
smitten with her shuttle for a dagger.*

*Pining in their misery, they bewailed their cruel doom,
those sons of a mother hapless in her marriage; but she
traced her descent from the ancient line of the Erechtheidae;
and in far-distant caves she was nursed amid her father's
storms, that child of Boreas, swift as a steed over the steep
hills, a daughter of gods; yet upon her also the gray Fates
bore hard, my daughter.*

(TEIRESIAS *is led in by a* BOY.)

TEIRESIAS. Prince of Thebes, we have come with linked steps,
both served by the eyes of one; for so, by a guide's help, the
blind must walk.

CREON. And what, aged Teiresias, are your tidings?

TEIRESIAS. I will tell you, and do you hearken to the seer.

CREON. Indeed, it has not been my wont to slight your counsel.

TEIRESIAS. And so you steered our city's course aright.

CREON. I have felt and can attest your benefits.

TEIRESIAS. Mark that now, once more, you are standing on
fate's fine edge.

CREON. What does this mean? How I shudder at your message!

TEIRESIAS. You will learn when you hear the warnings of my
art. As I took my place on my old seat of augury, where all

birds have been wont to gather within my ken, I heard a
strange voice among them. They were screaming with dire,
feverish rage that drowned their language in a jargon, and I
knew that they were rending each other with their talons,
murderously; the whir of wings told no doubtful tale.

Forthwith, in fear, I essayed burnt-sacrifice on a duly
kindled altar, but from my offerings the Fire-god showed no
flame. A dank moisture oozing from the thigh-flesh trickled
forth upon the embers and smoked and sputtered; the gall
was scattered to the air; and the streaming thighs lay bared
of the fat that had been wrapped round them.

Such was the failure of the rites by which I vainly asked
a sign, as from this boy I learned; for he is my guide, as I am
guide to others. And it is your counsel that has brought this
sickness on our state. For the altars of our city and of our
hearths have been tainted one and all by birds and dogs with
carrion from the hapless corpse, the son of Oedipus. Therefore the gods no more accept prayer and sacrifice at our
hands, or the flame of meat-offering; nor does any bird give
a clear sign by its shrill cry, for they have tasted the fatness
of a slain man's blood.

Think, then, on these things, my son. All men are liable
to err; but when an error has been made, that man is no
longer witless or unblest who heals the ill into which he has
fallen and does not remain stubborn.

Self-will, we know, incurs the charge of folly. Nay, allow
the claim of the dead; do not stab the fallen. What prowess
is it to slay the slain anew? I have sought your good, and for
your good I speak. Never is it sweeter to learn from a good
counselor than when he counsels for your own gain.

CREON. Old man, you all shoot your shafts at me as archers at
the butts. You must needs practice on me with seercraft also.
Aye, the seer-tribe has long trafficked in me and made me
their merchandise. Gain your gains, drive your trade, if you
like, in the silver-gold of Sardis and the gold of India; but
you shall not hide that man in the grave—no, though the ea-
gles of Zeus should bear the carrion morsels to their master's throne—no, not for dread of that defilement will I

suffer his burial; for well I know that no mortal can defile
the gods. But, aged Teiresias, the wisest fall with a shameful fall when they clothe shameful thoughts in fair words for
lucre's sake.

TEIRESIAS. Alas! Does any man know, does any consider—

CREON. What? What general truth are you announcing?

TEIRESIAS. How precious, above all wealth, is good counsel.

CREON. As folly, I think, is the worst mischief.

TEIRESIAS. Yet you are tainted with the distemper.

CREON. I would not answer the seer with a taunt.

TEIRESIAS. But you do, in saying that I prophesy falsely.

CREON. Well, the prophet-tribe was ever fond of money.

TEIRESIAS. And the race bred of tyrants loves base gain.

CREON. Do you know that your speech is spoken of your king?

TEIRESIAS. I do know it; for through me you have saved
Thebes.

CREON. You are a wise seer, but you love evil deeds.

TEIRESIAS. You will rouse me to utter the dread secret in my
soul.

CREON. Out with it! Only speak it not for gain.

TEIRESIAS. I am sure I shall not—as touching you.

CREON. Know that you shall not trade on my resolve.

TEIRESIAS. Then know you, and know it well, that you shall not
live through many more courses of the sun's swift chariot
before one begotten of your own loins shall have been given
by you a corpse for corpses, because you have thrust children of the sunlight to the shades and ruthlessly lodged a
living soul in the grave but keep in this world one who belongs to the Gods Infernal, a corpse unburied, unhonored,
all unhallowed. In such you have no part, nor have the gods
above, but this is a violence done to them by you. Therefore
the avenging destroyers lie in wait for you, the Furies of
Hades and of the gods, that you may be taken in these same
ills.

And mark well if I speak these things as a hireling. A
time not long to be delayed shall awaken the wailing of men
and of women in your house. And a tumult of hatred against

you stirs all the cities whose mangled sons had the burial rite from dogs or from wild beasts or from some winged bird that bore a polluting breath to each city that contains the hearths of the dead.

Such arrows for your heart, since you provoke me, have I launched at you, archerlike, in my anger, sure arrows of which you shall not escape the smart. Boy, lead me home, that he may spend his rage on younger men, and learn to keep a tongue more temperate, and to bear within his breast a better mind than now he bears. (*Exit.*)

CHORUS. The man has gone, O King, with dread prophecies. And, since the hair on this head once black has been white, I know that he has never been a false prophet to our city.

CREON. I too know it well and am troubled in soul. It is dire to yield; but by resistance to smite my pride with ruin—this too is a dire choice.

CHORUS. Son of Menoeceus, it behooves you to take wise counsel.

CREON. What shall I do, then? Speak and I will obey.

CHORUS. Go and free the maiden from her rocky chamber, and make a tomb for the unburied dead.

CREON. Is this your counsel? Would you have me yield?

CHORUS. Yes, King, and with all speed; for swift harms from the gods cut short the folly of men.

CREON. Ah me, it is hard, but I resign my cherished resolve; I obey. We must not wage a vain war with destiny.

CHORUS. Do you go and do these things; do not leave them to others.

CREON. Even as I am I'll go. On, on, my servants, each and all of you, take axes in your hands and hasten to the ground that you see yonder! Since our judgment has taken this turn I will be present to unloose her, as I myself bound her. My heart misgives me, it is best to keep the established laws, even to life's end.

CHORUS. *O thou of many names, glory of the Cadmeian bride, offspring of loud-thundering Zeus! thou who watchest over famed Italia, and reignest, where all guests are welcomed, in the sheltered plain of Eleusinian Deo! O Bacchus, dweller in Thebe, mother-city of Bacchants, by the softly-gliding stream of Ismenus, on the soil where the fierce dragon's teeth were sown!*

Thou hast been seen where torch-flames glare through smoke, above the crests of the twin peaks, where move the Corycian nymphs, thy votaries, hard by Castalia's stream.

Thou comest from the ivy-mantled slopes of Nysa's hills, and from the shore green with many-clustered vines, while thy name is lifted up on strains of more than mortal power, as thou visitest the ways of Thebe.

Thebe, of all cities, thou holdest first in honor, thou, and thy mother whom the lightning smote; and now, when all our people is captive to a violent plague, come thou with healing feet over the Parnassian height, or over the moaning strait!

O thou with whom the stars rejoice as they move, the stars whose breath is fire; O master of the voices of the night; son begotten of Zeus; appear, O King, with thine attendant Thyiads, who in nightlong frenzy dance before thee, the giver of good gifts, Iacchus!

MESSENGER (*enters*). Dwellers by the house of Cadmus and of Amphion, there is no estate of mortal life that I would ever praise or blame as settled. Fortune raises and Fortune humbles the lucky or unlucky from day to day, and no one can prophesy to men concerning those things which are established. For Creon was blest once, as I count bliss; he had saved this land of Cadmus from its foes; he was clothed with sole dominion in the land; he reigned, the glorious sire of princely children. And now all has been lost. For when a man has forfeited his pleasures, I count him not as living— I hold him but a breathing corpse. Heap up riches in your house, if you will; live in kingly state; yet, if there be no gladness therewith, I would not give the shadow of a vapor for all the rest, compared with joy.

CHORUS. And what is this new grief that you have to tell for our princes?

MESSENGER. Death; and the living are guilty for the dead.

CHORUS. Who is the slayer? Who the stricken? Speak.

MESSENGER. Haemon has perished; his blood has been shed by no stranger.

CHORUS. By his father's hand, or by his own?

MESSENGER. By his own, in wrath with his sire for the murder.

CHORUS. O prophet, how true have you proved your word!

MESSENGER. So these things stand; you must consider of the rest.

CHORUS. Look, I see unfortunate Eurydice, Creon's wife, approaching. She is coming from the house by chance, it may be, or because she knows the tidings of her son.

EURYDICE (*enters*). People of Thebes, I heard your words as I was going forth to salute the goddess Pallas with my prayers. Even as I was loosing the fastenings of the gate to open it, the message of a household woe smote my ear. I sank back, terror-stricken, into the arms of my handmaids and my senses fled. But say again what the tidings were; I shall hear them as one who is no stranger to sorrow.

MESSENGER. Dear lady, I will witness of what I saw and will leave no word of the truth untold. Why indeed should I soothe you with words in which I must presently be found false? Truth is ever best. I attended your lord as his guide to the furthest part of the plain, where the body of Polyneices, torn by dogs, still lay unpitied. We prayed the goddess of the roads, and Pluto, in mercy to restrain their wrath. We washed the dead with holy washing, and with freshly-plucked boughs we solemnly burned such relics as there were. We raised a high mound of his native earth. And then we turned away to enter the maiden's nuptial chamber with rocky couch, the caverned mansion of the bride of Death. From afar off one of us heard a voice of loud wailing at that bride's unhallowed bower, and came to tell our master Creon.

As the king drew nearer doubtful sounds of a bitter cry floated around him; he groaned and said in accents of anguish, "Wretched that I am, can my foreboding be true? Am I going on the woefulest way that ever I went? My son's

voice greets me. Go my servants, quickly nearer, and when
you have reached the tomb pass through the gap where the
stones have been wrenched away, to the cell's very mouth.
Look and see if it is Haemon's voice that I know, or if my ear
is cheated by the gods."

This search, at our despairing master's word, we went to
make. In the furthest part of the tomb we descried *her* hanging by the neck, slung by a thread-wrought halter of fine
linen; while *he* was embracing her with arms thrown around
her waist, bewailing the loss of his bride who is with the
dead, and his father's deeds, and his own ill-starred love.

His father, when he saw him, cried aloud with a dread
cry and went in, and called to him with a voice of wailing:
"Unhappy, what a deed you have done! What thought has
come to you? What manner of mischance has marred your
reason? Come forth, my child! I pray you, I implore!" But
the boy glared at him with fierce eyes, spat in his face, and
without a word of answer drew his cross-hilted sword. As
his father rushed forth in flight he missed his aim; then,
luckless man, angry with himself he straightway leaned
with all his weight against his sword and drove it, half its
length, into his side. While sense lingered he clasped the
maiden to his faint embrace, and as he gasped sent forth on
her pale cheek the swift stream of his oozing blood.

Corpse enfolding corpse he lies. He has won his nuptial
rites, poor youth, not here but in the halls of Death. And he
has witnessed to mankind that of all curses which cleave to
man ill counsel is the sovereign curse.

(*Exit* EURYDICE.)

CHORUS. What would you augur from this? The lady has
  turned back and is gone without a word, good or evil.
MESSENGER. I too am startled. Yet I nourish the hope that at
  these sad tidings of her son she cannot deign to give her sorrow public vent, but in the privacy of the house will set her
  handmaids to mourn the household grief. For she is not un-

taught of discretion, that she should err.

CHORUS. I do not know. To me, at least, a strained silence seems to portend evil, no less than vain abundance of lament.

MESSENGER. Well, I will enter the house and learn whether indeed she is not hiding some repressed purpose in the depths of a passionate heart. You say well: excess of silence, too, may have a perilous meaning. (*Exit.*)

(*Enter* CREON *with* ATTENDANTS *bearing the body of* HAEMON.)

CHORUS. Look, yonder the king himself draws near, bearing that which tells too clear a tale—the work of no stranger's madness, if we may say it, but of his own misdeeds.

CREON. *Woe for the sins of a darkened soul, stubborn sins, fraught with death! Behold us, the sire who has slain, the son who has perished! Woe is me for the wretched blindness of my counsels! Alas, my son, you have died in your youth, by a timeless doom, woe is me! Your spirit has fled not by your folly but by my own!*

CHORUS. *Ah me, how all too late you seem to see the right!*

CREON. *Ah me, I have learned the bitter lesson! But then, methinks, oh then, some god smote me from above with crushing weight and hurled me into ways of cruelty, woe is me, overthrowing and trampling on my joy! Woe, woe, for the troublous toils of men!*

(*Enter* MESSENGER *from palace.*)

MESSENGER. Sire, you have come, methinks, as one whose hands are not empty but who has store laid up besides. You bear yonder burden with you, and you are soon to look upon the woes within your house.

CREON. And what worse ill is yet to follow upon ills?

MESSENGER. Your queen has died, true mother of yonder corpse—ah, unhappy lady—by blows newly dealt.

CREON. *Oh Hades, all-receiving, whom no sacrifice can appease. Have you no mercy for me? You herald of bitter evil tidings,*

what word are you uttering? Alas, I was already as dead, and
you have smitten me anew! What are you saying, my son?
What is this new message that you bring—woe, woe is me!—
of a wife's doom, of slaughter heaped on slaughter?

CHORUS. *You can behold; it is no longer hidden within.*

(*The corpse of* EURYDICE *is revealed.*)

CREON. *Ah me, yonder I behold a new, a second woe! What*
destiny, ah what, can yet await me? I have but now raised
my son in my arms, and there again I see a corpse before
me! Alas, alas, unhappy mother! Alas, my child!

MESSENGER. There, at the altar, self-stabbed with a keen knife,
she suffered her darkening eyes to close, when she had
wailed for the noble fate of Megareus who died before, and
then for his fate who lies there, and when, with her last
breath, she had invoked evil fortunes upon you, the slayer of
her sons.

CREON. *Woe, woe! I thrill with dread. Is there none to strike me*
to the heart with two-edged sword? O miserable that I am,
and steeped in miserable anguish!

MESSENGER. Yes, both this son's doom, and that other's, were
laid to your charge by her whose corpse you see.

CREON. And what was the manner of the violent deed by
which she passed away?

MESSENGER. Her own hand struck her to the heart, when she
had learned her son's sorely lamented fate.

CREON. *Ah me, this guilt can never be fixed on any other of*
mortal kind, for my acquittal! I, even I, was your slayer,
wretched that I am—I own the truth. Lead me away, O my
servants, lead me hence with all speed, whose life is but
death!

CHORUS. Your counsels are good, if there can be good with
ills; briefest is best, when trouble is in our path.

CREON. *Oh, let it come, let it appear, that fairest of fates for*
me, that brings my last day—aye, best fate of all! Oh, let it
come, that I may never look upon tomorrow's light.

CHORUS. These things are in the future; present tasks claim our care: the ordering of the future rests where it should rest.

CREON. All my desires, at least, were summed in that prayer.

CHORUS. Pray no more; for mortals have no escape from destined woe.

CREON. *Lead me away, I pray you; a rash, foolish man; who have slain you, ah my son, unwittingly, and you too, my wife—unhappy that I am! I know not which way I should bend my gaze, or where I should seek support; for all is amiss with that which is in my hands—and yonder, again, a crushing fate has leapt upon my head. (Exit.)*

CHORUS. *Wisdom is the supreme part of happiness, and reverence toward the gods must be inviolate. Great words of prideful men are ever punished with great blows, and, in old age, teach the chastened to be wise.*

TRACHINIAN WOMEN

HERACLES HAD NEGLECTED HIS FAMILY FOR LONG stretches while he was engaged on his famous labors, but at his last departure from home he had left word that after fifteen months he would either have met his death or return to uninterrupted peace. As the play opens, the fifteen-month term has expired, and Heracles' wife Deianeira is troubled by his continued absence. She learns that he has sacked Oechalia, and presently discovers that he is enamored of its princess Iole, one of the captives he has sent home against his arrival. In order to regain his affection and preserve her home, Deianeira sends Heracles a garment treated with a salve the Centaur Nessus (whose good will she should have suspected) long ago gave her as a specific to prevent Heracles' love from straying. When she discovers, from her reproachful son Hyllus, that the salve is in fact lethal, she commits suicide.

Heracles, brought in bellowing in agony, recalls that his death is in accordance with a prophecy, insists that Hyllus marry Iole, and is then placed upon the pyre. Heracles' instruction to Hyllus is not a sign of repentance but an effort to retain Iole, despite her responsibility for Deianeira's death, in the only way possible—through his son. To the end he continues to be selfish and brutal to those dependent on him. But perhaps only so stark and willful a man could have achieved the labors which were beneficial to mankind. The circumstances of his death suggest that the good in Heracles outweighs the bad and that he does in fact merit the transfiguration bestowed upon him.

PERSONS

DEIANEIRA, *wife of Heracles*　　HERACLES
NURSE　　　　　　　　　　　　　AN OLD MAN
HYLLUS, *son of Heracles and*　　CHORUS OF TRACHINIAN
　　Deianeira　　　　　　　　　　MAIDENS
MESSENGER
LICHAS, *herald of Heracles*

SCENE: *Before the house of Heracles at Trachis.*

(*Enter* DEIANEIRA *and* NURSE.)

DEIANEIRA. There is a saying among men, put forth long ago,
　　that you cannot rightly judge whether a mortal's lot is good
　　or evil before he dies. But I know, even before I have passed
　　to the world of death, that my life is sorrowful and bitter.
　　While yet I dwelt at Pleuron, in the house of my father
　　Oeneus, I had such fear of bridals as never vexed any
　　maiden of Aetolia. For my wooer was a river-god, Achelous,
　　who was always asking me of my father in three shapes,
　　coming now as a bull in bodily form, now as a serpent with
　　shiny coils, now with trunk of man and face of ox, while
　　from his shaggy beard the streams of fountain-water flowed
　　abroad. With the fear of such a suitor before my eyes, I was
　　always praying in my wretchedness that I might die before I
　　should come near to such a bed.

　　But at last, to my joy, came the glorious son of Zeus and
　　Alcmena; he closed with him in combat and delivered me.
　　How the fight was waged I cannot clearly tell; I know not.
　　Anyone who may have watched that sight without terror
　　might describe it; I, as I sat there, was distraught with dread,

lest beauty should bring me sorrow in the end. But finally
the Zeus of battles ordained well—if well indeed it is. Since
I have been joined to Heracles as his chosen bride fear after
fear has haunted me on his account; one night brings a trouble, and the next night, in turn, drives it out. And then children were born to us, whom he has seen only as the farmer
sees his distant field, which he visits at seedtime and once
again at harvest. Such was the life that kept him journeying
to and fro, in the service of a certain master.

But now, when he has risen above those trials, now it is
that my anguish is sorest. Ever since he slew the valiant
Iphitus we have been dwelling here in Trachis, exiles from
our home and the guests of a stranger. Where he is no one
knows; I only know that he is gone, and has pierced my
heart with cruel pangs for him. I am almost sure that some
evil has befallen him; it is no short space that has passed but
ten long months and then five more—and still no message
from him. Yes, there has been some dreadful mishap; witness that tablet which he left with me before he went forth.
Often do I pray to the gods that I may not have received it for
my sorrow.

NURSE. Deianeira my mistress, many a time have I marked
your bitter tears and lamentations when you bewailed the
going forth of Heracles. But now—if it is proper to instruct
the freeborn with the advice of a slave and if I must say
what you should do—why, when you are so rich in sons, do
you not send one of them to seek your lord? Hyllus before
all might well go on that errand, if he cared for news about
his father's welfare. Look, there he comes, hurrying toward
the house with timely step. If you think my speech is seasonable you can use both my advice and the man.

(*Enter* HYLLUS.)

DEIANEIRA. My child, wise words may fall from humble lips,
it seems; this woman is a slave but she has spoken in the
spirit of the free.

HYLLUS. How, mother? Tell me, if it may be told.

DEIANEIRA. It brings you shame, she says, that when your father has been so long a stranger you have not tried to learn where he is.

HYLLUS. But I know—if rumor can be trusted.

DEIANEIRA. In what region does rumor place him, my child?

HYLLUS. Last year, they say, he toiled year long as bondman to a Lydian woman.

DEIANEIRA. If he endured that then no tidings can be surprising.

HYLLUS. He has been delivered from that, as I hear.

DEIANEIRA. Where then is he reported to be now—alive or dead?

HYLLUS. He is waging or planning a war, they say, upon Euboea, the realm of Eurytus.

DEIANEIRA. Do you know, son, that he has left sure oracles touching that land with me?

HYLLUS. What are they, mother? I do not know what you are speaking about.

DEIANEIRA. That he shall either meet his death or, having achieved this task, shall have rest thenceforward for all his days to come. So, my child, when his fate is trembling in the scale in this way, will you not go to help him? If he reaches safety we are saved, or else we perish with him.

HYLLUS. Yes, I will go, mother. If I had known the import of these prophecies I would have been there long since; as it was, my father's usual luck prevented me from feeling fear for him or being anxious about him. Now that I know, I will spare no pains to learn the whole truth in this matter.

DEIANEIRA. Then go, son; if the searcher be ever so late he is rewarded if he receives tidings of joy.

(*Exit* HYLLUS; *enter* CHORUS.)

CHORUS. *Thou whom Night brings forth at the moment when she is despoiled of her starry crown and lays to rest in thy splendor, tell me I pray thee, O Sun-god, tell me where abides Alcmena's son? Thou glorious lord of flashing light, say, is he threading the straits of the sea, or has he found an*

*abode on either continent? Speak, thou who seest as none
else can see!*

*For Deianeira, as I hear, hath ever an aching heart; she,
the battle-prize of old, is now like some bird lorn of its mate;
she can never lull her yearning nor stay her tears; haunted
by a sleepless fear for her absent lord, she pines on her anxious, widowed couch, miserable in her foreboding of mischance.*

*As one may see billow after billow driven over the wide
deep by the tireless south wind, or the north, so the trouble
of his life, stormy as the Cretan sea, now whirls back the son
of Cadmus, now lifts him to honor. But some god ever saves
him from the house of death and suffers him not to fail.*

*Lady, I praise not this thy mood; with all reverence will I
speak, yet in reproof. Thou dost not well, I say, to kill fair
hope by fretting; remember that the son of Cronus himself,
the all-disposing king, hath not appointed a painless lot for
mortals. Sorrow and joy come round to all, as the Bear
moves in his circling paths.*

*Yea, starry night abides not with men, nor tribulation,
nor wealth; in a moment it is gone from us, and another
hath his turn of gladness, and of bereavement. So would I
wish thee also, the Queen, to keep that prospect ever in thy
thoughts; for when hath Zeus been found so careless of his
children?*

DEIANEIRA. You have heard of my trouble, I think, and that has
brought you here; but the anguish which consumes my
heart—you are strangers to that, and never may you learn it
by suffering! Yes, the tender plant grows in those sheltered
regions of its own; and the Sun-god's heat vexes it not, nor
rain, nor any wind; but it rejoices in its sweet untroubled being, till such time as the maiden is called a wife, and finds
her portion of anxious thoughts in the night, brooding on
danger to husband or to children. Such a one could understand the burden of my cares; she could judge them by her
own.

Well, I have had many a sorrow to weep for before now;
but I am going to speak of one more grievous than them all.

When Heracles my lord was going from home on his last journey he left in the house an ancient tablet, inscribed with tokens which he had never brought himself to explain to me before, many as were the ordeals to which he had gone forth. He had always departed as if to conquer, not to die. But now, as if he were a doomed man, he told me what portion of his substance I was to take for my dower and how he would have his sons share their father's land amongst them. And he fixed the time, saying that when a year and three months should have passed since he had left the country then he was fated to die; or, if he should have survived that term, to live thenceforth an untroubled life.

Such, he said, was the doom ordained by the gods to be accomplished in the toils of Heracles, as the ancient oak at Dodona had spoken long ago, by the mouth of the two Peleiades. And this is the precise moment when the fulfillment of that word becomes due. That is why I start up from sweet slumber, my friends, stricken with terror at the thought that I must remain widowed of the noblest among men.

CHORUS. Hush—no more ill-omened words. I see a man approaching, wearing a wreath as if for joyous tidings.

MESSENGER (*enters*). Queen Deianeira, I shall be the first of messengers to free you from fear. Know that Alcmena's son lives and triumphs, and from battle brings the first-fruits to the gods of this land.

DEIANEIRA. What news is this, old man, that you have told me?

MESSENGER. That your lord, admired of all, will soon come to your house, restored to you in his victorious might.

DEIANEIRA. What citizen or stranger told you this?

MESSENGER. In the meadow, where oxen pasture in summer, the herald Lichas is proclaiming it to many. From him I heard it, and flew here, to be the first to give you the news, and so reap some reward from you and win your favor.

DEIANEIRA. Why is *he* not here if he brings good news?

MESSENGER. His task, lady, is no easy one. All the Malian folk have thronged around him with questions and he cannot move forward. Each and all are bent on learning what they desire and will not release him until they are satisfied. Thus their eagerness detains him against his will; but you will see him face to face presently.

DEIANEIRA. O Zeus, ruler of the meadows of Oeta which are sacred from the scythe, at last, though late, you have given us joy! Uplift your voices, you women within the house and you beyond our gates, for now we are gladdened by the light of this message which has risen beyond my hope!

CHORUS. *Let the maidens raise a joyous strain for the house, with songs of triumph at the hearth; and amidst them let the shout of the men go up with one accord for Apollo of the bright quiver, our Defender! And at the same time, ye maidens, lift up a paean, cry aloud to his sister, the Ortygian Artemis, smiter of deer, goddess of the twofold torch, and to the Nymphs, her neighbors!*

My spirit soars; I will not reject the wooing of the flute. O thou sovereign of my soul! Lo, the ivy's spell begins to work upon me! Evoe! Even now it moves me to whirl in the swift dance of Bacchanals!

Praise, praise unto the Healer! See, dear lady, see! Behold, these tidings are taking shape before thy gaze.

DEIANEIRA. I see it, dear maidens; my watchful eyes have not failed to note yonder company.

(*Enter* LICHAS, *followed by* CAPTIVE MAIDENS.)

All hail to the herald, whose coming has been so long delayed!—if indeed you bring anything that can give joy.

LICHAS. We are happy in our return and happy in your greeting, lady, which befits the deed achieved. When a man has fair fortune he needs must win good welcome.

DEIANEIRA. O best of friends, tell me first what first I would know—shall I receive Heracles alive?

LICHAS. Certainly I left him alive and well, in vigorous health, unburdened by disease.

DEIANEIRA. Where, tell me: at home or on foreign soil?

LICHAS. There is a headland of Euboea, where he is consecrat-

ing altars and the tribute of fruitful ground to Cenaean
Zeus.

DEIANEIRA. In payment of a vow? At the bidding of an oracle?

LICHAS. For a vow, made when he was seeking to conquer and
despoil the country of these women who are before you.

DEIANEIRA. And these—who are they pray, whose daughters?
They deserve pity, unless their plight deceives me.

LICHAS. These are captives whom he chose out for himself and
for the gods when he sacked the city of Eurytus.

DEIANEIRA. Was it war against that city which kept him away
so long, beyond all forecast, past all count of days?

LICHAS. Not so. The greater part of the time he was detained in
Lydia—no free man, as he declares, but sold into bondage.
No offense should attach to the word, lady, when the deed is
found to be of Zeus. So he passed a whole year, as he himself avows, in thralldom to Omphale the barbarian. So stung
was he by the disgrace that he bound himself by a solemn
oath that he would one day enslave, with wife and child, the
man who had brought the calamity upon him. Nor did he
speak the word in vain; when he had been purged he gathered an alien host and went against the city of Eurytus. That
man alone of mortals, he said, had a share in causing his
misfortune. For when Heracles, an old friend, came to his
house and hearth, Eurytus heaped upon him the taunts of a
bitter tongue and spiteful soul, saying, "You have unerring
arrows in your hands, and yet my sons surpass you in the
trial of archery"; "You are a slave," he cried, "a free man's
broken thrall"; and at a banquet, when his guest was full of
wine, he thrust him from his doors.

Such treatment enraged Heracles, and afterward when
Iphitus came to the hill of Tiryns in search of horses that
had strayed, Heracles seized a moment when the man's
thoughts wandered one way and his gaze another and hurled
him from a towerlike summit. But in anger at that deed Zeus
our lord, Olympian sire of all, sent him forth into bondage
and spared not, because this once he had taken a life by
guile. Had he wreaked his vengeance openly Zeus would

surely have pardoned him the righteous triumph; for the gods too have no love for insolence.

So those men who waxed so proud with bitter speech are themselves in the mansions of the dead, all of them, and their city is enslaved; while the women whom you see, fallen from happiness to misery, come here to you. Such was your lord's command which I, his faithful servant, perform. He himself, you may be sure, so soon as he shall have offered holy sacrifice to Zeus from whom he sprang, will be with you. After all the fair tidings that have been told, this, indeed, is the sweetest word to hear.

CHORUS. Now, O Queen, your joy is assured; part is with you, and you have promise of the rest.

DEIANEIRA. Yes, have I not the fullest reason to rejoice at these tidings of my lord's happy fortune? To such fortune such joy must needs respond. And yet a prudent mind can see room for misgivings lest he who prospers should one day suffer reverse. A strange pity has come over me, friends, at the sight of these ill-fated exiles, homeless and fatherless in a foreign land, once the daughters, it may be, of freeborn fathers but now doomed to the life of slaves. O Zeus, who turnest the tides of battle, never may I see child of mine thus visited by thy hand. If such visitation is to be, may it not fall while Deianeira lives! Such dread do I feel when I look upon these girls.

(*To* IOLE.) Ah, unhappy girl, tell me, who are you? A maiden or a mother? To judge by your looks, an innocent maiden, and of a noble race. Lichas, whose daughter is this stranger? Who is her mother, who her sire? Speak, I pity her more than all the rest when I look at her, for she alone shows a due feeling for her plight.

LICHAS. How should I know? Why should you ask me? Perhaps the offspring of not the meanest in yonder land.

DEIANEIRA. Can she be of royal race? Did Eurytus have a daughter?

LICHAS. I do not know; I did not ask many questions.

DEIANEIRA. And you have not heard her name from any of her companions?

LICHAS. No indeed; I went through my task in silence.

DEIANEIRA. Unhappy girl, let me, at least, hear it from your own mouth. It is indeed distressing not to know *your* name.

LICHAS. It will be unlike her former behavior, then, I can tell you, if she opens her lips. She has not uttered one word. She has been suffering with the burden of her sorrow continuously and weeping bitterly, poor girl, since she left her wind-swept home. Such a state is grievous for her, but claims our forbearance.

DEIANEIRA. Then let her be left in peace and pass under our roof as she wishes. Her present woes must not be crowned with fresh pains at my hands; she has enough already. Now let us all go in, so that you may start speedily on your return journey, while I make all things ready in the house.

(*Exit* LICHAS *and* CAPTIVES *into the house.*)

MESSENGER (*approaching* DEIANEIRA). First tarry here for a brief space so you may learn, apart from those people, whom you are taking to your hearth, and may learn the essentials which have not been told you. Of these I am in full possession.

DEIANEIRA. What does this mean? Why would you stay my departure?

MESSENGER. Pause and listen. My former story was worth your hearing, and so will this one be, I think.

DEIANEIRA. Shall I call those others back? Or will you speak before me and these maidens?

MESSENGER. To you and these I can speak freely; never mind the others.

DEIANEIRA. Well, they are gone; your story can proceed.

MESSENGER. Yonder man was not speaking the straightforward truth in anything that he has just told you. He has given false tidings now, or else his former report was dishonest.

DEIANEIRA. What are you saying? Explain your whole drift clearly; so far your words are riddles to me.

MESSENGER. I heard this man declare, before many witnesses, that for this maiden's sake Heracles overthrew Eurytus and the proud towers of Oechalia. Love alone of the gods wrought on him to do those deeds of arms, not the toilsome servitude to Omphale in Lydia nor the death to which Iphitus was hurled. But now the herald has thrust Love out of sight and tells a different tale.

Well, when he could not persuade her sire to give him the maiden for his paramour he devised some petty complaint as a pretext and made war upon her land—that in which, as he said, this Eurytus bore sway—and slew the prince her father and sacked her city. And now, as you see, he comes sending her to this house not in careless fashion, lady, nor like a slave. No, do not dream of that; it is not likely if his heart is kindled with desire.

I resolved therefore, O Queen, to tell you all that I had heard from yonder man. Many others were listening to it, as I was, in the public place where the Trachinians were assembled, and they can convict him. If my words are unwelcome I am grieved, but nevertheless I have spoken out the truth.

DEIANEIRA. Unhappy that I am! What is my situation? What secret bane have I received beneath my roof? Unlucky me! Is she nameless, then, as her escort swore?

MESSENGER. No, illustrious by name as by birth. She is the daughter of Eurytus and was once called Iole—she of whose parentage Lichas could say nothing because, forsooth, he asked no questions.

CHORUS. Accursed above other evildoers be the man whom deeds of treachery dishonor!

DEIANEIRA. Ah, maidens, what am I to do? These latest tidings have bewildered me!

CHORUS. Go and inquire from Lichas; perhaps he will tell the truth, if you constrain him to answer.

DEIANEIRA. Well, I will go; your counsel is not amiss.

MESSENGER. And I, shall I wait here? Or what is your pleasure?

DEIANEIRA. Stay; here he comes from the house of his own accord, without summons from me.

LICHAS (*enters*). Lady, what message shall I carry to Heracles? Give me your orders; as you see, I am going.

DEIANEIRA. How quickly you are rushing away, when your visit has been so long delayed—before we have had time for further talk.

LICHAS. If there is anything you would ask I am at your service.

DEIANEIRA. Will you indeed give me the honest truth?

LICHAS. Yes, be great Zeus my witness, in anything that I know.

DEIANEIRA. Who is the woman, then, whom you have brought?

LICHAS. She is Euboean; but of what birth I cannot say.

MESSENGER. You there, look at me: whom do you think you are speaking to?

LICHAS. And you—what do you mean by such a question?

MESSENGER. Deign to answer me, if you understand.

LICHAS. To the royal Deianeira, unless my eyes deceive me— daughter of Oeneus, wife of Heracles, and my queen.

MESSENGER. The very word that I wished to hear from you: you say that she is your queen?

LICHAS. Yes, as in duty bound.

MESSENGER. Well then, what are you prepared to suffer if found guilty of failing in that duty?

LICHAS. Failing in duty? What dark saying is this?

MESSENGER. 'Tis none; the darkest words are your own.

LICHAS. I will go—I was foolish to hear you so long.

MESSENGER. No, not till you have answered a brief question.

LICHAS. Ask what you will; you are not taciturn.

MESSENGER. That captive whom you have brought home—you know whom I mean?

LICHAS. Yes, but why do you ask?

MESSENGER. Well, did you not say your prisoner—she on whom your gaze now turns so vacantly—was Iole, daughter of Eurytus?

LICHAS. Said it to whom? Who and where is the man who will be your witness to hearing this from me?

MESSENGER. To many of our own folk you said it; in the public gathering of Trachinians a great crowd heard it from you.

LICHAS. Said they heard; but it is one thing to report a fancy and another to make the story good.

MESSENGER. A fancy! Did you not say on your oath that you were bringing her as a bride for Heracles?

LICHAS. I? Bringing a bride? In the name of the gods, dear mistress, tell me who this stranger may be?

MESSENGER. One who heard from your own lips that the conquest of the whole city was due to love for this girl; the Lydian woman was not its destroyer, but the passion which this maid has kindled.

LICHAS. Lady, let this fellow withdraw; to prate with the brain-sick befits not a sane man.

DEIANEIRA. Nay, I implore you by Zeus whose lightnings go forth over the high glens of Oeta, do not cheat me of the truth! For she to whom you will speak is not ungenerous, nor has she yet to learn that the human heart is inconstant to its joys. They are not wise, then, who stand forth to buffet against Love; for Love rules the gods as he will, and me; and why not another woman such as I am? So I am mad indeed if I blame my husband because that distemper has seized him; or this woman, his partner in a thing which is no shame to them and no wrong to me. Impossible! No; if he taught you to speak falsely 'tis not a noble lesson that you are learning; or if you are your own teacher in this you will be found cruel when it is your wish to prove kind. Tell me the whole truth. To a freeborn man the name of liar cleaves as a deadly brand. If your hope is to escape detection, that too is vain; there are many to whom you have spoken who will tell me.

And if you are afraid your fear is mistaken. *Not* to learn the truth—that indeed would pain me; but to know it—what is there terrible in that? Has not Heracles wedded others before now—ay, more than living man—and no one of them has had harsh word or taunt from me. Nor shall this girl, though her whole being should be absorbed in her passion; indeed, I felt a profound pity when I saw her, because her beauty has wrecked her life and she, luckless girl, all innocent, has brought her fatherland to ruin and to bondage.

Well, those things must go with wind and stream. To you I say deceive whom you will, but always speak the truth to me.

CHORUS. Hearken to her good counsel, and hereafter you shall have no cause to complain of this lady; our thanks too will be yours.

LICHAS. Ah then, dear mistress, since I see that you think as mortals should think and can allow for weakness, I will tell you the whole truth and hide nothing. Yes, the thing is as that man says. This girl inspired that overmastering love which long ago penetrated the soul of Heracles; for this girl's sake the desolate Oechalia, her home, was made the prey of his spear. And he—it is just to him to say so—never denied this, never told me to conceal it. But I, lady, fearing to wound your heart by such tidings, have sinned, if you count this in any sort a sin.

Now that you know the whole story, however, for both your sakes, for his and not less for your own, bear with the woman and be content that the words which you have spoken regarding her should bind you still. For he whose strength is victorious in all else has been utterly vanquished by his passion for this girl.

DEIANEIRA. Indeed my own thoughts move me so to act. Trust me, I will not add a new affliction to my burdens by waging a fruitless fight against the gods.

But let us go into the house so that you may receive my messages; and since gifts should be duly recompensed with gifts, that you may take these also. It is not right that you should go back with empty hands after coming with such a bountiful supply.

(*Exeunt* MESSENGER, LICHAS, DEIANEIRA.)

CHORUS. *Great and mighty is the victory which the Cyprian queen ever bears away. I stay not now to speak of the gods; I spare to tell how she beguiled the son of Cronus, and Hades, the lord of darkness, or Poseidon, shaker of the earth.*

*But when this bride was to be won, who were the valiant
rivals that entered the contest for her hand? Who went forth
to the ordeal of battle, to the fierce blows and the blinding
dust?*

*One was a mighty river-god, the dread form of a horned
and four-legged bull, Achelous from Oeniadae; the other
came from Thebe dear to Bacchus, with curved bow and
spears and brandished club, the son of Zeus. Then they met
in combat, fain to win a bride, and the Cyprian goddess of
nuptial joy was there with them, sole umpire of their strife.*

*Then was there clatter of fists and clang of bow, and the
noise of a bull's horns therewith; then were there close-
locked grapplings and deadly blows from the forehead and
loud deep cries from both.*

*Meanwhile she in her delicate beauty sat on the side of
a hill that could be seen afar, awaiting the husband that
should be hers.*

*[So the battle rages] as I have told; but the fair bride who
is the prize of the strife abides the end in piteous anguish.
And suddenly she is parted from her mother, as when a
heifer is taken from its dam.*

DEIANEIRA (*enters, carrying a casket containing a robe*). Dear
friends, while our visitor is saying his farewell to the captive
girls in the house I have stolen forth to you, partly to tell you
what these hands have devised and partly to crave your sympathy with my sorrow.

A maiden—or no longer a maiden but a mistress, as I
think—has found her way into my house, as a freight comes
to a mariner, a merchandise to make shipwreck of my
peace. And now we two are to share the same marriage-bed,
the same embrace. Such is the reward that Heracles has sent
me—he whom I called true and loyal—for guarding his
home through all that weary time. I have no thought of
anger against him, often as he is vexed with this distemper.
But then to live with her, sharing the same union—what
woman could endure it? For I see that the flower of her age
is blossoming while mine is fading; and the eyes of men
love to cull the bloom of youth, but they turn aside from

the old. This, then, is my fear—lest Heracles, in name my spouse, should be the younger's mate.

But, as I said, anger ill beseems a woman of understanding. I will tell you, friends, the way by which I hope to find deliverance and relief. I had a gift, given me long ago by a monster of olden time and stored in an urn of bronze, a gift which while yet a girl I took up from the shaggy-breasted Nessus—from his lifeblood as he lay dying; Nessus who used to carry men in his arms for hire across the deep waters of the Evenus, using no oar to waft them nor sail of ship.

I too was carried on his shoulders when, by my father's sending, I first went forth with Heracles as his wife. When I was in midstream he touched me with wanton hands. I shrieked; the son of Zeus turned quickly round and shot a feathered arrow. It whizzed through his breast to the lungs, and in his mortal faintness the Centaur spoke: "Child of aged Oeneus, you shall have at least this profit of my ferrying, if you will hearken, because you were the last whom I conveyed. If you gather with your hands the blood clotted round my wound, at the place where the Hydra, Lerna's monstrous growth, has tinged the arrow with black gall, this shall serve you as a charm for the soul of Heracles, so that he shall never look upon any woman to love her more than you."

I bethought me of this, my friends—for after his death I had kept it carefully locked up in a secret place; and I have anointed this robe, doing everything to it as he enjoined while he lived. The work is finished. May deeds of wicked daring be ever far from my thoughts and from my knowledge—as I abhor the women who attempt them! But if in any wise I may prevail against this girl by love-spells and charms used on Heracles, the means to that end are ready; unless, indeed, I seem to be acting rashly: if so I will desist at once.

CHORUS. No, if these measures give any ground of confidence we think your design is not amiss.

DEIANEIRA. This is how the matter stands: there is a fair promise, but I have not yet essayed the proof.

CHORUS. Knowledge must come through action. You can have
no test which is not fanciful except by trial.

DEIANEIRA. Well, we shall know presently. There I see the man
already at the doors, and he will soon be going. Only may
my secret be well kept by you! While your deeds are hidden,
even though they be not seemly, you will never be brought
to shame.

LICHAS (*enters*). What are your commands? Give me my
charge, daughter of Oeneus, for already I have tarried over-
long.

DEIANEIRA. Indeed, I have just been seeing to this for you,
Lichas, while you were speaking to the stranger maidens in
the house. Take for me this long robe, woven by my own
hand, a gift to my absent lord.

When you give it charge him that he and no other shall be
the first to wear it; that it shall not be seen by the light of the
sun nor by the sacred precinct nor by the fire at the hearth,
until he stand forth, conspicuous before all eyes, and show
it to the gods on a day when bulls are slain.

I had vowed that if I should ever see or hear that he had
come safely home I would duly clothe him in this robe, and
so present him to the gods newly radiant at their altar in new
garb. As proof you shall carry a token, which he will
quickly recognize within the circle of this seal.

Now go your way; and first, remember the rule that messengers should not be meddlers; next, so conduct yourself
that my thanks may be joined to his, doubling the grace
which you shall win.

LICHAS. If I ply this heraldcraft of Hermes with any sureness I
will never trip in doing your errand. I will not fail to deliver
this casket as it is, and to add your words in attestation of
your gift.

DEIANEIRA. You may be going now, for you know well how
things are with us in the house.

LICHAS. I know, and will report that all has prospered.

DEIANEIRA. And then you have seen the greeting given to the
stranger maiden—you know how I welcomed her?

LICHAS. So that my heart was filled with wondering joy.

DEIANEIRA. What more then is there for you to tell? I am afraid that it would be too soon to speak of the longing on my part, before we know if I am longed for there.

(*Exeunt,* LICHAS *with casket,* DEIANEIRA *into the house.*)

CHORUS. *O ye who dwell by the warm springs between haven and crag and by Oeta's heights, O dwellers by the land-locked waters of the Malian sea, on the shore sacred to the virgin-goddess of the golden shafts, where the Greeks meet in famous council at the Gates—*

Soon shall the glorious voice of the flute go up for you again, resounding with no harsh strain of grief, but with such music as the lyre makes to the gods! For the son whom Alcmena bore to Zeus is hastening homeward, with the trophies of all prowess.

He was lost utterly to our land, a wanderer over the sea, while we waited through twelve long months and knew nothing; and his loving wife, sad dweller with sad thoughts, was ever pining amid her tears. But now the War-god, roused to fury, has delivered her from the days of her mourning.

May he come, may he come! Pause not the many-oared ship that carries him till he shall have reached this town, leaving the island altar where, as rumor says, he is sacrificing! Thence may he come, full of desire, steeped in love by the specious device of the robe, on which Persuasion has spread her sovereign charm!

DEIANEIRA (*enters, agitated*). Friends, how I fear that I may have gone too far in all that I have been doing just now!

CHORUS. What has happened, Deianeira daughter of Oeneus?

DEIANEIRA. I do not know, but feel misgivings that I shall presently be found to have worked a great mischief, resulting from high hopes.

CHORUS. It is nothing, surely, that concerns your gift to Heracles?

DEIANEIRA. It is indeed. And henceforth I would say to everyone: do not act with zeal if you act without light.

CHORUS. Tell us the cause of your fear, if it may be told.

DEIANEIRA. Such a thing has happened, friends, that if I tell it
you will hear a marvel of which no one could have dreamed.

What I was lately anointing the festal robe with, a white
tuft of fleecy sheep's wool, has disappeared—not consumed
by anything in the house, but self-devoured and self-
destroyed, as it crumbled down from the surface of a stone.
But I must tell the story more fully, so that you may know
exactly how this thing happened.

I neglected no part of the precepts which the savage
Centaur gave me when the bitter barb was rankling in his
side; they were in my memory like the graven words which
no hand may wash from a tablet of bronze. These were his
orders, and I obeyed them: to keep this unguent in a secret
place, always remote from fire and from the sun's warm ray,
until I should apply it, newly spread, where I wished. So I
had done. And now when the moment for action had come I
performed the anointing privately in the house, with a tuft of
soft wool which I had plucked from a sheep of our flock;
then I folded up my gift and laid it, unvisited by sunlight,
within its casket, as you saw.

But as I was going back into the house I saw a thing too
wonderful for words and passing the wit of man to understand. I happened to have thrown a shred of the wool with
which I had been preparing the robe into the full blaze of
sunshine. As it grew warm it shriveled all away and quickly
crumbled to powder on the ground, like nothing so much as
the dust shed from a saw's teeth where men work timber. In
such a state it lies as it fell. And from the earth where it was
strewn clots of foam seethed up, as when the rich juice of
the blue fruit from the vine of Bacchus is poured upon the
ground.

So I do not know, unlucky me, where to turn my
thoughts; I only see that I have done a fearful deed. Why or
wherefore should the monster, in his death-throes, have
shown good will to me, on whose account he was dying?
Impossible! No, he was cajoling me, in order to slay the
man who had smitten him; and I know this too late, when it

is of no help. Yes, I alone—unless my foreboding prove false—I, wretched woman, must destroy him! For I know that the arrow which made the wound harmed even the god Cheiron, and it kills all beasts that it touches. And since it is this same black venom in the blood that has passed out through the wound of Nessus, must it not kill my lord also? I believe it must.

Nevertheless I am resolved that if he is to fall, I shall be swept from life at the same time. No woman could bear to live with an evil name if she rejoices that her nature is not evil.

CHORUS. Mischief must needs be feared, but it is not well to abandon hope before the event.

DEIANEIRA. Unwise counsels leave no room even for a hope which can lend courage.

CHORUS. Yet towards those who have erred unwittingly men's anger is softened; and so it should be toward you.

DEIANEIRA. No, such words are not for one who has borne a part in the ill deed, but only for him who has no trouble at his own door.

CHORUS. Better to refrain from further speech, unless you wish to inform your own son; here he is, returned from seeking his sire.

HYLLUS (*enters*). O mother, would that one of three things had befallen you! Would that you were dead, or if living no mother of mine, or that some new and better spirit had passed into your bosom.

DEIANEIRA. Ah, my son, what cause have I given you to abhor me?

HYLLUS. I tell you that your husband—yes, my father—has been done to death by you this day!

DEIANEIRA. Oh, what word has passed your lips, my child!

HYLLUS. A word that shall not fail of fulfillment. Who can undo what has come to pass?

DEIANEIRA. What have you said, my son? Who is your warranty for charging me with so terrible a deed?

HYLLUS. I have seen my father's grievous fate with my own eyes; I do not speak from hearsay.

DEIANEIRA. Where did you find him? Where did you stand at his side?

HYLLUS. If you are to hear it then all must be told. After sacking the famous town of Eurytus he went his way with the trophies and first-fruits of victory. There is a sea-washed headland of Euboea, Cape Cenaeum, where he dedicated altars and a sacred grove to the Zeus of his fathers; there I first beheld him, with the joy of yearning love.

He was about to celebrate a great sacrifice, when his own herald, Lichas, came to him from home, bearing your gift, the deadly robe. This he put on, according to your precept, and then began his offering with twelve bulls, free from blemish, the first-fruits of the spoil. Altogether he brought to the altar a hundred victims, large and small.

At first, unfortunate man, he prayed with serene soul, rejoicing in his handsome garb. But when the blood-fed flame began to blaze from the holy offerings and from the resinous pine, a sweat broke forth upon his flesh, and the tunic clung to his sides, at every joint, close-glued, as if by a craftsman's hand. There came a biting pain that racked his bones, and then the venom, as of some deadly, cruel viper, began to devour him.

Thereupon he shouted for the unhappy Lichas—in no way to blame for your crime—asking what treason had moved him to bring that robe. Knowing nothing, the unlucky man said that he had brought the gift from you alone, as it had been sent. When his master heard this, as a piercing spasm clutched his lungs, he caught him by the foot, where the ankle turns in the socket, and hurled him at a surf-beaten rock in the sea; he made the white brain ooze from the hair, as the skull was dashed to splinters and spattered with blood.

All the people lifted up a cry of awestruck grief when they saw that one man was in a frenzy and the other slain; and no one dared come before the man. The pain dragged him to earth, or made him leap into the air, with yells and shrieks, till the cliffs rang around, steep headlands of Locris and Euboean capes.

But when he was spent with often throwing himself on the ground in his anguish and often making loud lament—cursing his fatal marriage with vile you and his alliance with Oeneus, saying that he had found in it the ruin of his life—then from out of the shrouding altar-smoke he lifted up his wildly-rolling eyes and saw me in the great crowd, weeping. He turned his gaze on me and called me: "Son, draw near, do not fly from my trouble, even though you must share my death. Come, carry me out and set me, if you can, in a place where no man shall see me. Or if your pity forbids, at least convey me with all speed out of this land and let me not die where I am."

That command sufficed. We laid him in midship and brought him—but hardly brought him—to this shore, moaning in his torments. You shall presently behold him, alive or lately dead.

Such, mother, are the designs and deeds against my sire of which you have been found guilty. May avenging Justice and the Erinys visit you for them! Yes, if it be right, that is my prayer. And right it is, for I have seen you trample on the right by slaying the noblest man of all the world, whose like you shall never see again!

(DEIANEIRA *moves toward the house.*)

CHORUS. Why do you depart in silence? Do you not know that such silence pleads for your accuser?

HYLLUS. Let her depart. A fair wind speed her far from my sight! Why should the name of mother bring her a semblance of respect when she is all unlike a mother in her deeds? No, let her go. Farewell to her, and may such joy as she gives my sire become her own.

CHORUS. *See, maidens, how suddenly the divine word of the old prophecy has come upon us, which said that when the twelfth year should have run through its full tale of months, it should end the series of toils for the trueborn son of Zeus! And that promise is wafted surely to its fulfillment. For how shall he who beholds not the light have toilsome servitude any more beyond the grave?*

If a cloud of death is around him, and the doom wrought by the Centaur's craft is stinging his sides, where cleaves the venom which Thanatos begat and the gleaming serpent nourished, how can he look upon tomorrow's sun—when that appalling Hydra-shape holds him in its grip, and those murderous goads, prepared by the wily words of black-haired Nessus, have started into fury, vexing him with tumultuous pain?

Of such things this hapless lady had no forebodings; but she saw a great mischief swiftly coming on her home from the new marriage. Her own hand applied the remedy. But for the outcome of a stranger's counsel, given at a fatal meeting—for this, I think, she makes a despairing lament, shedding the tender dew of plenteous tears. And the coming fate foreshadows a great misfortune, contrived by guile.

Our streaming tears break forth. Alas, a plague is upon him more piteous than any suffering that foemen ever brought upon that glorious hero.

Ah, thou dark steel of the spear foremost in battle, by whose might yonder bride was lately borne so swiftly from Oechalia's heights! But the Cyprian goddess, ministering in silence, hath been plainly proved the doer of these deeds.

FIRST SEMICHORUS. *Is it fancy, or do I hear some cry of grief just passing through the house? What is this?*

SECOND SEMICHORUS. *No uncertain sound, but a wail of anguish from within. The house has some new trouble.*

CHORUS. *Mark how sadly, with what a cloud upon her brow, that aged woman approaches, to give us tidings.*

NURSE (*enters*). *Ah, my daughters, great indeed were the sorrows that we were to reap from the gift sent to Heracles!*

CHORUS. *Aged woman, what new mischance have you to tell?*

NURSE. *Deianeira has departed on the last of all her journeys, departed without stirring foot.*

CHORUS. *You are not speaking of death?*

NURSE. *My tale is told.*

CHORUS. *Dead, the poor woman?*

NURSE. *Again you hear it.*

CHORUS. *The poor woman, lost! Speak, what was the manner of her death?*

NURSE. *Oh, a cruel deed was there!*

CHORUS. *Speak out, how did she meet her doom?*

NURSE. *She died by her own hand.*

CHORUS. *What fury, what pangs of frenzy have cut her off by the edge of a dire weapon? How did she contrive this death upon death, all wrought by her alone?*

NURSE. *By the stroke of the sword that causes sorrow.*

CHORUS. *Did you see the violent deed? Poor helpless woman!*

NURSE. *I saw it; yes, I was standing near.*

CHORUS. *Whence did it come? How was it done? Oh, speak!*

NURSE. *It was the work of her own mind and her own hand.*

CHORUS. *What are you telling us?*

NURSE. *The sure truth.*

CHORUS. *The first-born, the first-born of that new bride is a dread Erinys for this house!*

NURSE. Too true. Had you been an eyewitness of the action surely your pity would have been yet deeper.

CHORUS. Could a woman's hand dare to do such deeds?

NURSE. Yes, with dread daring. You shall hear and then you will bear me witness.

When she came alone into the house, and saw her son preparing a deep litter in the court, to take it back and meet his father, she hid herself where none could see. She fell before the altars and wailed aloud that they were left desolate. When she touched any household thing that she had habitually used in the past, poor lady, her tears would flow; or when, roaming here and there through the house, she saw the figure of any well-loved servant, she wept at the sight, unfortunate woman, crying aloud upon her own fate and that of the household, which would thenceforth be in the power of others.

But when this ceased, suddenly I saw her rush into the chamber of Heracles. I watched her from a secret lookout, and saw her spreading coverings on the couch of her lord. When she had done this she sprang upon it and sat in the middle of the bed. Her tears burst forth in burning streams and she spoke: "Ah, bridal bed and bridal chamber, farewell now and forever; never more shall you receive me to rest upon this couch." She said no more, but with a vehement hand loosed her robe, where the gold-wrought brooch lay above her breast, baring all her left side and arm. Then I ran with all my strength and warned her son of her intent. But see, in the space between my going and our return she had driven a two-edged sword through her side to the heart.

At that sight her son uttered a great cry; for he knew, alas, that in his anger he had driven her to that deed, and he had learned too late, from the servants in the house, that she had acted without knowledge, by the prompting of the Centaur. And now in his misery the youth bewailed her with all passionate lament. He knelt and showered kisses on her lips; he threw himself at her side upon the ground, bitterly crying that he had rashly smitten her with a slander, weeping, that he must now live bereaved of both mother and father alike.

Such are the fortunes of this house. Rash indeed is the man who reckons on the morrow or on days beyond it, for tomorrow is not until today is safely past.

CHORUS. *Which woe shall I bewail first, which misery is the greater? Alas, it is hard for me to tell.*

One sorrow may be seen in the house, for one we wait with foreboding; and suspense has a kinship with pain.

Oh that some strong breeze might come with wafting power unto our hearth, to bear me far from this land, lest I die of terror when I look but once upon the mighty son of Zeus!

For they say that he is approaching the house in torments from which there is no deliverance, a wonder of unutterable woe.

Ah, it was not far off but close to us, that woe of which my lament gave warning, like the nightingale's piercing note!

Men of an alien race are coming yonder. And how, then,

are they bringing him? In sorrow, as for some loved one, they move on their mournful, noiseless march.

Alas, he is brought in silence! What are we to think, that he is dead, or sleeping?

(*Enter* HYLLUS *and* OLD MAN, *with attendants bearing* HERACLES.)

HYLLUS. *Woe is me for you, my father, woe is me for you, wretched that I am! Where shall I turn? What can I do? Ah me!*

OLD MAN. *Hush, my son! Do not rouse the cruel pain that infuriates your father! He is alive, though prostrated. Oh, put a stern restraint upon your lips!*

HYLLUS. *What are you saying, old man, is he alive?*

OLD MAN. *You must not awake the slumberer! You must not rouse and revive the dread frenzy that visits him, my son!*

HYLLUS. *Oh, but I am crushed with this weight of misery— there is madness in my heart!*

HERACLES (*awaking*). *O Zeus, to what land have I come? Who are these among whom I lie, tortured with unending agonies? Wretched, wretched, that I am! Oh, that dire pest is gnawing me once more!*

OLD MAN (*to* HYLLUS). *Did I not know how much better it was that you should keep silence, instead of scaring slumber from his brain and eyes?*

HYLLUS. *But I cannot be patient when I see this misery.*

HERACLES. *O you Cenaean rock upon which my altars rose, what a cruel reward you have won me for those fair offerings—be Zeus my witness! Ah, to what ruin have you brought me, to what ruin! Would that I had never seen you for your sorrow! Then I would never have come face to face with this fiery madness which no spell can soothe! Where is the charmer, where is the cunning healer, save Zeus alone, that shall lull this plague to rest? I should marvel if he ever came within my ken!*

Ah! Leave me, the unfortunate, to my rest, leave me to my last rest!

Where are you touching me? Which way would you turn me? You will kill me; you will kill me! If there is any pang that slumbers you have aroused it!

It has seized me, oh, the pest comes again! Where are you from, most ungrateful of all the Greeks? I wore my troubled days out in ridding Greece of pests, on the deep and in the forests; and now when I am stricken will no man succor me with merciful fire or sword?

Oh, will no one come and sever the head, at one fierce stroke, from this wretched body? Woe, woe is me!

OLD MAN. *Son of Heracles, this task exceeds my strength. Do you help, for you have enough strength not to need my aid in his relief.*

HYLLUS. *My hands are helping; but no resource, in myself or from another, can avail to make his life forget its anguish. Such is the doom appointed by Zeus!*

HERACLES. *O my son, where are you? Raise me, take hold of me—so, so! Alas my destiny!*

Again, again the cruel pest leaps forth to rend me, the fierce plague with which none may cope!

O Pallas, Pallas, it tortures me again! Alas, my son, pity your father—draw a blameless sword and strike beneath my collar-bone and heal this pain with which your godless mother has made me wild! So may I see her fall, exactly as she has destroyed me! Sweet Hades, brother of Zeus, give me rest, give me rest, end my woe by a swift doom!

CHORUS. I shudder, friends, to hear these sorrows of our lord. What a man is here, and what torments afflict him!

HERACLES. Ah, full often fierce, and grievous not in name alone, have been the labors of these hands, the burdens borne upon these shoulders! But no toil ever laid on me by the wife of Zeus or by the hateful Eurystheus was like this thing which the daughter of Oeneus, fair and false, has fastened upon my back, this woven net of the Furies in which I perish! Glued to my sides, it has eaten my flesh to the inmost parts. It is always with me, sucking the channels of my breath. Already it has drained my fresh lifeblood, and my whole body is wasted, a captive to these unutterable bonds.

Not the warrior on the battlefield, not the Giants' earth-born host, nor the might of savage beasts, has ever done the like to me, not Hellas, nor the land of the alien, nor any land to which I have come as a deliverer. No, a woman, a weak woman, not born to the strength of a man, all alone has vanquished me, without stroke of sword!

Son, show yourself my son indeed and do not honor a mother's name above a father's: bring forth the woman that bore you, and with your own hands give her into my hand, so that I may know of a truth which sight grieves you most, my tortured frame or hers, when she suffers her righteous doom!

Go, my son, do not shrink; show your pity for me, whom many might deem pitiful, for me moaning and weeping like a girl. The man does not live who can say that he ever saw me do the like before; no, without complaining I still went wherever my evil fortune led. But now, alas, the strong man has been found a woman.

Approach, stand near your father and see what a fate it is that has brought me to this pass, for I will lift the veil. Look! All of you look on this miserable body; see how wretched, how piteous is my plight!

Ah, woe is me! The burning throe of torment is there anew, it darts through my sides—I must wrestle once more with that cruel devouring plague!

Lord of the dark realm, receive me! Smite me, O fire of Zeus! Hurl down your thunderbolt, O King, send it, O father, upon my head! For again the pest is consuming me; it has blazed forth, it has started into fury! O hands, my hands, O shoulders and breast and trusty arms, you now in this plight are the same whose force of old subdued the dweller in Nemea, the scourge of herdsmen, the lion, a creature that no man might approach or confront. You tamed the Lernaean Hydra, and that monstrous host of double form, man joined to steed, a race with whom none may commune, violent, lawless, of surpassing might; you tamed the Erymanthian beast, and the three-headed whelp of Hades underground, a resistless terror, offspring of the dread

Echidna; you tamed the dragon that guarded the golden fruit in the utmost places of the earth.

These toils and countless others have I proved, nor has any man vaunted a triumph over my prowess. But now, with joints unhinged and with flesh torn to shreds, I have become the miserable prey of an unseen destroyer—I who am called the son of noblest mother, I whose reputed sire is Zeus, lord of the starry sky.

But you may be sure of one thing: though I am as nought, though I cannot move a step, yet she who has done this deed shall feel my heavy hand even now. Let her only come, and she shall learn to make this message known to all, that in my death as in my life I chastised the wicked.

CHORUS. Ah, unhappy Greece! What mourning do I foresee for her if she must lose this man!

HYLLUS. Father, since your pause permits an answer, hear me, afflicted though you are. I will ask you for no more than is my due. Accept my advice in a calmer mood than that to which this anger stings you, else you cannot learn how vain is your desire for vengeance, and how causeless your resentment.

HERACLES. Say what you will and be done. In this pain of mine I understand nothing of all your riddling words.

HYLLUS. I come to tell you of my mother, how it is now with her, and how she sinned unwittingly.

HERACLES. Villain! What, have you dared to breathe again in my hearing the name of the mother who has slain your father?

HYLLUS. Yes, such is her state that silence is unfitting.

HERACLES. Unfitting truly, in view of her past crimes.

HYLLUS. And also of her deeds this day, as you will own.

HERACLES. Speak—but give heed that you be not found a traitor.

HYLLUS. These are my tidings. She is dead, lately slain.

HERACLES. By whose hand? A wonderful message, from a prophet of ill-omened voice!

HYLLUS. By her own hand and no stranger's.

HERACLES. Alas, before she could die by mine, as she deserved!

HYLLUS. Even your wrath would be turned if you could hear all.

HERACLES. A strange preamble. But unfold your meaning.

HYLLUS. The sum is this; she erred, with a good intent.

HERACLES. Is it a good deed, you wretch, to have killed your father?

HYLLUS. She meant to use a love-charm for your heart when she saw the new bride in the house, but missed her aim.

HERACLES. What Trachinian deals in spells so potent?

HYLLUS. Nessus the Centaur persuaded her long ago to inflame your desire with such a charm.

HERACLES. Alas, alas, miserable that I am! Woe is me, I am lost—undone, undone! No more for me the light of day! Alas, now I see in what a plight I stand! Go, my son—for your father's end has come—summon, I pray you, all your brothers; summon too the luckless Alcmena, in vain the bride of Zeus, so that you may learn from my dying lips what oracles I know.

HYLLUS. But your mother is not here; as it happens she has her abode at Tiryns by the sea. Some of your children she has taken to live with her there, and others, you will find, are living in Thebe's town. But we who are with you, my father, will tender all service that is needed, at your bidding.

HERACLES. Hear your task, then; now is the time to show what stuff is in you, who are called my son.

It was foreshown me by my sire of old that I should perish by no creature that had the breath of life but by one that had passed to dwell with Hades. So I have been slain by this savage Centaur, the living by the dead, even as the divine will had been foretold.

And I will show you how later oracles tally therewith, confirming the old prophecy. I wrote them down in the grove of the Selli, dwellers on the hills, whose couch is on the ground; they were given by my father's oak of many tongues, and declared that at this present time my release from the toils laid upon me should be accomplished. I looked for prosperous days; but the meaning, it seems, was only that I should die, for the dead have no more toil.

　　Since those words are clearly finding their fulfillment, my son, you on your part must lend me your aid. You must not delay and so provoke me to bitter speech; you must consent and help with good grace, as one who has learned that best of laws, obedience to a father.

HYLLUS. Yes, father. Though I fear the issue to which our talk has brought me, I will do your good pleasure.

HERACLES. First of all, lay your right hand in mine.

HYLLUS. For what purpose do you insist upon this pledge?

HERACLES. Give your hand at once, do not disobey me!

HYLLUS. There it is; you shall not be gainsaid.

HERACLES. Now swear by the head of Zeus my sire!

HYLLUS. To do what deed? May this be told?

HERACLES. To perform for me the task that I shall enjoin.

HYLLUS. I swear it, with Zeus for witness of the oath.

HERACLES. And pray that if you break this oath you may suffer.

HYLLUS. I shall not suffer, for I shall keep it. Yet so I pray.

HERACLES. Well, you know the summit of Oeta, sacred to Zeus?

HYLLUS. Yes, I have often stood at his altar on that height.

HERACLES. To that summit you must carry me with your own hands, aided by what friends you will. You shall lop many branches from the deep-rooted oak and hew many faggots also from the sturdy stock of the wild-olive; on these you shall lay my body and kindle it with flaming pine-torch.

　　And let no tear of mourning be seen there; no, do this without lament and without weeping, if you are indeed my son. But if you do not do it, then even from the world below my curse and my wrath shall wait on you forever.

HYLLUS. Alas, my father, what have you spoken? How have you dealt with me!

HERACLES. I have spoken what you must perform; if you will not get you some other sire and be called my son no more!

HYLLUS. Woe, woe is me! What a deed you require of me,

father—that I should become your murderer, guilty of your blood!

HERACLES. Not so, in truth, but healer of my sufferings, sole physician of my pain!

HYLLUS. How shall I heal your body by kindling it?

HERACLES. If that thought dismays you, at least perform the rest.

HYLLUS. The service of carrying you shall not be refused.

HERACLES. And the heaping of the pyre, as I have bidden?

HYLLUS. Yes, save that I will not touch it with my own hand. All else I will do, and you shall have no hindrance on my part.

HERACLES. Well, so much shall be enough. But add one small boon to your large benefits.

HYLLUS. Be the boon never so large it shall be granted.

HERACLES. Do you know the girl whose sire was Eurytus?

HYLLUS. It is of Iole you speak, if I mistake not.

HERACLES. It is. This in brief is the charge I give you, my son. When I am dead, if you would show a pious remembrance of your oath to your father disobey me not but take this woman to be your wife. Let no other marry the woman who has lain at my side, but do you, my son, make that marriage-bond your own. Consent; after loyalty in great matters, to rebel in less is to cancel the grace that had been won.

HYLLUS. Ah me, it is not well to be angry with a sick man; but who could bear to see him in such a mind?

HERACLES. Your words show no desire to do my bidding.

HYLLUS. What! When she alone is to blame for my mother's death, and for your present plight besides? Does the man live who would make such a choice, unless he were maddened by avenging fiends?

It would be better, father, for me to die too rather than be united to the worst of our foes!

HERACLES. He will render no reverence, it seems, to my dying prayer. But be sure that the curse of the gods will attend you for disobedience to my voice.

HYLLUS. Ah, you will soon show, I think, how distempered you are!

HERACLES. Yes, for you are breaking the slumber of my plague.

HYLLUS. Unlucky me, what perplexities surround me!

HERACLES. Yes, since you do not deign to hear your father.

HYLLUS. But must I then learn to be impious, father?

HERACLES. It is not impiety if you will gladden my heart.

HYLLUS. Then do you command me to do this deed as a clear duty?

HERACLES. I do command you—the gods bear me witness!

HYLLUS. Then I will do it and not refuse—calling upon the gods to witness your action. I can never be condemned for loyalty to you, father.

HERACLES. Your conclusion is good. To these words, my son, quickly add the gracious deed; lay me on the pyre before any pain returns to rend or sting me.

Come, make haste and lift me! This in truth is rest from troubles; this is the end, the last end, of Heracles!

HYLLUS. Nothing now hinders the fulfillment of your wish, since your command constrains us, my father.

HERACLES. *Come then. Before you arouse this plague, O my stubborn soul, give me a curb as of steel on lips set like stone to stone and let no cry escape them. The deed which you are to do, though done perforce, is yet worthy of your joy!*

HYLLUS. *Lift him, men! And grant me full forgiveness for this, but mark the great cruelty of the gods in what is being done. They beget children, they are hailed as fathers, and yet they can look upon such sufferings.*

(HERACLES *is raised to the litter and moved off as* HYLLUS *chants the closing lines to the* CHORUS.)

No man foresees the future; but the present is fraught with mourning for us, and with shame for the powers above, and verily with anguish beyond compare for him who endures this doom.

Maidens, come ye also, nor linger at the house; ye who have lately seen a dread death, with sorrows manifold and strange. In all this there is nought but Zeus.

PHILOCTETES

PHILOCTETES CENTERS UPON TWO PERENNIALLY interesting and interrelated themes, the balance between the claims of the individual and of his society, and the process of maturation from the idealism of adolescence to the responsibilities of adult citizenship. Philoctetes has been badly, and in his judgment unfairly, used by his society, and is determined never to cooperate with it again. While directing his fellow chieftains to a particular altar on the voyage to Troy he was bitten by a snake, and his cries of anguish and the stench of his wound so disturbed his shipmates that, under Odysseus' direction, they marooned him on the deserted island of Lemnos. For ten years the solitary cripple has brooded over the injustice until the Greeks receive an oracle that Troy can be taken only with the help of Philoctetes and his bow. Odysseus, whom Philoctetes hates most of all men, and Neoptolemus, son of Achilles, unknown to Philoctetes, are sent to fetch them.

Neoptolemus has been nurtured on tales of his late father's chivalry and now finds his first assignment is to cheat a helpless cripple, who actually entrusts the bow to him during a paroxysm of pain. Presently conscience moves him to restore the bow, and he pleads with Philoctetes to come to Troy of his own good will—in vain. When Odysseus enters to threaten force, Philoctetes is on the point of using the bow against him. Heracles (who used the bow in the service of society) appears *ex machina* and persuades Philoctetes to go to Troy, where he will recover health and win glory. Both Philoctetes and Neoptolemus have learned that personal preferences must sometimes be compromised for the benefit of the group. The bow itself is a symbol of the responsibility which goes with special capacities. Odysseus is not a corrupter of innocence but (as elsewhere in Sophocles) a spokesman for the interests of the state. That the theme of man and society is central in this play (it is at least incidental in others of Sophocles) is clear from the circumstance that Lemnos is represented as uninhabited when everyone at that time knew that it was in fact inhabited and was so represented in (lost) plays on Philoctetes by Aeschylus and Euripides.

PERSONS

ODYSSEUS
NEOPTOLEMUS
PHILOCTETES
MERCHANT, *follower of*
  Odysseus in disguise

HERACLES
CHORUS, *sailors of*
  Neoptolemus

SCENE: *Rocky cliff on Lemnos.*

(*Enter* ODYSSEUS *and* NEOPTOLEMUS.)

ODYSSEUS. This is the shore of the sea-girt land of Lemnos, untrodden of men and desolate. Neoptolemus, true-bred son of Achilles, you whose sire was the noblest of the Greeks, here long ago I put ashore the Malian, son of Poeas (as I was bidden by my chiefs to do), his foot all ulcerous with a gnawing sore, because we could attempt neither drink-offering nor sacrifice in peace; with his fierce ill-omened cries he filled the whole camp continually, shrieking, moaning. But what need to speak of that? This is no time for many words; if he learn that I am here I shall waste the whole plan by which I expect to take him soon.

Come, to work! it is for you to help in what remains. Seek where in this region is a cave with twofold mouth, such that in cold weather either front offers a sunny seat, but in summer a breeze wafts sleep through the tunneled grotto. And a little below, on the left hand, you might see a spring if it has not failed.

Move toward the place silently, and signify to me whether he is still living there or is to be sought elsewhere, so that our further course may be explained by me and heard by you and sped by the joint work of both.

NEOPTOLEMUS. King Odysseus, the task that you set lies not far off; I think I see such a cave as you have described.

ODYSSEUS. Above you or below? I do not see it.

NEOPTOLEMUS. Here, high up. Of footsteps not a sound.

ODYSSEUS. See whether he is not lodged there, asleep.

NEOPTOLEMUS. I see an empty chamber, no man in it.

ODYSSEUS. And no provision for man's abode?

NEOPTOLEMUS. Yes, a mattress of leaves, as if for someone who lives here.

ODYSSEUS. All else bare? Nothing else beneath the roof?

NEOPTOLEMUS. Just a rude cup of wood, the work of a sorry craftsman, and with it this tinder stuff.

ODYSSEUS. His is the household you describe.

NEOPTOLEMUS. Ha! Here are also some rags drying in the sun, stained with matter from some grievous sore.

ODYSSEUS. The man dwells in these regions, clearly, and is somewhere not far off; how could a man go far afield with foot maimed by that inveterate plague? No, he has gone forth in quest of food or perhaps of some soothing herb that he has noted somewhere. Send your attendant, therefore, to keep watch, lest the foe come on me unawares; for he would rather take me than all the Greeks beside.

NEOPTOLEMUS. Enough, the man is going and the path shall be watched. And now, if you would say more, proceed.

ODYSSEUS. Son of Achilles, you must be loyal to your mission, and not with your body alone. If you should hear some new thing, some plan unknown to you till now, you must help it; for to help is your part here.

NEOPTOLEMUS. What is your bidding?

ODYSSEUS. You must beguile the mind of Philoctetes by a story told in your conversation with him. When he asks you who and whence you are, say the son of Achilles—there must be no deception touching that. But say you are home-ward bound: you have left the fleet of the Achaean warriors and have conceived a deadly hatred for them, because, when they had moved you by their prayers to come from home (since this was their only hope of taking Ilium), they deemed you not worthy of the arms of Achilles, did not deign to give them to you when you came and claimed them by right, but made them over to Odysseus. Of me say what you will, the vilest of vile reproaches; by that you will cost me no pang. But if you fail to do this deed you will bring sorrow on all our host. For if yonder man's bow is not to be taken, never can you sack the realm of Dardanus.

And mark why your intercourse with him may be free from mistrust or danger while mine cannot. *You* have come to Troy under no oath to any man and by no constraint, nor had you any part in the earlier voyage; but none of these things can I deny. And so if he shall perceive me while he is still master of his bow I am lost, and you as my comrade will share my doom. No, the thing that must be plotted is just this—how you may win the resistless arms by stealth. I well know, my son, that by nature you are not apt to utter or contrive such guile, yet seeing that victory is a sweet prize to gain bend your will to it; our honesty shall be shown forth another time. But now lend yourself to me for one little knavish day, and then, through all your days to come, be called the most righteous of mankind.

NEOPTOLEMUS. When counsels pain my ear, son of Laertes, then I abhor to aid them with my hand. It is not in my nature to compass anything by evil arts, nor was it, as men say, in my sire's. But I am ready to take the man by force, not by fraud; having the use of one foot only he cannot prevail in fight against us who are so many. And yet, having been sent to act with you, I am loth to be called traitor. But my wish, O King, is to do right and miss my aim rather than succeed by evil ways.

ODYSSEUS. Son of brave sire, time was when I too, in my youth, had a slow tongue and a ready hand; but now, when I come forth to the proof, I see that words, not deeds, are ever the masters among men.

NEOPTOLEMUS. What then is your command? What but that I should lie?

ODYSSEUS. I say that you are to take Philoctetes by guile.

NEOPTOLEMUS. And why by guile rather than by persuasion?

ODYSSEUS. He will never listen; and by force you cannot take him.

NEOPTOLEMUS. Has he such dread strength to make him bold?

ODYSSEUS. Shafts unavoidable and winged with death.

NEOPTOLEMUS. May none dare even to approach that foe?

ODYSSEUS. Not unless you take him by guile, as I say.

NEOPTOLEMUS. You think it no shame then to speak falsehoods?

ODYSSEUS. No, if the falsehood brings deliverance.

NEOPTOLEMUS. How have the face to speak those words?

ODYSSEUS. When your deed promises gain it is unmeet to shrink.

NEOPTOLEMUS. What gain is it for me that he should come to Troy?

ODYSSEUS. With these shafts alone can Troy be taken.

NEOPTOLEMUS. Then *I* am not to be the conqueror, as you said?

ODYSSEUS. Neither you apart from these, nor these from you.

NEOPTOLEMUS. It would seem that we must try to win them, if it stands thus.

ODYSSEUS. Know that if you do this thing two prizes are yours.

NEOPTOLEMUS. What are they? Tell me, and I will not refuse the deed.

ODYSSEUS. You will be called at once wise and valiant.

NEOPTOLEMUS. Come what may, I'll do it, and cast off all shame.

ODYSSEUS. Are you mindful, then, of the counsels that I gave?

NEOPTOLEMUS. Be sure of it, now that once I have consented.

ODYSSEUS. Stay here, then, in wait for him; I will go away, not to be seen with you, and will send our watcher back to the ship. If you seem to be tarrying at all beyond the due time I will send that same man here again, disguised as the captain of a merchant ship, so secrecy may help us. Then, my son, as he tells his artful story take such hints as may help you from the tenor of his words.

Now I will go to the ship, having left this charge with you. May speeding Hermes, the lord of stratagem, lead us

on, and Victory, even Athena Polias, who saves me ever!
(*Exit.*)

CHORUS (*enters*). *A stranger in a strange land, what am I to
hide, what am I to speak, O Master, before a man who will
be swift to think evil? You be my guide; his skill excels all
other skill, his counsel has no peer, with whom is the sway
of the godlike scepter given by Zeus. And to you, my son,
that sovereign power has descended from of old; tell me,
therefore, wherein I am to serve you.*

NEOPTOLEMUS. *For the present you may survey fearlessly the
place where he lives at the ocean's edge; but when the dread
wayfarer who has left this dwelling shall return, come forward at my beck from time to time and try to help as the moment may require.*

CHORUS. *Long have I been careful of that care, my prince, that
my eye should be watchful for your good before all else.
Now tell me, in what manner of shelter has he made his
abode? In what region is he? It were not unseasonable for
me to learn, lest he surprise me from some quarter. What is
the place of his wandering, or of his rest? Where does he
plant his steps, within his dwelling or abroad?*

NEOPTOLEMUS. *Here you see his home with its two portals, his
rocky cell.*

CHORUS. *And its luckless inmate—where is he gone?*

NEOPTOLEMUS. *I doubt not but he is trailing his painful steps
somewhere near this spot, in quest of food. Rumor says that
in this fashion he lives, seeking prey with his winged shafts,
all-wretched that he is. No healer of his woe comes near
him.*

CHORUS. *I pity him, to think how, with no man to care for him,
and seeing no companion's face, suffering, always lonely,
he is vexed by fierce disease and bewildered by each want as
it rises. How, how does he endure in his misery? Alas, the
dark dealings of the gods! Alas, hapless races of men, whose
destiny exceeds due measure!*

*This man, noble, perchance, as any scion of the noblest
house, reft of all life's gifts, lies lonely, apart from his fel-
lows, with the dappled or shaggy beasts of the field, piteous*

*alike in his torments and his hunger, bearing anguish that
finds no cure; while the mountain nymph, babbling Echo,
appearing afar, makes answer to his bitter cries.*

NEOPTOLEMUS. *Nothing of this is a marvel to me. By heavenly
ordinance, if such as I may judge, those first sufferings came
on him from relentless Chryse. The woes that now he bears,
with none to tend him, surely he bears by the providence of
some god, that so he might not bend against Troy the resistless shafts divine till the time be fulfilled when, as men say,
Troy is fated by those shafts to fall.*

CHORUS. *Hush, peace, my son!*

NEOPTOLEMUS. *What now?*

CHORUS. *A sound rose on the air such as might haunt the lips
of a man in weary pain. From this point it came I think—or
this. It smites, it smites indeed upon my ear—the voice of
one who creeps painfully on his way. I cannot mistake that
grievous cry of human anguish from afar—its accents are
too clear.*

Then turn, my son—

NEOPTOLEMUS. *Say where?*

CHORUS. *—to new counsels; the man is not far off but near.
Not with music of the reed does he come, like a shepherd in
the pastures, no, but with far-sounding moan as he stum-
bles, perhaps from stress of pain, or as he gazes on the
haven that has no ship for guest. Loud is his cry and dread.*

PHILOCTETES (*enters*). O strangers! Who may you be and from
what country have you put into this land that is harborless
and desolate? What should I deem to be your city or your
race?

The fashion of your garb is Greek, most welcome to my
sight, but I would like to hear your speech. Do not shrink
from me in fear or be scared by my wild looks; nay, in pity
for one so wretched and so lonely, for a sufferer so desolate
and so friendless, speak to me, if indeed you have come as
friends. Oh, answer! It is not meet that I should fail of this,
at least, from you, or you from me.

NEOPTOLEMUS. Then know this first, good sir, that we are
Greeks, since you are eager to learn that.

PHILOCTETES. O well-loved sound! Ah, that I should indeed be greeted by such a man, after so long a time! What quest, my son, has drawn you toward these shores and to this spot? What enterprise? What kindliest of winds? Speak, tell me all, so I may know who you are.

NEOPTOLEMUS. My birthplace is the sea-girt Scyros; I am sailing homeward; Achilles was my sire; my name is Neoptolemus. You know all.

PHILOCTETES. O son of well-loved father and dear land, foster child of aged Lycomedes, on what errand have you touched this coast? Whence are you sailing?

NEOPTOLEMUS. It is from Ilium that I hold my present course.

PHILOCTETES. What? You were not, certainly, our shipmate at the beginning of the voyage to Ilium?

NEOPTOLEMUS. Had you indeed a part in that emprise?

PHILOCTETES. O my son, then you do not know who is before you?

NEOPTOLEMUS. How should I know one whom I had never seen before?

PHILOCTETES. Then you have not even heard my name or any rumor of those miseries by which I was perishing?

NEOPTOLEMUS. Be assured that I know nothing of what you ask.

PHILOCTETES. O wretched indeed that I am, O abhorred of heaven, that no word of this my plight should have won its way to my home or to any home of Greeks! No, the men who wickedly cast me out keep their secret and laugh, while my plague still rejoices in its strength and grows to more!

O my son, O boy whose father was Achilles, behold, I am he of whom you may have heard as lord of the bow of Heracles. I am the son of Poeas, Philoctetes, whom the two chieftains and the Cephallenian king foully cast upon this solitude when I was wasting with a fierce disease, stricken down by the furious bite of the destroying serpent. With that plague for sole companion, O my son, those men put me out here and were gone, when from sea-girt Chryse they touched at this coast with their fleet. They were glad when they saw me asleep, after much tossing on the waves; they abandoned me in the shelter of a cave upon the shore, first putting out a few rags, good enough for such a wretch, and also a scanty dole of food: may heaven give them the like!

Think now, my son, think what a waking was mine when they had gone and I rose from sleep that day! What bitter tears started from my eyes, what miseries were those that I bewailed when I saw that the ships with which I had sailed were all gone, and that there was no man in the place, not one to help, not one to ease the burden of the sickness that vexed me, when, looking all around, I could find no provision, save for anguish—but of that a plenteous store, my son!

So time went on for me, season by season; and alone in this narrow house I was content to meet each want by my own service. For hunger's needs this bow provided, bringing down the winged doves; and whatever my string-sped shaft might strike I would crawl to it myself, luckless me, trailing my wretched foot just so far. Or if, again, water had to be fetched, or if, when the frost was out, as happens often in winter, a bit of firewood had to be broken, I would creep forth, poor wretch, and manage it. Then fire would be lacking; but by rubbing stone on stone I would at last draw forth the hidden spark; and this it is that keeps life in me from day to day. Indeed, a roof over my head, and with it fire, gives all that I want—save release from my disease.

Come now, my son, you must learn what manner of isle this is. No mariner approaches it by choice; there is no anchorage; there is no seaport where he can find a gainful market or a kindly welcome. This is not a place to which prudent men make voyages. Well, suppose that someone has put in against his will; such things may often happen in the long course of a man's life. These visitors when they come have compassionate words for me, and perhaps they are moved by pity to give me a little food or some raiment; but there is one thing that no one will do when I speak of it—take me safe home. No, this is now the tenth year that I am wearing out my wretched days, in hunger and in misery, feeding the plague that is never sated with my flesh.

Thus have the Atreidae and the proud Odysseus dealt with me, my son: may the Olympian gods some day give them the like sufferings in requital for mine!

CHORUS. I too pity you, son of Poeas, in like measure with your former visitors.

NEOPTOLEMUS. And I am myself a witness to your words; I know that they are true, for I have felt the villainy of the Atreidae and the proud Odysseus.

PHILOCTETES. What, have you too a grief against the accursed sons of Atreus, a cause to resent ill-usage?

NEOPTOLEMUS. Oh that it might be mine one day to wreak my hatred with my hand, that so Mycenae might learn, and Sparta, that Scyros also is a mother of brave men.

PHILOCTETES. Well said, my son! Now why have you come in this fierce wrath which you denounce against them?

NEOPTOLEMUS. Son of Poeas, I will speak out—and yet it is hard to speak—concerning the outrage that I suffered from them at my coming. When fate decreed that Achilles should die—

PHILOCTETES. Ah me! Tell me no more until I first know this: are you saying that the son of Peleus is dead?

NEOPTOLEMUS. Dead—by no mortal hand, but by a god's; laid low, as men say, by the arrow of Phoebus.

PHILOCTETES. Well, noble alike are the slayer and the slain! I scarcely know, my son, which I should do first, inquire into your wrong or mourn the dead.

NEOPTOLEMUS. Your own sorrows, I think, are enough for you, without mourning for the woes of your neighbor.

PHILOCTETES. You speak the truth. Resume your story, then, and tell me in what way they wronged you.

NEOPTOLEMUS. They came for me in a ship with gaily decked prow—princely Odysseus and he who watched over my father's youth—saying (whether truly or falsely I do not know) that since my father had perished fate now forbade that the towers of Troy should be taken by any hand but mine.

Saying that these things were so, my friend, they made me pause not long before I set forth in haste, chiefly through my yearning toward the dead, that I might see him before burial—for I had never seen him. Besides, there was a charm in their promise if, when I went, I should sack the towers of Troy.

It was now the second day of my voyage when, sped by breeze and oar, I drew nigh to cruel Sigeum. And when I landed straightway all the host thronged about me with greetings, vowing that they saw their lost Achilles once more alive.

He then lay dead; and I, unlucky me, when I had wept for him, presently went to the Atreidae—to friends, as I might well suppose—and claimed my father's arms with all else that had been his. O, it was a shameless answer that they made! "Seed of Achilles, you can take all else that was your sire's; but of the arms another man is now lord, the son of Laertes." The tears came into my eyes, I sprang up in passionate anger, and I said in my bitterness, "Wretch! What, have you dared to give my arms to another man, without my leave?" Then said Odysseus, for he chanced to be near, "Yes, boy, this award of theirs is just; I saved the arms and their master at his need." Then straightway in my fury I began to hurl all manner of taunts at him and spared not one, if I was indeed to be robbed of my arms by him. At this point, stung by the abuse though not prone to wrath, he answered, "You were not here with us but absent from your duty. And since you must talk so saucily, you shall never carry those arms back to Scyros."

Thus upbraided, thus insulted, I am sailing for home, despoiled of my own by that worst offspring of an evil breed, Odysseus. And yet he, I think, is less to blame than the rulers. For an army, like a city, hangs wholly on its leaders, and when men do lawless deeds it is the counsel of their teachers that corrupts them. My tale is told; and may the foe of the Atreidae have the favor of heaven as he has mine!

CHORUS. *Goddess of the hills, all-fostering Earth mother of Zeus most high, thou through whose realm the great Pactolus rolls golden sands—there also, dread Mother, I called upon thy name when all the insults of the Atreidae*

*were being heaped upon this man—when they were giving
his sire's armor, that peerless marvel, to the son of Laertes—
hear it, thou immortal one, who ridest on bull-slaughtering
lions!*

PHILOCTETES. It seems that you have come to me, friends, well
commended by a common grief; your story is of a like
strain with mine, so that I can recognize the work of the
Atreidae and of Odysseus. Well I know that he would lend
his tongue to any base pretext, to any villainy, if thereby he
could hope to compass some dishonest end. No, it is not at
this that I wonder, but rather that the elder Ajax, if he was
there, could endure to see it.

NEOPTOLEMUS. Ah, friend, he was no more; I should never
have been thus plundered while he lived.

PHILOCTETES. How do you say? Is he too dead and gone?

NEOPTOLEMUS. Think of him as one who sees the light no
more.

PHILOCTETES. Woe is me! But the son of Tydeus and the offspring of Sisyphus that was bought by Laertes—they will
not die, for they ought not to live.

NEOPTOLEMUS. Not they, be sure of it. No, they are now prospering full greatly in the Argive host.

PHILOCTETES. And what of my brave old friend Nestor of
Pylos—is he not alive? *Their* mischiefs were often baffled
by his wise counsels.

NEOPTOLEMUS. He has trouble now; death has taken Antil-
ochus, the son that was at his side.

PHILOCTETES. Ah me! These two again whom you have named
are men of whose death I had least wished to hear. Alas!
What are we to look for when these have died and here
again Odysseus lives—when he should have been numbered with the dead in their place?

NEOPTOLEMUS. A clever wrestler he; but even clever schemes,
Philoctetes, are often tripped up.

PHILOCTETES. Now tell me, pray, where was Patroclus in your
need, he whom your father loved so well?

NEOPTOLEMUS. He too was dead. To be brief I would tell you
this: war takes no evil man by choice but good men always.

PHILOCTETES. I bear you witness. For that same reason I will ask you how fares a man of little worth but shrewd of tongue and clever—

NEOPTOLEMUS. Surely this will be no one but Odysseus?

PHILOCTETES. I did not mean him; there was one Thersites, who could never be content with brief speech though all men chafed. Do you know if he is alive?

NEOPTOLEMUS. I did not see him, but heard that he still lives.

PHILOCTETES. It was his due. No evil thing has been known to perish; no, the gods take a tender care of such and have a strange joy in turning back from Hades all things villainous and knavish, while they are ever sending the just and the good out of life. How am I to imagine these things or wherein shall I praise them when, praising the ways of the gods, I find that the gods are evil?

NEOPTOLEMUS. Son of Oetaean sire, I at least shall be on my guard henceforth against Ilium and the Atreidae, nor look on them save from afar. Where the worse man is stronger than the good, where honesty fails and the dastard bears sway—among such men I will never make my friends. No, rocky Scyros shall suffice for me henceforth, nor shall I ask a better home.

Now to my ship! And you, son of Poeas, farewell, heartily farewell; may the gods deliver you from your sickness, even as you would! But we must be going, so that we may set forth whenever the god permits our voyage.

PHILOCTETES. Are you starting now, my son?

NEOPTOLEMUS. Aye, prudence bids us watch the weather near our ship rather than from afar.

PHILOCTETES. Now by your father and by your mother, my son, by all that is dear to you in your home, solemnly I implore you, leave me not thus forlorn, helpless amid these miseries in which I live, such as you see and many that you have heard! Nay, spare a passing thought to me. Great is the discomfort, I well know, of such a freight, yet bear with it. To noble minds baseness is hateful and a good deed is glorious. Forsake this task and your fair name is sullied; perform it, my son, and a rich meed of glory will be yours if I return alive to Oeta's land. Come, the trouble does not last one whole day; make the effort, take and thrust me where you will, in hold, in prow, in stern, wherever I shall least annoy my shipmates.

O consent, by the great Zeus of suppliants, my son, be persuaded! I supplicate you on my knees, infirm as I am, poor wretch and maimed! Do not leave me thus desolate, far from the steps of men! Bring me safely to your own home, or to Euboea, Chalcodon's seat; from there it will be no long journey for me to Oeta and the Trachinian heights and the fair-flowing Spercheius, that you may show me to my beloved sire. I have long feared that he may have gone from me. Often have I summoned him by those who came, with imploring prayers that he would himself send a ship and fetch me home. But either he is dead, or else, I suppose, my messengers—as was likely—made small account of my concerns and hastened on their homeward voyage.

Now, however, since in you I have found one who can carry at once my message and myself, do you save me, do you show me mercy, seeing how all human destiny is full of the fear and the peril that good fortune may be followed by evil. He who stands clear of trouble should beware of dangers; and when a man lives at ease, then it is that he should look most closely to his life, lest ruin come on it by stealth.

CHORUS. *Have pity, O King; he has told of a struggle with sufferings manifold and grievous; may the like befall no friend of mine! And if, my prince, you hate the hateful Atreidae, then turning their misdeeds to this man's gain I would waft him in your good swift ship to the home for which he yearns, that so you flee the just wrath of Heaven.*

NEOPTOLEMUS. Beware lest, though now as a spectator you are pliant, yet when wearied of his malady by consorting with it you be found no longer constant to these words.

CHORUS. No indeed; never will you have cause to utter that reproach against me!

NEOPTOLEMUS. Nay then, it would be shameful for the stranger to find me less prompt than you are to serve him at his need. Come, if it please you, let us sail. Let the man set forth at once; our ship for her part will carry him and will not refuse. Only may the gods convey us safely out of this land, and hence to our haven, wherever it be!

PHILOCTETES. O most joyful day! O kindest friend, and you, good sailors, would that I could prove to you in deeds what love you have won from me! Let us be going, my son, when you and I have made a solemn farewell to the homeless home within, so that you may learn by what means I sustained life and how stout a heart has been mine. I believe that the bare sight would have deterred any other man from enduring such a lot; but I have been schooled by necessity to patience.

(NEOPTOLEMUS *is about to follow* PHILOCTETES *into the cave.*)

CHORUS. Stay, let us give heed. Two men are coming, one a seaman of your ship, the other a stranger. You should hear their tidings before you go in.

MERCHANT (*enters*). Son of Achilles, I asked my companion here—who with two others was guarding your ship—to tell me where you might be, since I have fallen in with you, when I did not expect it, by the chance of coming to anchor off the same coast. Sailing in trader's wise with no great company, homeward bound from Ilium to Peparethus with its cluster-laden vines, when I heard that the sailors were all of your crew, I resolved not to go on my voyage in silence without first giving you my news and reaping due reward. You know nothing, I suspect, of your own affairs, the new designs that the Greeks have concerning you, nay, not designs merely but deeds in progress and no longer tarrying.

NEOPTOLEMUS. Truly sir, the grace shown me by your forethought, if I should not be unworthy, shall live in my grateful thoughts. But tell me just what it is of which you have spoken, that I may learn what strange design on the part of the Greeks you are announcing to me.

MERCHANT. Pursuers have started in quest of you with ships, the aged Phoenix and the sons of Theseus.

NEOPTOLEMUS. To bring me back by force or by fair words?

MERCHANT. I do not know, but I have come to tell you what I have heard.

NEOPTOLEMUS. Can Phoenix and his comrades be showing such zeal on such an errand to please the Atreidae?

MERCHANT. The errand is being done, I assure you, and without delay.

NEOPTOLEMUS. Why then was not Odysseus ready to sail for this purpose and to bring the message himself? Or did some fear restrain him?

MERCHANT. Oh, he and the son of Tydeus were setting forth in pursuit of another man as I was leaving port.

NEOPTOLEMUS. Who was this other in quest of whom Odysseus himself was sailing?

MERCHANT. There was a man . . . But tell me first who that is yonder—and whatever you say do not speak loud.

NEOPTOLEMUS. Sir, you see the renowned Philoctetes.

MERCHANT. Ask me no more, then, but convey yourself with all speed out of this land.

PHILOCTETES. What is he saying, my son? Why is the sailor trafficking with you about me in these dark whispers?

NEOPTOLEMUS. I do not know his meaning yet, but whatever he would say he must say openly to you and me and these men.

MERCHANT. Seed of Achilles, do not accuse me to the army of saying what I should not. I receive many benefits from them for my services, as a poor man may.

NEOPTOLEMUS. I am the foe of the Atreidae, and this man is my best friend because he hates them. Since then you have come with a kindly purpose toward me you must not keep from us any part of the tidings that you have heard.

MERCHANT. Watch what you are doing, my son.

NEOPTOLEMUS. I am well aware.

MERCHANT. I will hold you accountable.

NEOPTOLEMUS. Do so, but speak.

MERCHANT. I obey. It is in quest of this man that those two are sailing that I named to you, the son of Tydeus and mighty Odysseus, sworn to bring him, either by winning words or by constraining force. All the Achaeans heard this plainly from Odysseus, for his confidence of success was higher than his comrade's.

NEOPTOLEMUS. Why, after so long a time, did the Atreidae turn their thoughts toward this man, whom they had long since cast forth? What was the yearning that came to them, what compulsion, or what vengeance from gods who requite evil deeds?

MERCHANT. I can expound all that to you, since it seems that you have not heard it. There was a seer of noble birth, a son of Priam, Helenus by name, whom this guileful Odysseus, of whom all shameful and dishonoring words are spoken, made his prisoner. Leading him in bonds, he showed him publicly to the Achaeans, a goodly prize. Helenus then prophesied to them whatever else they asked and also that they would never sack the towers of Troy unless by winning words they should bring this man from the island upon which he now dwells.

And the son of Laertes, when he heard the seer say this, straightway promised that he would bring this man and show him to the Achaeans—most likely, he thought, as a willing captive, but if reluctant, then by force; adding that should he fail whoso wished might have his head. You have heard all, my son, and I commend speed to you and to any man for whom you care.

PHILOCTETES. Luckless that I am! Has he, that utter pest, sworn to bring me by persuasion to the Achaeans? As soon shall I be persuaded, when I am dead, to come up from Hades to the light, as his father came!

MERCHANT. I know nothing about that. But I must go to ship, and may Heaven be with you both for all good. (*Exit.*)

PHILOCTETES. Now is not this wonderful, my son, that the offspring of Laertes should have hoped by means of soft words to lead me forth from his ship and show me amidst the Greeks? No! Sooner would I hearken to that deadliest of my foes, the viper which made me the cripple that I am! But there is nothing that *he* would not say or dare; and now I know that he will be here. Come, my son, let us be moving, that a wide sea may part us from the ship of Odysseus. Let us go: good speed in good season brings sleep and rest when toil is over.

NEOPTOLEMUS. We will sail, then, as soon as the head wind falls; at present it is adverse.

PHILOCTETES. 'Tis ever fair sailing when you flee from evil.

NEOPTOLEMUS. Nay, but this weather is against them also.

PHILOCTETES. No wind comes amiss to pirates when there is a chance to steal or rob by force.

NEOPTOLEMUS. Well, let us be going if you will, when you have taken from within whatever you need or desire most.

PHILOCTETES. Yes, there are some things that I need, though the choice is not large.

NEOPTOLEMUS. What is there that will not be found aboard my ship?

PHILOCTETES. I keep by me a certain herb with which I can always best assuage this wound, till it is wholly soothed.

NEOPTOLEMUS. Fetch it then. Now what else would you take?

PHILOCTETES. Any of these arrows that may have been forgotten and may have slipped away from me, lest I leave it to be another's prize.

NEOPTOLEMUS. Is that indeed the famous bow which you are holding?

PHILOCTETES. This and no other, that I carry in my hand.

NEOPTOLEMUS. Is it lawful for me to have a nearer view of it, to handle it and salute it as a god?

PHILOCTETES. To you, my son, this shall be granted, and anything else in my power that is for your good.

NEOPTOLEMUS. I certainly long to touch it, but my longing is on this wise: if it be lawful, I should be glad; if not, think no more of it.

PHILOCTETES. Your words are reverent and your wish, my son, is lawful. You alone have given to my eyes the light of life, the hope to see the Oetean land, to see my aged father and my friends; when I lay beneath the feet of my foes, you have lifted me beyond their reach. Be of good cheer; the bow shall be yours, to handle and to return to the hand that gave it. You shall be able to vaunt that in reward of your kindness you alone of mortals have touched it; for it was by a good deed that I myself won it.

NEOPTOLEMUS. I rejoice to have found you and to have gained your friendship; a man who knows how to render benefit for benefit must prove a friend above price. Go in, I pray you.

PHILOCTETES. Yes, and I will lead you in, for my sick estate craves the comfort of your presence. (*Exeunt.*)

CHORUS. *I have heard in story, but seen not with mine eyes, how he who once came near the bed of Zeus was bound upon a swift wheel by the almighty son of Cronus; but of no other mortal know I, by hearsay or by sight, that hath encountered a doom so dreadful as this man's; who, though he had wronged none by force or fraud, but lived at peace with his fellow-men, was left to perish thus cruelly.*

Verily I marvel how, as he listened in his solitude to the surges that beat around him, he kept his hold upon a life so full of woe; where he was neighbor to himself alone—powerless to walk—with no one in the land to be near him while he suffered, in whose ear he could pour forth the lament, awaking response, for the plague that gnawed his flesh and drained his blood; no one to assuage the burning flux, oozing from the ulcers of his envenomed foot, with healing herbs gathered from the bounteous earth, so often as the torment came upon him.

Then would he creep this way or that, with painful steps, like a child without kindly nurse, to any place whence his need might be supplied, whenever the devouring anguish abated; gathering not for food the fruit of holy Earth, nor aught else that we mortals gain by toil; save when haply he found wherewith to stay his hunger by winged shafts from his swift-smiting bow. Ah, joyless was his life, who for ten years never knew the gladness of the winecup, but still bent his way toward any stagnant pool that he could descry as he gazed around him.

But now, after these troubles, he shall be happy and mighty at the last; for he hath met with the son of a noble race, who in the fulness of many months bears him on sea-cleaving ship to his home, haunt of Malian nymphs, and to

the banks of the Spercheius; where, above Oeta's heights,
the lord of the brazen shield drew near to the gods, amid the
splendor of the lightnings of his sire.

(*Enter* NEOPTOLEMUS *and* PHILOCTETES.)

NEOPTOLEMUS. I pray you, come on. Why are you so silent? Why do you halt, as if dismayed, without a cause?

PHILOCTETES. Alas, alas!

NEOPTOLEMUS. What is the matter?

PHILOCTETES. Nothing serious. Go on, my son.

NEOPTOLEMUS. Are you in pain from the disease that vexes you?

PHILOCTETES. No indeed. No, I think I am better just now. Ye gods!

NEOPTOLEMUS. Why are you groaning so and calling on the gods?

PHILOCTETES. That they may come to us with power to save and soothe. Ah me! ah me!

NEOPTOLEMUS. What ails you? Speak, do not persist in this silence. It is plain that something is amiss with you.

PHILOCTETES. I am lost, my son. I can never hide my trouble from you. Ah, it pierces me, it pierces! O misery, O wretched that I am! I am undone, my son, it devours me. Oh, for the gods' love, if you have a sword ready to your hand, strike at my heel, shear it off straightway, do not heed my life! Quick, quick, my son!

NEOPTOLEMUS. What new thing has come on you so suddenly that you are bewailing yourself with such loud laments?

PHILOCTETES. You know, my son.

NEOPTOLEMUS. What is it?

PHILOCTETES. You know, boy.

NEOPTOLEMUS. What is the matter with you? I do not know.

PHILOCTETES. How can you help knowing? Oh, oh!

NEOPTOLEMUS. Dread indeed is the burden of the malady.

PHILOCTETES. Yes, dread beyond telling. Oh, pity me!

NEOPTOLEMUS. What shall I do?

PHILOCTETES. Do not forsake me in fear. This visitant comes

but now and then, when she has been sated, perchance, with
her roamings.

NEOPTOLEMUS. Ah, luckless man! Luckless indeed are you
found in all manner of woe! Shall I take hold of you, or lend
you a helping hand?

PHILOCTETES. No, no. But take this bow of mine, I pray you,
as you asked of me just now, and keep if safe until this present access of my disease is past. For indeed sleep falls on
me when this plague is passing away, nor can the pain cease
sooner; but you must allow me to slumber in peace. And if
meanwhile those men come, I charge you by Heaven that in
no wise, willingly or unwillingly, you give up this bow to
them, lest you bring destruction at once on yourself and on
me who am your suppliant.

NEOPTOLEMUS. Have no fears as to my caution. The bow shall
pass into no hands but yours and mine. Give it to me, and
may good luck come with it!

PHILOCTETES. There it is, my son. Pray the jealous gods that it
may not bring you troubles such as it brought to me and to
him who was its lord before me.

NEOPTOLEMUS. Ye gods, grant this to us two! Grant us a voyage prosperous and swift, whithersoever the god approves
and our purpose tends!

PHILOCTETES. Nay, my son, I fear that your prayers are vain.
Once more the dark blood oozes drop by drop from the
depths, and I look for worse to come. Ah me, oh, oh! You
wretched foot, what torment will you work for me! It creeps
on me, it is drawing near! Woe, woe is me! You know it now;
do not flee, I pray you!

O Cephallenian friend, would that this anguish might
cleave to you and transfix your breast! Ah me! Ah me! O
you chieftains both, Agamemnon, Menelaus, would that
you instead of me might have this malady upon you and for
as long! Ah me! Ah me! O Death, Death, when I am thus
ever calling you, day by day, why can you never come? O
my son, generous youth, come, seize me, burn me up, true-
hearted friend, in yonder fire famed as Lemnian; I too once
deemed it lawful to do the same to the son of Zeus, for the

meed of these same arms which are now in your keeping.
What do you say, boy, what do you say? Why are you silent?
Where are your thoughts, my son?

NEOPTOLEMUS. I have long been grieving in my heart for your
load of pain.

PHILOCTETES. Nay, my son, have good hope nevertheless. This
visitor comes sharply but goes quickly. Only, I beseech you,
do not leave me alone.

NEOPTOLEMUS. Fear not, we will remain.

PHILOCTETES. You will remain?

NEOPTOLEMUS. Be sure of it.

PHILOCTETES. Well, I do not ask to put you on your oath, my
son.

NEOPTOLEMUS. Rest satisfied. It is not lawful for me to go
without you.

PHILOCTETES. Your hand for pledge!

NEOPTOLEMUS. I give it, to stay.

PHILOCTETES. Now take me yonder, yonder—

NEOPTOLEMUS. Where do you mean?

PHILOCTETES. Up yonder—

NEOPTOLEMUS. What is this new frenzy? Why are you gazing
on the vault above us?

PHILOCTETES. Let me go, let me go!

NEOPTOLEMUS. Where?

PHILOCTETES. Let me go, I say!

NEOPTOLEMUS. I will not.

PHILOCTETES. You will kill me if you touch me.

NEOPTOLEMUS. There, then; I release you, since you are calmer.

PHILOCTETES. O Earth, receive me as I die, here and now! The
pain no longer suffers me to stand upright.

NEOPTOLEMUS. Sleep is likely to come to him before long. See,
his head sinks backward; yes, a sweat is bathing his whole
body, and a thin stream of dark blood has broken forth from
his heel.

 Come, friends, let us leave him in quietness, that he may
fall on slumber.

CHORUS. *Sleep, stranger to anguish, painless Sleep, come at
our prayer, with gentle breath, come with benison, O King,*

*and keep before his eyes such light as is spread before them
now. Come, I pray you, come with power to heal!*

*O son, bethink you where you will stand and to what
counsels you will next turn our course. You see how it is
now! Why should we delay to act? Opportunity, arbiter of
all action, often wins a great victory by one swift stroke.*

NEOPTOLEMUS. Nay, though he hears nothing, I see that in vain
we have made this bow our prize if we sail without him. He
must be the crown. It would be a foul shame for us to boast
of deeds in which failure has waited on fraud.

CHORUS. *Nay, my son, the god will look to that. But when you
answer me again, softly, softly, whisper your words, my son.
Sick men's restless sleep is ever quick of vision..*

*But I pray you, use your utmost care to win that prize,
that great prize, by stealth. For if you maintain your present
purpose toward this man—you know of what purpose I
speak—a prudent mind can foresee troubles most grievous.*

*Now, my son, now the wind is fair for you. Sightless and
helpless the man lies stretched in darkness—sleep in the
heat is sound—with no command of hand or foot, but reft of
all his powers, like one who rests with Hades.*

*Take heed, look if your counsels be seasonable. So far as
my thoughts can seize the truth, my son, the best strategy is
that which gives no alarm.*

NEOPTOLEMUS. Hush, I say, and let not your wits forsake you.
Yonder man opens his eyes and lifts his head.

PHILOCTETES. Ah, sunlight following on sleep, ah, you friendly
watchers, undreamed of by my hopes! Never, my son, could
I have dared to look for this, that you should have patience to
wait so tenderly upon my sufferings, staying beside me and
helping to relieve me. The Atreidae certainly, those valiant
chieftains, had no heart to bear this burden so lightly. But
your nature, my son, is noble and of noble breed; and so you
have made little of all this, though loud cries and noisome
odors vexed your senses.

And now, since the plague seems to allow me a space of
forgetfulness and peace at last, raise me yourself, my son,

set me on my feet, so that when the faintness shall at length
release me we may set forth to the ship and not delay to sail.

NEOPTOLEMUS. Right glad am I to see you, beyond my hope,
living and breathing, free from pain; judged by the sufferings that afflict you, your symptoms seemed to speak of
death. But now lift yourself, or if you prefer it these men
will carry you; the trouble would not be grudged, since you
and I are of one mind.

PHILOCTETES. Thanks, my son, and help me to rise, as you say.
But do not trouble these men, so that they may not suffer
from the noisome smell before the time. It will be trial
enough for them to live on board with me.

NEOPTOLEMUS. So be it. Now stand up, and take hold of me
yourself.

PHILOCTETES. Do not fear; the old habit will help me to my feet.

NEOPTOLEMUS. Alack! What am I to do next!

PHILOCTETES. What is the matter, my son? Where is your
speech straying?

NEOPTOLEMUS. I do not know how I should turn my faltering
words.

PHILOCTETES. Faltering? Do not say so, my son.

NEOPTOLEMUS. Indeed, perplexity has now brought me to that
pass.

PHILOCTETES. It cannot be that the offense of my disease has
changed your purpose of receiving me in your ship?

NEOPTOLEMUS. All is offense when a man has forsaken his
true nature and is doing what does not befit him.

PHILOCTETES. Nay, you, at least, are not departing from your
sire's example in word or deed by helping one who deserves it.

NEOPTOLEMUS. I shall be found base; this is the thought that
torments me.

PHILOCTETES. Not in your present deeds. But the presage of
your words disquiets me.

NEOPTOLEMUS. O Zeus, what shall I do? Must I be found twice
a villain, by disloyal silence as well as by shameful speech?

PHILOCTETES. If my judgment is not mistaken, that man means
to betray me and forsake me and go his way!

NEOPTOLEMUS. Forsake you, no; but take you, perhaps, on a bitter voyage. That is the pain that haunts me.

PHILOCTETES. What do you mean, my son? I do not understand.

NEOPTOLEMUS. I will tell you all. You must sail to Troy, to the Achaeans and the host of the Atreidae.

PHILOCTETES. Oh, what have you said?

NEOPTOLEMUS. Do not lament until you learn—

PHILOCTETES. Learn what? What would you do to me?

NEOPTOLEMUS. Save you, first, from this misery, then go and ravage Troy's plains with you.

PHILOCTETES. And this is indeed your purpose?

NEOPTOLEMUS. A stern necessity ordains it; do not be angry to hear it.

PHILOCTETES. I am lost, luckless one, betrayed! What have you done to me, stranger? Restore my bow at once!

NEOPTOLEMUS. I cannot; duty and policy alike constrain me to obey my chiefs.

PHILOCTETES. You fire, you utter monster, you hateful master-piece of subtle villainy—how have you dealt with me, how have you deceived me! And you are not ashamed to look upon me, you wretch, the suppliant who turned to you for pity? In taking my bow you have despoiled me of my life. Restore it, I beseech you, restore it, I implore you, my son! By the gods of your fathers, do not rob me of my life! Ah me! No, he speaks to me no more; he looks away. He will not give it up!

O you creeks and headlands, O you wild creatures of the hills with whom I dwell, O you steep cliffs!—to you—for to whom else can I speak?—to you, my wonted listeners I be-wail my treatment by the son of Achilles. He swore to con-vey me home—to Troy he carries me; he clinched his word with the pledge of his right hand—yet has he taken my bow, the sacred bow once borne by Heracles son of Zeus, and keeps it, and is eager to show it to the Argives as his own.

He drags me away, as if he had captured a strong man, and does not see that he is slaying a corpse, the shadow of a vapor, a mere phantom. In my strength he would not have taken me, no, nor as I am, save by guile. But now I have been tricked, unhappy that I am. What shall I do? Nay, give it back, return, even now, to your true self! What do you say? Silent? Woe is me, I am lost!

Ah, you cave with twofold entrance, familiar to my eyes, once more I must return to you—but disarmed and without the means to live. Yes, in yonder chamber my lonely life shall fade away. No winged bird, no beast that roams the hills shall I slay with yonder bow. Rather I myself, wretched one, shall make a feast for those who fed me and become a prey to those on whom I preyed. Alas, I shall render my lifeblood for the blood which I have shed, the victim of a man who seemed innocent of evil! Perish! No, not yet, till I see if you will still change your purpose; if you will not may you die accursed!

CHORUS. What shall we do? It now rests with you, O Prince, whether we sail or hearken to that man's prayer.

NEOPTOLEMUS. A strange pity for him has smitten my heart— and not now for the first time but long ago.

PHILOCTETES. Show mercy, my son, for the love of the gods; do not give men cause to reproach you for having ensnared me.

NEOPTOLEMUS. Ah me, what shall I do? Would I had never left Scyros! so grievous is my plight.

PHILOCTETES. You are no villain, but you seem to have come here as one schooled by villains to a base part. Now leave that part to others whom it befits, and sail away—when you have given me back my arms.

NEOPTOLEMUS. What shall we do, friends?

ODYSSEUS (appears suddenly). Wretch, what are you doing? Back with you, and give that bow to me!

PHILOCTETES. Ah, who is this? Do I hear Odysseus?

ODYSSEUS. Odysseus, be sure of it, me whom you see.

PHILOCTETES. Ah me, I am betrayed, lost! He it was, then, that entrapped me and robbed me of my arms.

ODYSSEUS. I, surely, and no other; I avow it.

PHILOCTETES. Give me back my bow, give it up, my son.

ODYSSEUS. That he shall never do, even if he would. Moreover you must come along with it or they will bring you by force.

PHILOCTETES. What, you basest and boldest of villains, are these men to take *me* by force?

ODYSSEUS. Unless you come of your free will.

PHILOCTETES. O Lemnian land, and you all-conquering flame whose kindler is Hephaestus, is this indeed to be borne, that yonder man should take me from your realm by force?

ODYSSEUS. It is Zeus, let me tell you, Zeus who rules this land, Zeus whose pleasure this is; and I am his servant.

PHILOCTETES. Hateful wretch, what pleas you can invent! Sheltering yourself behind gods, you make those gods liars.

ODYSSEUS. No, true prophets. Our march must begin.

PHILOCTETES. Never!

ODYSSEUS. But I say Yes. There is no help for it.

PHILOCTETES. Woe is me! Plainly, then, my father begot me to be a slave and no free man.

ODYSSEUS. No, but to be the peer of the bravest, with whom you are destined to take Troy by storm and raze it to the dust.

PHILOCTETES. No, never—though I must suffer the worst— while I have this isle's steep crags beneath me!

ODYSSEUS. What would you do?

PHILOCTETES. Throw myself straightway from the rock and shatter this head upon the rock below!

ODYSSEUS. Seize him, both of you! Put it out of his power!

PHILOCTETES. Ah, hands, how ill you fare for lack of the bow that you loved to draw, yonder man's close prisoners! O you who cannot think one honest or one generous thought, how have you once more stolen upon me, how have you snared me, taking this boy for your screen, a stranger to me, too good for your company but meet for mine, who had no thought but to perform your bidding, and who already shows remorse for his own errors and for my wrongs. But your base soul, ever peering from some ambush, had well trained him, all unapt and unwilling as he was, to be cunning in evil.

And now, wretch, you purpose to bind me hand and foot and take me from this shore where you flung me forth, friendless, helpless, homeless, dead among the living!

Alas!

Perdition seize you! So have I often prayed for you. But since the gods grant nothing sweet to me you live and are glad, while life itself is pain to me, steeped in misery as I am, mocked by you and by the sons of Atreus, the two chieftains for whom you are doing this errand. Yet you sailed with them only when brought under their yoke by stratagem and constraint; but I, thrice wretched that I am, joined the fleet of my own accord, with seven ships, and then was spurned and cast out—by *them* as you say, or as they say, by you.

And now, why would you take me? why carry me with you? for what purpose? I am nothing; for you I have long been dead. Wretch abhorred of heaven, how is it that you no longer find me lame and noisome? How, if I sail with you, can you burn sacrifices to the gods or make drink-offerings any more? That was your pretext for casting me forth.

Miserably may you perish! And perish you shall, for the wrong that you have wrought against me, if the gods regard justice. But I know that they regard it, for you would never have come on this voyage in quest of one so wretched unless some heaven-sent yearning for me had goaded you on.

O my fatherland and you watchful gods, bring your vengeance, bring your vengeance on them all, at last though late, if you see anything to pity in my lot! Yes, a piteous life is mine; but if I saw those men overthrown I could dream that I was delivered from my plague.

CHORUS. Bitter with his soul's bitterness are the stranger's words, Odysseus; he does not bend before his woes.

ODYSSEUS. I could answer him at length if leisure served, but now I can say one thing only. Such as the time needs, such am I. Where the question is of just men and good, you will find no man more scrupulous. Victory, however, is my aim in every field—save in regard to you—to you, in this case, I will gladly give way.

Yes, release him, lay no finger upon him more, let him stay here. Indeed we have no further need of you, now that these arms are ours. Teucer is there to serve us, well-skilled in this craft, and I, who can wield this bow no worse than you, I think, and point it with as true a hand. What need then of you? Pace your Lemnos and joy be with you! We must be going. Perhaps your treasure will bring to me the honor which ought to have been your own.

PHILOCTETES. Ah, unhappy that I am, what shall I do? Shall *you* be seen among the Argives graced with the arms that are mine?

ODYSSEUS. Bandy no more speech with me; I am going.

PHILOCTETES. Son of Achilles, will you too speak no more to me but depart without a word?

ODYSSEUS (*to* NEOPTOLEMUS). Come on. Do not look at him, generous though you are, lest you mar our fortune.

PHILOCTETES (*to* CHORUS). Will you also, friends, indeed leave me thus desolate and show no pity?

CHORUS. This youth is our commander; whatever he says to you, that answer is ours also.

NEOPTOLEMUS (*to* CHORUS). I shall be told by my chief that I am too softhearted. Yet tarry here, if yonder man will have it so, until the sailors have made all ready on board and we have offered our prayers to the gods. Meanwhile, perhaps, he may come to a better mind concerning us. So we two will be going; when we call you, you are to set forth with speed.

(*Exeunt* ODYSSEUS *and* NEOPTOLEMUS.)

PHILOCTETES. *You hollow of the caverned rock, now hot now icy-cold—so then it was my unlucky destiny never to leave you! No, you are witness to my death also. Woe, woe is me! Ah, you sad dwelling, so long haunted by the pain of my presence, what shall be my daily portion henceforth? Where and whence, wretched that I am, shall I find a hope of sustenance? Above my head the timorous doves will go their way through the shrill breeze, for I can arrest their flight no more.*

CHORUS. *It is you, it is you yourself, ill-fated man, that have so decreed. This fortune to which you are captive comes not from without or from a stronger hand, for when it was in your power to show wisdom your choice was to reject the better fate and accept the worse.*

PHILOCTETES. *Ah, luckless, luckless then that I am and broken by suffering! Henceforth I must dwell here in my misery, with no man for companion in days to come, and waste away— woe, woe is me—no longer bringing food to my home, no longer gaining it with the winged weapons held in my strong hands.*

But the unsuspected deceits of a treacherous soul beguiled me. Would that I might see him, the contriver of this plot, doomed to my pangs, and for as long a time!

CHORUS. *Fate, heaven-appointed fate has come upon you in this, not any treachery to which my hand was lent. Do not point your dread and baneful curse at me! I am eager that you should not reject my friendship.*

PHILOCTETES. *Ah me, ah me! Sitting on the margin of the white waves he mocks me, I suppose, brandishing the weapon that sustained my luckless life, the weapon which no other living man had borne! Ah, you well-loved bow, ah, you that have been torn from loving hands, surely if you can feel you see with pity that the comrade of Heracles is never to use you again! You have found a new and wily master; by him are you wielded. Foul deceits you see, and the face of that abhorred foe by whom countless mischiefs springing from vile arts have been contrived against me—be you, O Zeus, my witness!*

CHORUS. *It is the part of a man ever to assert the right; but when he has done so, to refrain from stinging with rancorous taunts. Odysseus was only the agent of the host, and at their mandate achieved a public benefit for his friends.*

PHILOCTETES. *Ah, my winged prey and you tribes of bright-eyed beasts that this place holds in its upland pastures, start no more in flight from your lairs, for I do not bear in my hands those shafts which were my strength of old—ah, wretched that I now am! Nay, roam at large—the place now has no more terrors for you, no more! Now is the moment to take blood for blood, to glut yourselves at will on my discolored flesh! Soon I shall pass out of life, for where shall I find the means to live? Who can feed on the winds when he no longer commands anything that life-giving earth supplies?*

CHORUS. *For the love of the gods, if you have any regard for a friend who draws near to you in all kindness, approach him. Consider, consider well—it is in your own power to escape from this plague. Cruel is it to him on whom it feeds, and time cannot teach patience under the countless woes that dwell with it.*

PHILOCTETES. *Again, again, you have recalled the old pain to my thoughts, kindest though you are of all who have visited this shore. Why have you afflicted me? What have you done to me?*

CHORUS. *How do you mean?*

PHILOCTETES. *It was your hope to take me to that Trojan land which I abhor.*

CHORUS. *So I deemed it best.*

PHILOCTETES. *Leave me, then, begone!*

CHORUS. *Welcome is your word, right welcome. I am not loth to obey. Come, let us be going, each to his place in the ship!*

PHILOCTETES. *By the Zeus who hears men's curses, do not depart, I implore you!*

CHORUS. *Be calm.*

PHILOCTETES. *Friends, in the gods' name, stay!*

CHORUS. *Why do you call?*

PHILOCTETES. *Alas, alas! My doom, my doom! Luckless, I am undone! O foot, foot, what shall I do with you, wretched that I am, in the days to come? O friends, return!*

CHORUS. *What would you have us do different from the purport of your former bidding?*

PHILOCTETES. *It is no just cause for anger if one who is distraught with stormy pain speaks frantic words.*

CHORUS. *Come then, unhappy man, as we exhort you.*

PHILOCTETES. *Never, never—of that be assured—no, though the lord of the fiery lightning threaten to wrap me in the blaze of his thunderbolts! Perish Ilium and the men before its walls who had the heart to spurn me from them, thus crippled! But oh, my friends, grant me one boon!*

CHORUS. *What would you ask?*

PHILOCTETES. *A sword, if you can find one, or an ax, or any weapon—oh, bring it to me!*

CHORUS. *What rash deed would you do?*

PHILOCTETES. *Mangle this body utterly, hew limb from limb with my own hand! Death, death is my thought now—*

CHORUS. *What does this mean?*

PHILOCTETES. *I would seek my sire—*

CHORUS. *In what land?*

PHILOCTETES. *In the realm of the dead; he is in the sunlight no more. Ah, my home, city of my fathers! Would I might behold you! Misguided indeed I was when I left your sacred stream and went forth to help the Danai, my enemies. Undone, undone!*

CHORUS. Long since I should have left you, and should now have been near my ship, had I not seen Odysseus approaching, and the son of Achilles too, coming here to us.

(*Enter* NEOPTOLEMUS, *followed by* ODYSSEUS.)

ODYSSEUS. Will you not tell me on what errand you are returning in such hot haste?

NEOPTOLEMUS. To undo the fault that I committed before.

ODYSSEUS. A strange saying. And what was the fault?

NEOPTOLEMUS. When, obeying you and all the host—

ODYSSEUS. What deed did you do that did not become you?

NEOPTOLEMUS. When I ensnared a man with base fraud and guile.

ODYSSEUS. Whom? Alas!—can you be planning some rash act?

NEOPTOLEMUS. Rash, no; but to the son of Poeas—

ODYSSEUS. What will you do? A strange fear comes over me.

NEOPTOLEMUS. —from whom I took this bow, to him again—

ODYSSEUS. Zeus! What would you say? You will not give it back?

NEOPTOLEMUS. Yes, I have gotten it basely and without right.

ODYSSEUS. In the name of the gods, are you saying this to mock me?

NEOPTOLEMUS. If it be mockery to speak the truth.

ODYSSEUS. What do you mean, son of Achilles? What have you said?

NEOPTOLEMUS. Must I repeat the same words twice and thrice?

ODYSSEUS. I should have wished not to hear them at all.

NEOPTOLEMUS. Rest assured that I have nothing more to say.

ODYSSEUS. There is a power, I tell you, that shall prevent your deed.

NEOPTOLEMUS. What do you mean? Who is to hinder me in this?

ODYSSEUS. The whole host of the Achaeans—and I for one.

NEOPTOLEMUS. Wise though you be, your words are void of wisdom.

ODYSSEUS. Your speech is not woe, nor yet your purpose.

NEOPTOLEMUS. But if just, that is better than wise.

ODYSSEUS. How is it just to give up what you have won by my counsels?

NEOPTOLEMUS. My fault has been shameful, and I must seek to retrieve it.

ODYSSEUS. Have you no fear of the Achaean host in doing this?

NEOPTOLEMUS. With justice on my side, I do not fear your terrors.

ODYSSEUS. But I will compel you.

NEOPTOLEMUS. Nay, not even to your force do I yield obedience.

ODYSSEUS. Then we shall fight, not with the Trojans but with you.

NEOPTOLEMUS. Come then what must.

ODYSSEUS. Do you see my right hand on my sword-hilt?

NEOPTOLEMUS. You shall see me doing the same, and that promptly.

ODYSSEUS. Well, I will take no more heed of you; I will go and tell this to all the host, and by them you shall be punished.

NEOPTOLEMUS. You have come to your senses, and if you are thus prudent henceforth perhaps you may keep clear of trouble. (*Exit* ODYSSEUS.) But you, O son of Poeas, Philoctetes, come forth, leave the shelter of your rocky home!

PHILOCTETES (*within*). What means this noise of voices rising once more beside my cave? Why do you call me forth? What would you have of me, sirs? (PHILOCTETES *appears at the mouth of the cave and sees* NEOPTOLEMUS.) Ah me! this bodes no good. Can you have come as heralds of new woe for me to crown the old?

NEOPTOLEMUS. Fear not, but hearken to the words that I bring.

PHILOCTETES. I am afraid. Fair words brought me evil fortune once before, when I believed your promises.

NEOPTOLEMUS. Is there no room, then, for repentance?

PHILOCTETES. Just such were you in speech when seeking to steal my bow, a trusty friend with treason in his heart.

NEOPTOLEMUS. But not so now. I wish to learn whether your resolve is to abide here and endure or to sail with us.

PHILOCTETES. Stop, speak no more! All that you can say will be said in vain.

NEOPTOLEMUS. You are resolved?

PHILOCTETES. More firmly, believe me, than speech can tell.

NEOPTOLEMUS. Well, I could have wished that you had listened to my words. But if I am not speaking in season I have done.

PHILOCTETES. Yes, all you will say is in vain. Never can you win the amity of my soul, you who have taken the stay of my life by fraud and robbed me of it, and have then come here to give me counsel, you most hateful offspring of a noble sire! Perdition seize you all, the Atreidae first, and next the son of Laertes, and you!

NEOPTOLEMUS. Utter no more curses, but receive these weapons from my hand.

PHILOCTETES. What are you saying? Am I being tricked a second time?

NEOPTOLEMUS. No, I swear it by the pure majesty of Zeus most high!

PHILOCTETES. O welcome words—if your words are true!

NEOPTOLEMUS. The deed shall soon prove the word. Come, stretch forth your right hand and be master of your bow!

ODYSSEUS (*appears*). But I forbid it—be the gods my witnesses—in the name of the Atreidae and all the host!

PHILOCTETES. My son, whose voice was that? Did I hear Odysseus?

ODYSSEUS. Be sure of it, and you see him at your side. I will carry you to the plains of Troy perforce, whether the son of Achilles will or no.

PHILOCTETES. But to your cost if this arrow fly straight.

NEOPTOLEMUS (*seizing his arm*). Ah, for the gods' love, forbear, do not launch your shaft.

PHILOCTETES. Unhand me, in Heaven's name, dear youth!

NEOPTOLEMUS. I will not.

PHILOCTETES. Alas! why have you disappointed me of slaying my hated enemy with my bow!

NEOPTOLEMUS. It suits not with my honor, nor with yours.

(*Exit* ODYSSEUS.)

PHILOCTETES. Well, you may be sure of one thing. The chiefs of the host, the lying heralds of the Greeks, though brave with words are cowards in fight.

NEOPTOLEMUS. Good. The bow is yours and you have no cause of anger or complaint against me.

PHILOCTETES. I grant it. You have shown the race, my son, from which you spring; no child, you, of Sisyphus but of Achilles, whose fame was fairest when he was with the living, as it is now among the dead.

NEOPTOLEMUS. Sweet to me is your praise of my sire, and of myself. But hear the boon I wish to win from you. Men must needs bear the fortunes given by the gods; but when they cling to self-inflicted miseries as you do, no one can justly excuse or pity them. You have become intractable. You can tolerate no counselor. If anyone advises you, speaking with good will, you hate him, deeming him a foe who wishes you ill. Yet I will speak, calling Zeus to witness, who hears men's oaths, and do you mark these words and write them in your heart.

You suffer this sore plague by a heaven-sent doom, because you drew near Chryse's watcher, the serpent, secret warder of her home, that guards her roofless sanctuary. Know that relief from this grievous sickness can never be your portion, so long as the sun still rises in the east and sets in the west, until you come of your own free will to the plains of Troy, where you shall meet with the sons of Asclepius, our comrades, and shall be eased of this malady; and, with this bow's aid and mine, shall achieve the capture of the Ilian towers.

I will tell you how I know that these things are so ordained. We have a Trojan prisoner, Helenus, foremost among seers; he says plainly that all this must come to pass. He says further that this present summer must see the utter overthrow of Troy, or else he is willing that his life be forfeit if this word of his prove false.

Now that you know this, therefore, yield with a good grace. It is a glorious heightening of your gain to be singled out as bravest of the Greeks—first to come into healing hands, then to take Troy of many tears, and so to win a matchless renown.

PHILOCTETES. O hateful life, why do you keep me in the light of day instead of suffering me to seek the world of the dead? Ah me, what shall I do? How can I be deaf to this man's words, who has counseled me with kindly purpose? But shall I yield, then? How, after doing so, shall I come into men's sight, wretched that I am? Who will speak to me? You eyes that have beheld all my wrongs, how could you endure to see me consorting with the sons of Atreus, who wrought my ruin, or with the accursed son of Laertes?

It is not the resentment for the past that stings me: I seem to foresee what I am doomed to suffer from these men in the future; for when the mind once becomes a parent of evil it teaches men to be evil thenceforth. And in you too this conduct moves my wonder. It behooved you never to revisit Troy yourself and to hinder me from going there. Those men have done you outrage by wresting from you the honors of your sire, when, in their award of your father's arms, they adjudged unlucky Ajax inferior to Odysseus. After that, will you go to fight at their side, and would you constrain me to do likewise?

Nay, do not do so, my son; but rather, as you have sworn to me, convey me home; and yourself abiding in Scyros, leave those evil men to their evil doom. So shall you win double thanks from me, as from my sire, and you shall not seem, through helping bad men, to be like them in nature.

NEOPTOLEMUS. There is reason in what you say; nevertheless I would have you put your trust in the gods and in my words, and sail forth from this land with me, my friend.

PHILOCTETES. What! to the plains of Troy, and to the abhorred son of Atreus—with this wretched foot?

NEOPTOLEMUS. Nay, but to those who will free you and your ulcered limb from pain and will heal your sickness.

PHILOCTETES. You giver of dire counsel, what can you mean?

NEOPTOLEMUS. What I see is fraught with the best issue for us both.

PHILOCTETES. Have you no shame that the gods should hear these words?

NEOPTOLEMUS. Why should a man be ashamed of benefiting his friends?

PHILOCTETES. Is this benefit to the Atreidae, or for me?

NEOPTOLEMUS. For you, I believe; I am your friend and speak in friendship.

PHILOCTETES. How so, when you would give me up to my foes?

NEOPTOLEMUS. I pray you, learn to be less defiant in misfortune.

PHILOCTETES. You will ruin me, I know you will, with these words.

NEOPTOLEMUS. *I* will not; but I say that you do not understand.

PHILOCTETES. Do I not know that the Atreidae cast me out?

NEOPTOLEMUS. They cast you out, but look if they will not restore you to welfare.

PHILOCTETES. Never—if I must first consent to visit Troy.

NEOPTOLEMUS. What am I to do, then, if my pleading cannot win you to anything I urge? The easiest course for me is that I should cease from speech and that you should live, as you do now, without deliverance.

PHILOCTETES. Let me bear the sufferings that are my portion, but the promise which you made me, with hand laid in mine—to bring me home—that promise fulfill, my son. Do not tarry, and do not speak any more of Troy, for the measure of lamentation is full.

NEOPTOLEMUS. If you will, let us be going.

PHILOCTETES. O generous word!

NEOPTOLEMUS. Now plant your steps firmly.

PHILOCTETES. To the utmost of my strength.

NEOPTOLEMUS. But how shall I escape blame from the Achaeans?

PHILOCTETES. Do not heed it.

NEOPTOLEMUS. What if they ravage my country?

PHILOCTETES. I will be there—

NEOPTOLEMUS. And what help will you render?

PHILOCTETES. With the shafts of Heracles—

NEOPTOLEMUS. What is your meaning?

PHILOCTETES. I will keep them afar.

NEOPTOLEMUS. Take your farewell of this land and set forth.

HERACLES (*appears*). *Nay, not yet, till you have hearkened to my words, son of Poeas. Know that the voice of Heracles sounds in your ears and you look upon his face.*

For your sake I have come from the heavenly seats, to show you the purpose of Zeus, and to stay the journey upon which you are departing. Give heed to my counsel.

First I would tell you of my own fortunes, how, after enduring many labors to the end, I have won deathless glory, as you see. And for you, be sure, the destiny is ordained that through these sufferings of yours you should glorify your life.

You shall go with yonder man to the Trojan city, where, first, you shall be healed of your sore malady. Then, chosen out as foremost in prowess of the host, with my bow you shall slay Paris, the author of these ills. You shall sack Troy; the prize of valor shall be given to you by our warriors; and you shall carry the spoils to your home, for the joy of Poeas your sire, even to your own Oetaean heights. And whatever spoils you receive from the host, take from them a thank-offering for my bow to my pyre.

These my counsels are for you too, son of Achilles, for you cannot subdue the Trojan realm without his help, nor he without yours. You are like two lions that roam together; each of you guards the other's life.

For the healing of your sickness I will send Asclepius to Troy, since it is doomed to fall a second time before my arrows. But of this be mindful when you lay waste the land: show reverence toward the gods. All things else are of less account in the sight of our father Zeus. Piety dies not with men; in their life and in their death it is immortal.

PHILOCTETES. Ah, you whose accents I had yearned to hear, you whose form is seen after many days, I will not disobey your words!

NEOPTOLEMUS. I too consent.

HERACLES. Tarry not long, then, before you act. Occasion urges, and the fair wind yonder at the stern. (*Exit.*)

PHILOCTETES. *Come, then, let me greet this land as I depart. Farewell, chamber that has shared my watches, farewell, nymphs of stream and meadow, and you, deep voice of the sea-lashed cape—where, in the cavern's inmost recess, my head was often wetted by the south-wind's blasts, and where often the Hermaean mount sent an echo to my mournful cries, in the tempest of my sorrow!*

But now, you springs and you Lycian fount, I am leaving you, leaving you at last, I who had never attained to such a hope!

Farewell, you sea-girt Lemnos. Speed me with fair course, for my contentment, to that haven whither I am borne by mighty fate, and by the counsel of friends, and by the all-subduing god who has brought these things to fulfillment.

CHORUS. *Now let us all set forth together, when we have made our prayer to the nymphs of the sea, that they come to us for the prospering of our return.*

OEDIPUS AT COLONUS

AFTER THE EVENTS DESCRIBED IN *OEDIPUS THE King,* Oedipus started on his wanderings as a blind beggar, leaving Iocasta's brother Creon as regent of Thebes. The kingship was to be held alternately by Oedipus' sons Eteocles and Polyneices; but when it came Polyneices' turn to rule, Eteocles refused to yield the throne and Polyneices enlisted six Argive chieftains to support his war against Thebes. Meanwhile an oracle has advised Thebes that success will fall to the party which has the grave of Oedipus in its possession. In his wanderings over the years Oedipus, attended by his daughter Antigone, has reached Colonus, a suburb of Athens, and there has won the sympathy of Theseus, King of Athens.

The action of *Oedipus at Colonus* is simple. First Creon by dint of force and then Polyneices by supplication try to win Oedipus over, but he rejects them both and goes to die at a predestined spot in Colonus. But though its action is simple, *Oedipus at Colonus* is a rich and spiritually moving play. Written at the end of Sophocles' long life (and presented posthumously), it is his farewell to the stage and to Athens. Its scene, described with affection, is where Sophocles grew up and its characters those with whom he had won his greatest successes. Athens was in decline, and its beloved hero Theseus is brought in to exemplify its generous nobility and to envision a happier future. Oedipus himself, poor and old and blind, is still the stark, self-assured character he was in *Oedipus the King;* indeed, he can now insist that he was more sinned against than sinning. And his claim is vindicated, for amidst claps of thunder which signify divine approval he walks erect and unaided to the spot of his transfiguration, which will thenceforth be a seat of blessing for Athens.

PERSONS

OEDIPUS
ANTIGONE } *his daughters*
ISMENE
STRANGER, *a man of*
    Colonus
THESEUS, *King of Athens*

CREON, *of Thebes*
POLYNEICES, *elder son of*
    Oedipus
MESSENGER
CHORUS, *elders of Colonus*

SCENE: *Colonus, near Athens, before a grove sacred to the Erinyes.*

(*Enter* OEDIPUS, *blind, led by* ANTIGONE.)

OEDIPUS. Daughter of the blind old man, to what region have we come, Antigone, or what city of men? Who will entertain the wandering Oedipus today with scanty gifts? Little do I crave, and win yet less than that little, and therewith am content; for patience is the lesson of suffering, and of the years in our long fellowship, and lastly of a noble mind. My child, if you see any resting-place, whether on profane ground or by the groves of the gods, halt me and set me down, that we may inquire where we are: for we stand in need to learn, as strangers of natives, and to perform their bidding.

ANTIGONE. Father, toil-worn Oedipus, the towers that guard the city, to judge by sight, are far off; and this place is sacred, to all seeming—thick-set with laurel, olive, vine; and in its heart a feathered choir of nightingales makes music. So sit here on this unhewn stone; you have traveled a long way for an old man.

OEDIPUS. Seat me, then, and watch over the blind.

ANTIGONE. If time can teach I do not need to learn that.

OEDIPUS. Can you tell me now where we have arrived?

ANTIGONE. Athens I know, but not this place.

OEDIPUS. Aye, so much every wayfarer told us.

ANTIGONE. Well, shall I go and learn how the spot is called?

OEDIPUS. Yes, child—if indeed it is habitable.

ANTIGONE. Inhabited it surely is, but I think there is no need;
    yonder I see a man near us.

OEDIPUS. Coming this way? Starting?

ANTIGONE. He is at our side already. Speak as the moment
    prompts you, for the man is here.

(*Enter* STRANGER.)

OEDIPUS. Stranger, hearing from this maiden, who has sight
    for herself and for me, that you have drawn nigh with timely
    quest for the solving of our doubts—

STRANGER. Now before you question me at large quit this seat,
    for you are on ground which it is not lawful to tread.

OEDIPUS. And what is this ground? Sacred to what deity?

STRANGER. Ground inviolable, on which none may dwell; for
    the dread goddesses hold it, the daughters of Earth and
    Darkness.

OEDIPUS. Who may they be, whose awful names I am to hear
    and invoke?

STRANGER. The all-seeing Eumenides the folk here would call
    them; but other names please in other places.

OEDIPUS. Then graciously may they receive their suppliant!
    For I will never more depart from my rest on this land.

STRANGER. What does this mean?

OEDIPUS. It is the watchword of my fate.

STRANGER. For my part I do not dare remove you without war-
    rant from the city before I report what I am doing.

OEDIPUS. Now for the gods' love, stranger, do not refuse me,
    hapless wanderer that I am, the knowledge which I beg.

STRANGER. Speak; from me you shall find no refusal.

OEDIPUS. What then is the place that we have entered?

STRANGER. All that *I* know you shall learn from my mouth.
    This whole place is sacred. Awful Poseidon holds it, and in

it is the fire-fraught god, the Titan Prometheus. As for the spot on which you tread, it is called the "Brazen Threshold" of this land, the stay of Athens. The neighboring fields claim yonder knight Colonus for their primal lord, and all the people bear his name in common for their own. Such you may know, stranger, are these haunts, not honored in story but rather in the life that loves them.

OEDIPUS. Are there indeed dwellers in this region?

STRANGER. Yes surely, the namesakes of yonder god.

OEDIPUS. Have they a king? Or does speech rest with the people?

STRANGER. These parts are ruled by the king in the city.

OEDIPUS. And who is this sovereign in counsel and in might?

STRANGER. Theseus he is called, son of Aegeus who was before him.

OEDIPUS. Could a messenger go for him from among you?

STRANGER. With what aim? To speak or to prepare his coming?

OEDIPUS. That by small service he may find a great gain.

STRANGER. What help can come from one who does not see?

OEDIPUS. In all that I speak there shall be sight.

STRANGER. Mark me now, friend, I would not have you come to harm, for you are noble if one may judge by your looks, leaving your fortune aside; stay here where I found you till I go and tell these things to the people in this spot, not in the town. They will decide for you whether you should abide or retire. (*Exit.*)

OEDIPUS. My child, say, is the stranger gone?

ANTIGONE. He is gone, and so you can utter what you will, father, in quietness, knowing that I alone am near.

OEDIPUS. Queens of dread aspect, since your seat is the first in this land at which I have bent the knee, do not show yourselves ungracious to Phoebus or to myself. When Phoebus proclaimed that doom of many woes he spoke of *this* as a rest for me after long years: on reaching my goal in a land where I should find a seat of the Awful Goddesses and a hospitable shelter, there I should close my weary life, with benefits, through my having dwelt in it, for my hosts, but ruin for those who sent me forth, who drove me away. And he went on to warn me that signs of these things should come in earthquake or thunder, perhaps, or in the lightning of Zeus.

Now I perceive that in this journey some faithful omen from you has surely led me home to this grove; never else could I have met with you, first of all, in my wanderings, I the austere with you who take no delight in wine, or taken this solemn seat not shaped by man.

Then, goddesses, according to the word of Apollo, give me at last some way to accomplish and close my course—unless perchance I seem beneath your grace, thrall that I am evermore to woes the sorest on the earth. Hear, sweet daughters of primeval Darkness! Hear, you that are called the city of great Pallas, Athens, of all cities most honored! Pity this poor wraith of Oedipus—for verily it is the man of old no more.

ANTIGONE. Hush! Here come some aged men, I think to spy out your resting-place.

OEDIPUS. I will be mute. Hide me in the grove apart from the road till I learn how these men will speak; for in knowledge is the safeguard of our course.

(*Exeunt; enter* CHORUS.)

CHORUS. *Give heed—who was he then? Where is he lodging? Whither has he rushed from this place, insolent above all who live? Scan the ground, look well, urge the quest in every part.*

A wanderer that old man must have been, a wanderer, not a dweller in the land; else he would never have advanced into this untrodden grove of the maidens with whom none may strive, whose name we tremble to speak, by whom we pass with eyes turned away, moving our lips without sound or word in still devotion.

But now it is rumored that one has come who in no wise reveres them; him I cannot yet discern, though I look round all the holy place, nor know I where to find his lodging.

OEDIPUS (*stepping forward with* ANTIGONE). *Behold the man whom you seek! For in sound is my sight as the saying has it.*

CHORUS. *O! O! Dread to see and dread to hear!*

OEDIPUS. *Do not regard me, I entreat you, as a lawless man.*

CHORUS. *Zeus defend us! Who may the old man be?*

OEDIPUS. *Not wholly of the best fortune that you should envy him, you guardians of this land! It is plain; else I would not be walking thus by the eyes of others and buoying my strength upon weakness.*

CHORUS. *Alas! Were you sightless even from your birth? Evil have been your days, and many to all seeming; but at least if I can help you shall not add this curse to your doom. You are going too far, too far! Retire, withdraw, lest your rash steps intrude on the sward of yonder voiceless glade, where the bowl of water blends its stream with the flow of honied offerings—be well aware of such trespass! A wide space parts us: do you hear, toil-worn wanderer? If you have anything to say in converse with us leave forbidden ground and speak where it is lawful for all; but till then refrain.*

OEDIPUS. *Daughter, to what counsel shall we incline?*

ANTIGONE. *Father, we must conform to the customs of the land, yielding where it is meet and hearkening.*

OEDIPUS. *Then give me your hand.*

ANTIGONE. *It is laid in yours.*

OEDIPUS. *Strangers, let me not suffer wrong when I have trusted in you and have passed from my refuge! (Moves forward; pauses.) Further then?*

CHORUS. *Come still further.*

OEDIPUS. *Further?*

CHORUS. *Lead him onward, maiden, for you understand.*

[*Lacuna of three verses.*]

ANTIGONE. . . . *Come, follow me this way with your dark steps, father, as I lead you.*

[*Lacuna of one verse.*]

CHORUS. *A stranger in a strange land, hapless man, incline your heart to abhor what the city holds in settled hate and to reverence what she loves.*

OEDIPUS. *Then do you lead me, child, to a spot where I may speak and listen within piety's domain, and let us not wage war with necessity.*

CHORUS. *There! Do not bend your steps beyond that floor of native rock.*

OEDIPUS. *This far?*

CHORUS. *Enough, I tell you.*

OEDIPUS. *Shall I sit down?*

CHORUS. *Yes, move sideways and crouch low on the edge of the rock.*

ANTIGONE. *Father, this is my task. Knit step to quiet step—*

OEDIPUS. *Ah me! Ah me!*

ANTIGONE. *—and lean your aged frame upon my loving arms.* (Seats OEDIPUS.)

CHORUS. *Ah, hapless one, since you now have ease speak: Whence are you sprung? In what name are you led on your weary way? What is the fatherland of which you can tell us?*

OEDIPUS. *Strangers, I am an exile—but forbear—*

CHORUS. *What is this that you forbid, old man?*

OEDIPUS. *—forbear, forbear to ask me who I am. Seek, probe, no further!*

CHORUS. *What does this mean?*

OEDIPUS. *Dread the birth—*

CHORUS. *Speak!*

OEDIPUS. (to ANTIGONE). *My child, alas, what shall I say?*

CHORUS. *What is your lineage, stranger, speak, and who your sire?*

OEDIPUS. *Woe is me!—What will become of me, my child?*

ANTIGONE. *Speak, for you are driven to the verge.*

OEDIPUS. *Then speak I will; I have no way to hide it.*

CHORUS. *You two make a long delay. Come, haste!*

OEDIPUS. *Do you know a son of Laius . . . O!* (The CHORUS utter a cry.) *. . . and the race of the Labdacidae? . . .*

CHORUS. *O Zeus!*

OEDIPUS. *The hapless Oedipus? . . .*

CHORUS. *You are he?*

OEDIPUS. *Have no fear of any words that I speak—* (CHORUS *cry out and turn away.*) *—Unhappy that I am!* (*The clamor continues.*) *—Daughter, what is about to befall?*

CHORUS. *Out with you! Forth from the land!*

OEDIPUS. *And your promise—to what fulfillment will you bring it?*

CHORUS. *No man is visited by fate if he requites deeds which were first done to himself; deceit on the one part matches deceits on the other, and gives pain instead of benefit for reward. And you—back with you! Out from these seats! Begone! Away from my land with all speed, lest you fasten some heavier burden on my city!*

ANTIGONE. *Strangers of reverent soul, since you have not borne with my aged father—knowing as you do the rumor of his unpurposed deeds—pity at least my hapless self, I implore you. I supplicate you for my sire alone, supplicate you with eyes that can still look on your own; pity me as though I were sprung from your own blood, that the sufferer may find compassion.*

On you as on a god we depend in our misery. Hear us! Grant the boon for which we scarce dare hope! By everything sprung from you that you held dear I implore you, by child, by wife, or treasure, or gold! Look well and you will not find the mortal who could escape if a god should lead him on.

CHORUS. Be sure, daughter of Oedipus, we pity you and him alike for your fortune; but dreading the judgment of the gods, we could not say anything beyond what has now been said to you.

OEDIPUS. What good comes, then, of repute or fair fame if it ends in idle breath, seeing that Athens, as men say, has the perfect fear of Heaven, and the power above all cities to shelter the vexed stranger, and the power above all to succor him?

Where do I find these things when, after making me rise up from these rocky seats, you then drive me from the land, afraid of my name alone? Not, surely, afraid of my person or of my acts, since my acts, at least, have been in suffering rather than in doing—were it seemly that I should tell you the story of my mother or my father, by reason of which you dread me; that I know full well.

And yet in *nature* how was I evil? I who was but requiting a wrong, so that had I been acting with knowledge, even then I could not be accounted wicked; but as it was, all unknowing I went—where I went—while they who wronged me knowingly sought my ruin.

Therefore, strangers, I beseech you by the gods, even as you made me leave my seat so protect me, and do not, while you honor the gods, refuse to give those gods their due. Rather deem that they look on the god-fearing among men and on the godless, and that never yet has escape been found for an impious mortal on the earth.

With the help of those gods, spare to cloud the bright fame of Athens by ministering to unholy deeds; but as you have received the suppliant under your pledge, rescue me and guard me to the end. Do not scorn me when you look on this face unlovely to behold; for I have come to you as one sacred and pious and fraught with comfort for this people. But when the master has come, whosoever he is that is your chief, then you shall hear and know all. Meanwhile never show yourself false.

CHORUS. The thoughts urged on your part, old man, must needs move awe; they have been set forth in no light words. I am content that the rulers of our country should judge in this cause.

OEDIPUS. And where, strangers, is the lord of this realm?

CHORUS. He is at the city of his father in our land; and the messenger who sent us here has gone to fetch him.

OEDIPUS. Do you think he will have any regard or care for the blind man, so as to come here himself?

CHORUS. Yes surely, so soon as he learns your name.

OEDIPUS. Who is there to bring him that message?

CHORUS. The way is long, and many rumors from wayfarers are wont to go abroad; when he hears them he will soon be with us, do not fear. For your name, old man, has been

mightily noised through all lands, so that even if he is taking his ease and slow to move, when he hears of *you* he will
arrive with speed.

OEDIPUS. Well, may he come with a blessing to his own city as
to me! What good man is not his own friend?

ANTIGONE. O Zeus! What shall I say, what shall I think, father?

OEDIPUS. What is it, Antigone my child?

ANTIGONE. I see a woman coming toward us, mounted on a colt
of Etna; she wears a Thessalian bonnet to screen her face from
the sun. What shall I say? Is it she or is it not? Is fancy cheat-
ing me? Yes—no—I cannot tell—ah me! It is no other—
yes!—she greets me with bright glances as she draws nigh,
and shows that Ismene and no other is before me.

OEDIPUS. What are you saying, my child?

ANTIGONE. That I see your daughter and my sister; you can
know her straightway by her voice.

ISMENE (*enters*). Father and sister, names most sweet to me!
How hardly have I found you! And now I can scarcely see
you for my tears.

OEDIPUS. My child, you have come?

ISMENE. Ah, father, sad is your fate to see!

OEDIPUS. You are with us, my child!

ISMENE. And it has cost me toil.

OEDIPUS. Touch me, my daughter!

ISMENE. I give a hand to each.

OEDIPUS. Ah, children—ah, you sisters!

ISMENE. Alas, twice-wretched life!

OEDIPUS. Her life and mine?

ISMENE. And mine, hapless, with you two.

OEDIPUS. Child, why have you come?

ISMENE. Through care for you, father.

OEDIPUS. Through longing to see me?

ISMENE. Yes, and to bring you tidings by my own mouth—with
the only faithful servant that I had.

OEDIPUS. Where are the young men your brothers at our need?

ISMENE. They are—where they are; it is their dark hour.

OEDIPUS. O, true image of the ways of Egypt that they show in
their spirit and their life! For there the men sit weaving in

the house but the wives go forth to win the daily bread. And in your case my daughter, those to whom these toils belonged keep the house at home like girls, while you in their stead bear your father's hapless burdens.

One, from the time when her tender age was past and she came to a woman's strength has always been the old man's guide in weary wanderings, often roaming hungry and barefoot through the wild wood, often sore-vexed by rains and scorching heat, but not regarding the comforts of home if so her father should have tendance.

And you, my child, in former days came forth bringing your father, unknown of the Cadmeans, all the oracles that had been given touching Oedipus; you took upon yourself the office of a faithful watcher in my behalf when I was being driven from the land. And now what new tidings have you brought your father, Ismene? On what mission have you set forth from home? You do not come empty-handed, well I know, or without some word of fear for me.

ISMENE. The sufferings I bore in seeking where you were living, father, I will pass by; I would not renew the pain in the recital. But the ills that now beset your ill-fated sons—it is of these that I have come to tell you.

At first it was their desire that the throne should be left to Creon and the city spared pollution, when they thought calmly on the blight of the race from of old and how it has clung to your ill-starred house. But now, moved by some god and by a sinful mind, an evil rivalry has seized them, thrice infatuate!—to grasp at rule and kingly power.

The hotbrained youth, the younger born, has deprived the elder, Polyneices, of the throne, and has driven him from his fatherland. But he, as the general rumor says among us, has gone as exile to hill-girt Argos and is taking up a new kinship and warriors for his friends, as deeming that Argos shall soon possess the Cadmean land in honor or lift that land's praise to the stars.

These are no vain words, my father, but deeds terrible. Where the gods will have pity on your griefs I cannot tell.

OEDIPUS. What, had you come to hope that the gods would ever look on me for my deliverance?

ISMENE. Yes, that is my hope, father, from the present oracles.

OEDIPUS. What are they? What has been prophesied, my child?

ISMENE. That you shall yet be desired, alive and dead, by the men of that land, for their welfare's sake.

OEDIPUS. Who could have good of such a one as I?

ISMENE. Their power, it is said, comes to be in *your* hand.

OEDIPUS. When I am nothing, then in that hour I am a man?

ISMENE. Yes, for the gods lift you now, but before they were working your ruin.

OEDIPUS. It is little to lift age when youth was ruined.

ISMENE. Know, at least, that Creon will come to you in this cause, and rather soon than late.

OEDIPUS. With what purpose, daughter? Explain to me.

ISMENE. To plant you near the Cadmean land so that they may have you in their grasp; but you may not set foot on their borders.

OEDIPUS. And how can I advantage them while I rest beyond their gates?

ISMENE. Your tomb has a curse for them, if all is not well with it.

OEDIPUS. It needs no god to help our wit so far.

ISMENE. Well, therefore they wish to acquire you as neighbor, in a place where you shall not be your own master.

OEDIPUS. Will they also shroud me in Theban dust?

ISMENE. No, the guilt of a kinsman's blood debars you, father.

OEDIPUS. Then never shall they become my masters.

ISMENE. Some day, then, this shall be a grief for the Cadmeans.

OEDIPUS. In what conjuncture of events, my child?

ISMENE. By force of your wrath, when they take their stand at your tomb.

OEDIPUS. And who has told you what you tell, my child?

ISMENE. Sacred envoys, from the Delphian hearth.

OEDIPUS. Phoebus has indeed spoken thus concerning me?

ISMENE. So say the men who have come back to Thebes.

OEDIPUS. Has either of my sons heard this?

ISMENE. Yes, both have heard and know it well.

OEDIPUS. And those base ones, aware of this, held the kingship dearer than the wish to recall me?

ISMENE. It grieves me to hear, but I must bear it.

OEDIPUS. Then may the gods not quench their fated strife, and may it become mine to decide this warfare to which they are now setting their hands, spear to spear! For then neither should he abide who now holds the scepter and the throne, nor should the banished one ever return; seeing that when I their father was being thrust so shamefully from my country, they did not hinder or defend me. No, they saw me sent forth homeless, they heard my doom of exile cried aloud.

You will say that it was my own wish then, and that the city merely granted me that boon. No indeed. In that first day when my soul was seething and my darling wish was for death, yes, death by stoning, no one was found to help me in that desire. But after a time when all my anguish was now assuaged and when I began to feel that my wrath had run too far in punishing those past errors, then it was that the city on her part went about to drive me perforce from the land, after all that time. And my sons when they might have brought help—sons to their father—would not do it. No; for lack of one little word from them I was left to wander, an outcast and a beggar forever.

It is to these sisters, girls as they are, that so far as nature enables them I owe my daily food and a shelter in the land and the offices of kinship; the brothers have bartered their sire for a throne and sceptered sway and rule of the realm. But they shall never win Oedipus for an ally, nor shall good ever come to them from this reign at Thebes. That I know when I hear this maiden's oracles and meditate the old prophecies stored in my own mind, which Phoebus has fulfilled for me at last.

Therefore let them send Creon to seek me, and anyone else powerful in Thebes. For if you, strangers—with the championship of the dread goddesses who dwell among your folk—are willing to succor me, you shall procure a great deliverer for this state and troubles for my foes.

CHORUS. Right worthy are you of compassion, Oedipus, you

and these maidens; and since to this plea you add your power to save our land, I would willingly advise you for your welfare.

OEDIPUS. Kind sir, be sure than that I will obey in all—do you be my friend.

CHORUS. Now make atonement to these deities to whom you have first come and on whose ground you have trespassed.

OEDIPUS. With what rites? Instruct me, strangers.

CHORUS. First, from a perennial spring fetch holy drink-offerings, borne in clean hands.

OEDIPUS. And when I have gotten this pure draught?

CHORUS. Bowls there are, the work of a cunning craftsman: crown their edges and the handles at either brim.

OEDIPUS. With branches, or woollen cloths, or in what way?

CHORUS. Take the freshly-shorn wool of a ewe-lamb.

OEDIPUS. Good; and then, to what last rite shall I proceed?

CHORUS. Pour your drink-offerings, with your face to the dawn.

OEDIPUS. With these vessels of which you speak shall I pour them?

CHORUS. Yes, in three streams; but empty the last vessel wholly.

OEDIPUS. With what shall I fill this before I set it? Tell me this also.

CHORUS. With water and honey; but add no wine.

OEDIPUS. And when the ground under the dark shade has drunk of these?

CHORUS. Lay on it thrice nine sprays of olive with both your hands, and make this prayer the while.

OEDIPUS. The prayer I fain would hear; it is of chief moment.

CHORUS. That, as we call them "Benign Powers," with hearts benign they may receive the suppliant for saving. Let this be your prayer, your own or his who prays for you. Speak inaudibly and do not lift up your voice; then retire without looking behind. Do thus, and I would be bold to stand by you; but otherwise, stranger, I would fear for you.

OEDIPUS. Daughters, do you hear these strangers who dwell near?

ANTIGONE. We have listened. You bid us what to do.

OEDIPUS. I cannot go for I am disabled by two evils, lack of

strength and lack of sight. But let one of you two go and do
these things. For I think that one soul suffices to pay this
debt for ten thousand, if it come to the shrine with good will.
Act, then, with speed, yet do not leave me alone, for strength
would fail me to move without help or guiding hand.

ISMENE. Then I will go and perform the rite. But where am I to
find the spot? This I wish to know.

CHORUS. On the further side of this grove, maiden. And if you
have need of anything there is a guardian of the place who
will direct you.

ISMENE. So to my task; but you, Antigone, watch our father
here. If toil there be in parents' cause, we must not reck of
toil. (*Exit.*)

CHORUS. *Dread it is, stranger, to arouse the old grief that has
so long been laid to rest; and yet I yearn to hear—*

OEDIPUS. *What now?*

CHORUS. *—of that grievous anguish, found cureless, wherewith you have wrestled.*

OEDIPUS. *By your kindness for a guest, do not bare the shame
that I have suffered!*

CHORUS. *Seeing, in truth, that the tale is widespread and does
not wane, I am eager, friend, to hear it aright.*

OEDIPUS. *Woe is me!*

CHORUS. *Be content, I pray you.*

OEDIPUS. *Alas, alas!*

CHORUS. *Grant my wish, as I have granted yours in its fullness.*

OEDIPUS. *I have suffered misery, strangers, suffered it through
unwitting deeds, and of those acts—be Heaven my witness!—no part was of my own choice.*

CHORUS. *But in what regard?*

OEDIPUS. *By an evil wedlock Thebes bound me, all unknowing,
to the bride that was my curse.*

CHORUS. *Can it be, as I hear, that you made your mother the
partner of your bed, for its infamy?*

OEDIPUS. *Woe is me! Cruel as death, strangers, are these
words in my ears. But those maidens begotten of me—*

CHORUS. *What will you say?*

OEDIPUS. *—two daughters, two curses—*

CHORUS. *O Zeus!*

OEDIPUS. *—sprang from the travail of the womb that bore me.*

CHORUS. *These then are at once your offspring and. . . .*

OEDIPUS. *—yes, very sisters of their father.*

CHORUS. *Oh, horror!*

OEDIPUS. *Horror indeed. Yes, horrors untold sweep back upon my soul!*

CHORUS. *You have suffered—*

OEDIPUS. *Suffered woes dread to bear—*

CHORUS. *You have sinned—*

OEDIPUS. *No willful sin—*

CHORUS. *How?*

OEDIPUS. *A gift was given to me—O, broken-hearted that I am, would I had never won from Thebes that reward for having served her!*

CHORUS. *Wretch! How then? Your hand shed blood?*

OEDIPUS. *Why this? What would you learn?*

CHORUS. *A father's blood?*

OEDIPUS. *Oh! Oh, a second stab! Wound on wound!*

CHORUS. *Slayer!*

OEDIPUS. *Yes, slayer. Yet I have a plea—*

CHORUS. *What can you plead?*

OEDIPUS. *—a plea in justice.*

CHORUS. *What?*

OEDIPUS. *You shall hear it. They whom I slew would have taken my own life; stainless before the law, void of malice, have I come to this pass!*

CHORUS. Look, yonder comes our prince, Theseus son of Aegeus, at your bidding, to do the part for which he was summoned.

THESEUS (*enters*). Hearing from many in time past concerning the cruel marring of your sight, I have recognized you, son of Laius; and now through hearsay in this my coming, I have fuller certainty. For your dress and that hapless face alike assure me of your name. In all compassion I would ask you, ill-fated Oedipus, what is your suit to Athens or to me that you have taken your place here, you and the hapless maiden at your side. Declare it; dire indeed must be the fortune you tell to make me stand aloof. For I know that I myself also was reared in exile, like yours, and in strange lands wrestled perils to my life, as no man beside. Never then would I turn aside from a stranger, such as you are now, or refuse to aid in his deliverance. For I know well that I am a man and that in the morrow my portion is no greater than yours.

OEDIPUS. Theseus, your nobleness has shown such grace in brief words that for me there is need to say but little. You have rightly said who I am, from what sire I spring, from what land I have come; and so nothing else remains for me but to speak my desire, and the tale is told.

THESEUS. Even so, speak that; I would like to hear.

OEDIPUS. I come to offer you my woe-worn body as a gift— not goodly to look upon, but the gains from it are better than beauty.

THESEUS. What gain do you claim to have brought?

OEDIPUS. You shall learn later; not yet, I think.

THESEUS. When then will your benefit be shown?

OEDIPUS. When I am dead and you have given me burial.

THESEUS. You crave life's boon; for all between you have no memory, or no care.

OEDIPUS. Yes, for by that boon I reap all the rest.

THESEUS. Nay, then, this grace which you crave from me has small compass.

OEDIPUS. Yet give heed; this issue is no light one, no indeed.

THESEUS. Do you mean as between your sons and me?

OEDIPUS. King, they wish to convey me to Thebes.

THESEUS. But if to your contentment then exile is not seemly for you.

OEDIPUS. But when *I* was willing *they* refused.

THESEUS. Foolish man, temper is not proper in misfortune.

OEDIPUS. When you have heard my story, chide; till then forbear.

THESEUS. Say on; I must not pronounce without knowledge.

OEDIPUS. I have suffered, Theseus, cruel wrong on wrong.

THESEUS. Will you speak of the ancient trouble of your race?

OEDIPUS. No; *that* is noised throughout Hellas.

THESEUS. What then is your grief that passes the griefs of man?

OEDIPUS. This is how it is with me. I have been driven from my country by my own offspring, and my doom is to return no more, as being guilty of a father's blood.

THESEUS. How then should they fetch you if you must dwell apart?

OEDIPUS. The mouth of the god will constrain them.

THESEUS. What prophesied woe do they fear?

OEDIPUS. That they may be smitten in this land.

THESEUS. And how should bitterness come between them and me?

OEDIPUS. Kind son of Aegeus, to the gods alone comes never old age or death, but all else is confounded by all-mastering time. Earth's strength decays, and the strength of the body; faith dies, distrust is born; and the same spirit is never steadfast among friends, or betwixt city and city; for, be it soon or be it late, men find sweet turn to bitter, and then once more to love.

And if now all is sunshine between Thebes and you, yet time in his untold course gives birth to days and nights untold, wherein for a small cause they shall sunder with the spear that plighted concord of today; when my slumbering and buried corpse, cold in death, shall one day drink their warm blood, if Zeus is still Zeus, and Phoebus the son of Zeus speaks true.

But since I would not break silence touching mysteries, suffer me to cease where I began. Only make your own word good, and never shall you say that you welcomed Oedipus to dwell in this realm in vain—unless the gods cheat my hope.

CHORUS. King, from the first yonder man has shown the mind to perform these promises, or the like, for our land.

THESEUS. Who then would reject the friendship of such a one? To him, first, the hearth of an ally is ever open, by mutual right among us; and then he has come as a suppliant to our gods, fraught with no light recompense for this land and for me. In reverence for these claims I will never spurn his grace but will establish him as a citizen in the land. And if it is the stranger's pleasure to abide here, I will charge you to guard him; or if to come with me be more pleasing—this choice or that, Oedipus, you can take; your will shall be mine.

OEDIPUS. O Zeus, may you be good to such men!

THESEUS. What is your wish, then? To come to my house?

OEDIPUS. Yes, if it were lawful; but *this* is the place—

THESEUS. What are you to do here? I will not thwart you. . . .

OEDIPUS. —where I shall vanquish those who cast me forth.

THESEUS. The boon promised from your presence would be great.

OEDIPUS. It shall be—if your pledge is kept with me indeed.

THESEUS. Do not fear touching me; I will never fail you.

OEDIPUS. I will not bind you with an oath, as one untrue.

THESEUS. You would win nothing more than by my word.

OEDIPUS. How will you act, then?

THESEUS. What might you fear?

OEDIPUS. Men will come—

THESEUS. These people will look to that.

OEDIPUS. Beware lest if you leave me—

THESEUS. Do not teach me my part.

OEDIPUS. Fear constrains—

THESEUS. My heart feels no fear.

OEDIPUS. You do not know the threats—

THESEUS. I know that none shall take you hence in my despite. Often have threats blustered, in men's wrath, with threatenings loud and vain; but when the mind is lord of himself once more the threats are gone. And for yonder men it may be—though they have waxed bold to speak dread things of bringing you back—the sundering waters will prove wide and hard to sail. Now I would have you be of good courage, apart from any resolve of mine, if indeed Phoebus has sent you on your way. Though I may not be here, my name, I think, will shield you from harm. (*Exit.*)

CHORUS. *Stranger, in this land of goodly steeds thou hast come to earth's fairest home, even to our white Colonus; where the nightingale, a constant guest, trills her clear note in the covert of green glades, dwelling amid the wine-dark ivy and the god's inviolate bowers, rich in berries and fruit, unvis-*

ited by sun, unvexed by wind of any storm; where the reveler Dionysus ever walks the ground, companion of the nymphs that nursed him.

And, fed of heavenly dew, the narcissus blooms morn by morn with fair clusters, crown of the Great Goddesses from of yore; and the crocus blooms with golden beam. Nor fail the sleepless founts whence the waters of Cephisus wander, but each day with stainless tide he moveth over the plains of the land's swelling bosom, for the giving of quick increase; nor hath the Muses' quire abhorred this place, nor Aphrodite of the golden rein.

And a thing there is such as I know not by fame on Asian ground, or as ever born in the great Dorian isle of Pelops— a growth unconquered, self-renewing, a terror to the spears of the foemen, a growth which mightily flourishes in this land—the gray-leafed olive, nurturer of children. Youth shall not mar it by the ravage of his hand, nor any who dwells with old age; for the sleepless eye of the Morian Zeus beholds it, and the gray-eyed Athena.

And another praise have I to tell for this the city our mother, the gift of a great god, a glory of the land most high; the might of horses, the might of young horses, the might of the sea.

For thou, son of Cronus, our lord Poseidon, hast throned her in this pride, since in these roads first thou didst show forth the curb that cures the rage of steeds. And the shapely oar, apt to men's hands, hath a wondrous speed on the brine, following the hundred-footed Nereids.

ANTIGONE. O land praised above all lands, now it is for you to make those bright praises seen in deeds!

OEDIPUS. What new thing has happened, daughter?

ANTIGONE. Yonder Creon draws near us—not without followers, father.

OEDIPUS. Ah, kind elders, now give me, I pray you, the final proof of my safety!

CHORUS. Have no fear, it shall be yours. If *I* am aged, this country's strength has not grown old.

CREON (*enters*). Sirs, noble dwellers in this land, I see that a sudden fear has troubled your eyes at my coming. Do not shrink from me; and let no ungentle word escape you.

I am here with no thought of force. I am old, and I know that the city to which I have come is mighty, if any in Hellas has might. No; I have been sent, in these my years, to plead with yonder man that he return with me to the land of Cadmus. I am not one man's envoy but have been charged by all our people, since it was mine, by kinship, to mourn his woes as no Theban beside.

Unhappy Oedipus, hear us and come home! Rightfully are you called by all the Cadmean folk, and in chief by me, for I—unless I am the basest of all men born—chiefly sorrow for your ills, old man, when I see you unhappily a stranger and a wanderer always, roaming in beggary, with one handmaid to support you. Alas, I had not thought that she could fall to such a depth of misery as that to which she has fallen, poor girl, while she constantly attends your dark life amid penury, in ripe youth but unwed, a prize for the first rude hand.

Is it not a cruel reproach—alas!—that I have cast at you, and me, and all our race? But indeed an open shame cannot be hid; then—in the name of your father's gods, hearken to me, Oedipus!—do *you* hide it by consenting to return to the city and the house of your fathers, after a kindly farewell to this state—for she is worthy: yet your own has the first claim on your piety, since it was she that nurtured you of old.

OEDIPUS. All-daring, who from any plea of right would draw a crafty device, why do you make such an attempt on me and seek once more to take me in the snare where capture would be sorest? In the old days, when I was distempered by self-wrought woes and yearned to be cast out of the land, your will did not meet mine to grant the boon. But when my fierce grief had spent its force and the seclusion of the house was sweet, *then* you were for thrusting me from the house and from the land. Kinship had no dearness for you then. And now again, when you see that I have kindly welcome from this city and from all her sons, you seek to pluck me away, wrapping hard thoughts in soft words. And yet what joy is there in kindness shown us against our will? As if a man should give you no gift, bring you no help, when you desired the boon; but after your soul's desire was sated should grant it then, when the grace could be gracious no more: would you not find that pleasure vain? Yet such are your own offers to me, good in name but in their substance evil.

I will declare it to these men also, to show you false. You have come to fetch me, not to take me home, but to plant me near your borders so your city may escape unscathed by troubles from this land. *That* portion is not for you but *this*—my curse upon the country, to abide there forever; and for my sons this heritage—room enough in my realm wherein—to die.

Am I not wiser than you in the fortunes of Thebes? Yes, wiser far, as the sources of my knowledge are truer, Phoebus and his father Zeus most high. But you have come here with fraud on your lips, yes, with a tongue keener than the edge of the sword; yet by your pleading you are like to reap more woe than weal. However, I know that I do not persuade you of this—go!—and suffer us to live here; for even in this plight our life would not be evil if we were content with it.

CREON. Which, do you think, most suffers in this parley, I by your course or you by your own?

OEDIPUS. For me it is enough that your pleading fails. As with me so with you there are men near.

CREON. Unhappy man, shall it be seen that not even your years have brought you sense? Must you live to be the reproach of age?

OEDIPUS. You have a ready tongue, but I do not know the honest man who has fair words for every cause.

CREON. Words may be many and yet may miss their aim.

OEDIPUS. As if yours, forsooth, were few but aimed aright.

CREON. No, truly, for one whose wit is such as yours.

OEDIPUS. Depart—I will say it in the name of yonder men also—and do not beset me with jealous watch in the place where I am destined to abide.

CREON. These men, not you, I call to witness. But as for the strain of your answer to your kindred, if ever I take you—

OEDIPUS. Who could take me in despite of these allies?

CREON. I promise you, you shall soon smart without that.

OEDIPUS. Where is the deed that warrants that blustering word?

CREON. One of your two daughters has just been seized by me and sent away; the other I will remove forthwith.

OEDIPUS. Woe is me!

CREON. You will soon find it more woeful.

OEDIPUS. You have my child?

CREON. And will have this one before long.

OEDIPUS. Alas! Friends, what will you do? Will you forsake me? Will you not drive the godless man from this land?

CHORUS. Out, stranger, out, begone! Unrighteous is your present deed, unrighteous the deed which you have done.

CREON (*to his* ATTENDANTS). It is time for you to lead yonder girl off perforce, if she will not go of her free will.

ANTIGONE. Wretched that I am! Whither shall I fly? Where find help from gods or men?

CHORUS (*threateningly, to* CREON). What do you want, stranger?

CREON. I will not touch yonder man but her who is mine.

OEDIPUS. O elders of the land!

CHORUS. Stranger, your deed is not just.

CREON. It is just.

CHORUS. How just?

CREON. I take my own.

OEDIPUS. *Hear, O Athens!*

CHORUS. *What are you about, stranger? Release her! Your strength and ours will soon be proved.*

CREON. *Stand back!*

CHORUS. *Not from you while this is your purpose.*

CREON. *It will be war with Thebes for you if you harm me.*

OEDIPUS. *Did I not say so?*

CHORUS. *Unhand the maid at once!*

CREON. *Do not command where you are not master.*

CHORUS. *Leave hold, I tell you!*

CREON (*to a guard who seizes* ANTIGONE). *And I tell you, begone!*

CHORUS. *To the rescue, men of Colonus, to the rescue! Athens, yes Athens, is outraged with the strong hand. Hither, hither to our help!*

ANTIGONE. They drag me away, ah me, friends, friends!

OEDIPUS. Where are you, my child?

ANTIGONE. I am taken by force—

OEDIPUS. Your hands, my child—

ANTIGONE. But I am helpless.

CREON (*to* GUARDS). Away with you!

OEDIPUS. Ah me, ah me!

(*Exeunt* GUARDS *with* ANTIGONE.)

CREON. So *those* two crutches shall never more prop your steps. But since it is your will to worst your country and your friends—whose mandate, though a prince, I here discharge—then let that victory be yours. Hereafter, I think, you will come to know all this—that now as in time past you have done yourself no good, when, in despite of friends, you have indulged anger, which is always your bane. (*Turns to follow his* GUARDS.)

CHORUS. Hold, stranger!

CREON. Hands off, I say!

CHORUS. I will not let you go unless you give back the maiden.

CREON. Then you will soon give Thebes a still dearer prize: I will seize more than those two girls.

CHORUS. What? Which way are you turning?

CREON. Yonder man shall be my captive.

CHORUS. A valiant threat!

CREON. It will forthwith be a deed.

CHORUS. Unless the ruler of this realm hinders you.

OEDIPUS. Shameless voice! Will you indeed touch me?

CREON. Be silent!

OEDIPUS. But may the powers of this place suffer me to utter yet this curse! Wretch, who when these eyes were dark have reft from me by force the helpless one who was my eyesight! Therefore to you and to your race may the Sun-god, the god who sees all things, yet grant an old age such as mine!

CREON. Do you see this, people of the land?

OEDIPUS. They see both me and you; they know that my wrongs are deeds, and my revenge—only breath.

CREON. I will not curb my wrath, no, alone though I am and slow with age. I'll take yonder man by force. (*Approaches* OEDIPUS.)

OEDIPUS. *Woe is me!*

CHORUS. *It is a bold spirit that you have brought with you, stranger, if you think to achieve this.*

CREON. *I do.*

CHORUS. *Then will I deem Athens a city no more.*

CREON. *In a just cause the weak vanquishes the strong.*

OEDIPUS. *Do you hear his words?*

CHORUS. *Yes, words which he shall not turn to deeds, Zeus knows!*

CREON. *Zeus may know; you do not.*

CHORUS. *Insolence!*

CREON. *Insolence which you must bear.*

CHORUS. *What ho, people, rulers of the land, ho, hither with all speed, hither! These men are on their way to cross our borders!*

THESEUS (*enters*). What does this shout mean? What is the trouble? What fear can have moved you to stay my sacrifice at the altar to the Sea-god, the lord of your Colonus? Speak, so that I may know all, since I have sped here with more than easy speed of foot for that reason.

OEDIPUS. Ah, friend—I know your voice—yonder man has only now done me foul wrong.

THESEUS. What is that wrong? Who has wrought it? Speak!

OEDIPUS. Creon, whom you see there, has torn away from me my two children, my all.

THESEUS. What are you telling me?

OEDIPUS. You have heard my wrong.

THESEUS (*to* ATTENDANTS). Hasten, one of you, to the altars yonder, make the folk leave the sacrifice and speed—footmen, horsemen all, with slack rein, to the region where the two highways meet, lest the maidens pass and I become a mockery to this stranger, as one despoiled by force. Away I

tell you, quick! (*Turning toward* CREON.) As for that man—
if my wrath went as far as he deserves—I would not have
suffered him to go scatheless from my hand. But now such
law as he himself has brought and no other shall be the rule
for his correction.—You shall not quit this land until you
bring those maidens and produce them in my sight; for your
deed is a disgrace to me and to your own race and to your
country. You have come to a city that observes justice and
sanctions nothing without law—yet you have put her lawful
powers aside, you have made this rude inroad, you are taking captives at your pleasure and snatching prizes by violence, as in the belief that my city was void of men or
manned by slaves, and I a thing of nought.

Yet it is not by Theban training that you are base; Thebes
is not wont to rear unrighteous sons, nor would she praise
you if she learned that you are despoiling me, yes, despoiling the gods, when by force you lead off their hapless suppliants. If my foot were on your soil I would never wrest or
plunder without license from the ruler of the land whoever
he might be—no, though my claim were the most just of all:
I should know how an alien ought to live among citizens.
But you are shaming a city that does not deserve it, your
own; and the fullness of your years brings you an old age
bereft of wit.

I have said, then, and I say it again—let the maidens be
brought here with all speed, unless you would sojourn in
this land by no free choice. This I tell you from my soul, as
with my lips.

CHORUS. Do you see your plight, stranger? You are deemed to
come of a just race, but your deeds are found evil.

CREON. Not counting this city void of manhood, son of Aegeus,
nor of counsel—as you say—have I wrought this deed; but
because I judged that its folk could never be so enamored of
my kinsfolk as to foster them against my will. And I knew
that this people would not receive a parricide, a polluted man,
a man with whom had been found the unholy bride of her
son. Such is the wisdom, I knew, that dwells on the Mount of
Ares in their land; which does not suffer such wanderers to

dwell within this realm. In that faith I sought to take this prize. And I would not have done so but that he was calling down bitter curses on me and on my race; being so wronged, I deemed that I had warrant for this requital. For anger knows no old age, till death comes; the dead alone feel no smart.

Therefore you shall act as seems good to you; for though my cause is just the lack of aid makes me weak. Yet old though I am, I will endeavor to meet deed with deed.

OEDIPUS. O shameless soul, where do you think this taunt of yours falls, on my age or on your own? Bloodshed, incest, misery, all this your lips have launched against me—all this I have borne, woe is me, by no choice of mine; for such was the pleasure of the gods, who may have been angry with my race from of old. Take me alone and you could find no sin to upbraid me with in requital for which I was driven so to sin against myself and against my kin. Tell me now, if an oracle had prophesied a divine doom coming upon my father, that he should die by a son's hand, how could you justly reproach me with it, me who was then unborn, whom no sire had yet begotten, no womb conceived? And if when born to woe— as I was born—I met my father in strife and slew him, all ignorant of what I was doing and to whom, how could you justly blame the unknowing deed?

And my mother—wretch, have you no shame in forcing me to speak of her nuptials when she was your sister and her nuptials such as I will now tell? Indeed I will not be silent when you have gone so far in impious speech. Yes, she was my mother, oh, misery, my mother! I did not know it nor did she, and for her shame she bore children to the son whom she had borne. But one thing at least I know: your will consents to revile her and me so, but not of my free will did I wed her, and not of free will do I speak now.

No, not in this marriage shall I be called guilty, nor in that slaying of my father which you keep urging against me with bitter reviling. Answer me but one thing that I ask you. If here and now one should come up and seek to slay you, you the righteous man, would you ask if the murderer was your father or would you deal with him straightway? I think, as you love your life, that you would requite the culprit and not look round you for your warrant. But such was the plight into which *I* came, led by gods. If my father could come back to life I think he would not gainsay me in this.

Yet *you*—for you are not a just man but one who thinks it proper to utter all things, knowing no barrier between speech and silence—*you* taunt me in this way before yonder men. And you find it timely to flatter the renowned Theseus and Athens, saying how well her state has been ordered; yet while giving such large praise you forget this, that if any land knows how to worship the gods with due rites this land excels in so doing; and from this land you had planned to steal me, the suppliant, the old man, and you sought to seize me, and have already carried off my daughters. Therefore I now call on yonder goddesses, I supplicate them, I adjure them with prayers to bring me help and fight in my cause, so that you may learn well by what manner of men this realm is guarded.

CHORUS. The stranger is a good man, O King. His fate has been accursed, but it is worthy of our succor.

THESEUS. Enough of words. The doers of the deed are in flight, while we the sufferers stand still.

CREON. What then would you have a helpless man do?

THESEUS. Show the way in their track, while I escort you, so that if you have the maidens we seek in these regions you yourself may discover them to me. But if your men are fleeing with the spoil in their grasp we may spare our trouble; the chase is for others, from whom they will never escape out of this land to thank their gods.

Come, forward! The spoiler has been spoiled, I tell you. Fate has taken the hunter in the toils; gains got by wrongful arts are soon lost. And you shall have no ally in your aim, for I know well that not without accomplice or resource have you gone to such a length of violence in the daring mood which has inspired you here. No, there was someone in whom you were trusting when you attempted these deeds. To this I must look, and not make this city weaker than one man. Do you take my drift? Or do these words seem

as vain as the warnings seemed when your deed was still
a-planning?

CREON. Say what you will while you are here; I will not cavil.
But at home I too will know how to act.

THESEUS. For the present threaten, but go forward. You,
Oedipus, stay here in peace, I pray you, with my pledge that,
unless I die before, I will not cease until I put you in possession of your children.

OEDIPUS. Heaven reward you, Theseus, for your nobleness and
your loyal care in my behalf. (*Exeunt.*)

CHORUS. *Oh to be where the foeman, turned to bay, will soon
join in the brazen clangor of battle haply by the shores loved
of Apollo, haply by that torch-lit strand where the Great
Goddesses cherish dread rites for mortals, on whose lips the
ministrant Eumolpidae have laid the precious seal of silence;
where, methinks, the war-waking Theseus and the captives
twain, the sister maids, will soon meet within our borders,
amid a warcry of men strong to save!*

*Or perchance they will soon draw nigh to the pastures on
the west of Oea's snowy rock, borne on horses in their flight,
or in chariots racing at speed.*

*Creon will be worsted! Terrible are the warriors of
Colonus, and the followers of Theseus are terrible in their
might. Yea, the steel of every bridle flashes—with slack
bridle-rein all the knighthood rides apace that worships our
Queen of Chivalry, Athena, and the earth-girdling Sea-god,
the son of Rhea's love.*

*Is the battle now, or yet to be? For somehow my soul
woos me to the hope that soon I shall be face to face with the
maidens thus sorely tried, thus sorely visited by the hand of
a kinsman.*

*Today, today, Zeus will work some great thing: I have
presage of victory in the strife. O to be a dove with swift
strength as of the storm, that I might reach an airy cloud,
with gaze lifted above the fray!*

*Hear, all-ruling lord of heaven, all-seeing Zeus! Enable
the guardians of this land, in might triumphant, to achieve
the capture that gives the prize to their hands! So grant thy*

daughter also, our dread Lady, Pallas Athena! And Apollo,
the hunter, and his sister, who follows the dappled, swift-
footed deer—fain am I that they should come, a twofold
strength, to this land and to her people.

Ah, wanderer friend, you will not have to tax the watcher
with false augury; yonder I see the maidens drawing near
with an escort.

OEDIPUS. Where, where? How? What are you saying?

(*Enter* ANTIGONE *and* ISMENE *with* THESEUS *and* ATTEN-
DANTS.)

ANTIGONE. O father, father, would that some god would suffer
your eyes to see this noble man who has brought us here to
you!

OEDIPUS. My child, you are really here?

ANTIGONE. Yes, for these strong arms have saved us, Theseus
and his trusty followers.

OEDIPUS. Come here, child, let me embrace you—restored beyond all hope!

ANTIGONE. Your wish shall be granted; we crave what we be-
stow.

OEDIPUS. Where, then, where are you?

ANTIGONE. Here, approaching you together.

OEDIPUS. My darlings!

ANTIGONE. A father loves his own.

OEDIPUS. Props of my age!

ANTIGONE. And sharers of your sorrow.

OEDIPUS. I hold my dear ones, and should I now die I would
not be wholly wretched, since you have come to me. Press
close to me on either side, children, cleave to your sire and
repose from this late roaming, so forlorn, so grievous! Tell
me what passed, as shortly as you may; brief speech suffices
for young maidens.

ANTIGONE. Here is our deliverer; from him you should hear the
story, father, since his is the deed; so my part shall be brief.

OEDIPUS. Sir, do not marvel if with such yearning I prolong my
words to my children, found again beyond my hope. Well I

know that this joy in respect of them has come to me from you and you alone. You have rescued them, and no man beside. May the gods deal with you after my wish, with you and with this land; for among you above all human kind I have found the fear of heaven and the spirit of fairness and the lips that do not lie. I know these things which with these words I requite; for what I have I have through you and no man else.

Stretch forth your right hand I pray you, O King, that I may touch it, and if it is lawful kiss your cheek. But what am I saying? Unhappy as I have become, how could I wish you to touch one with whom all stain of sin has made its dwelling? No, not I—nor allow you if you would. They alone can share this burden to whom it has come home. Receive my greeting where you stand; and in the future still give me your loyal care, as you have given it to me this hour.

THESEUS. It is no marvel to me if you have shown some mind to large discourse for joy in these your children, and if your first care has been for their words rather than for me; indeed, there is nothing to vex me in that. Not in words so much as deeds would I make the luster of my life. You have the proof; I have failed in nothing of my sworn faith to you, old man. Here I am with the maidens living, yes, unhurt by those threats. What need that I should idly boast how the fight was won when you will learn it from these maidens in conversation?

But there is a matter that has newly happened to me as I came here; lend me your counsel upon it, for though it be small it is food for wonder, and mortal man should deem nothing beneath his care.

OEDIPUS. What is it, son of Aegeus? Tell me; I myself know nothing of that whereof you ask.

THESEUS. A man, they say, not your countryman yet your kinsman, has somehow cast himself as a suppliant at our altar of Poseidon, where I was sacrificing when I first set out this way.

OEDIPUS. Of what land is he? What does he crave by the supplication?

THESEUS. I know one thing only; they say he asks brief speech with you which shall not irk you much.

OEDIPUS. On what theme? That suppliant posture is not trivial.

THESEUS. He asks no more, they say, than that he may confer with you, and return unharmed from his journey here.

OEDIPUS. Who can he be who thus implores the god?

THESEUS. Look if you have any kinsman at Argos who might crave this boon of you.

OEDIPUS. O friend! Say no word more!

THESEUS. What ails you?

OEDIPUS. Do not ask it of me—

THESEUS. Ask what? Speak!

OEDIPUS. By those words I know who the suppliant is.

THESEUS. Who can he be, that I should have a grief against him?

OEDIPUS. My son, O King, the hated son whose words would vex my ear as the words of no man beside.

THESEUS. What? Can you not listen without doing what you do not wish? Why should it pain you to hear him?

OEDIPUS. Most hateful, King, has that voice become to his sire. Do not lay constraint on me to yield in this.

THESEUS. But think whether his suppliant state constrains you. What if you have a duty of respect for the god?

ANTIGONE. Father, hearken to me, though I who counsel am young. Allow the king to gratify his own heart and to gratify the god as he wishes; and for your daughter's sake allow our brother to come. For he will not pluck you by force from your resolve—never fear—by such words as shall not be spoken for your good. But to hear him speak—what harm can be in that? Ill-devised deeds, you know, are often confounded by speech. You are his father, so that even if he were to wrong you with the most impious of wrongs, my father, it is not lawful for you to wrong him again.

O, let him come. Other men also have evil offspring and are swift to wrath; but they hear advice and are charmed from their mood by the gentle spells of friends.

Look to the past, not to the present, think of all that you have borne through father and mother; and if you consider those things I know well you will discern how evil is the end that waits on evil wrath. Your reasons to think on this are not slight, bereft as you are of the sight that returns no more.

Nay, yield to us! It is not seemly for just suitors to sue long; it is not seemly that a man should receive good and thereafter lack the mind to requite it.

OEDIPUS. My child, it is sore for me, this pleasure that you win from me by your pleading; but be it as you will. Only, if that man is to come here, friend, let no one ever become master of my life!

THESEUS. I need not hear such words more than once, old man. I would not boast, but be sure that your life is safe while god saves mine. (*Exit.*)

CHORUS. *Whoso craves the ampler length of life, not content to desire a modest span, him will I judge with no uncertain voice; he cleaves to folly.*

For the long days lay up full many things nearer to grief than to joy. But as for your delights, their place shall know them no more when a man's life has lapsed beyond the fitting term. The Deliverer comes at the last to all alike— when the doom of Hades is suddenly revealed, without marriage song or lyre or dance—even Death at the last.

Not to be born is past all prizing best; but when a man has seen the light this is next best by far, that with all speed he should go thither whence he has come.

For when he has seen youth go by, with its light follies, what troublous affliction is strange to his lot, what suffering is not therein?—envy, factions, strife, battles, and slaughters. And last of all age claims him for her own—age, dispraised, infirm, unsociable, unfriended, with whom all woe of woe abides.

In such years is yon hapless one, not I alone. As some cape that fronts the north is lashed on every side by the waves of winter, so he also is fiercely lashed evermore by the dread troubles that break on him like billows, some from the setting of the sun, some from the rising, some in the region of the noontide beam, some from the gloom-wrapped hills of the north.

ANTIGONE. Look, yonder, I think, I see the stranger coming this way—yes, without attendants, father—the tears streaming from his eyes.

OEDIPUS. Who is he?

ANTIGONE. The same who was in our thoughts from the first; Polyneices has come to us.

POLYNEICES (*enters*). Ah me, what shall I do? Shall I weep first for my own sorrows, sisters, or for my aged father's, as I see them yonder? I have found him in a strange land, an exile here with you two, clad in raiment of which the foul squalor has dwelt with that aged form so long, a very blight upon his flesh—while above the sightless eyes the unkempt hair flutters in the breeze; and matching with these things, it seems, the food that he carries, hapless one, against hunger's pinch.

Wretch that I am! I learn all this too late, and I bear witness that I am proved the vilest of men in all that touches care for you; from my own lips hear what I am. But seeing that Zeus himself in all that he does has mercy for the sharer of his throne, may she come to your side also, father; for the faults can be healed, but can never more be made worse.

Why are you silent? Speak, father; do not turn away from me. Have you not even an answer for me? Will you dismiss me in mute scorn, without telling why you are angry?

You his daughters, sisters mine, strive at least to move our father's implacable, inexorable silence, that he send me not away dishonored, who am the suppliant of the god, in such wise as this, with no word of response.

ANTIGONE. Tell him yourself, unhappy one, what you have come to seek. As words flow perhaps they will touch to joy, perhaps they glow with anger or with tenderness, and so they somehow give a voice to the dumb.

POLYNEICES. Then I will speak boldly—for you admonish me well—first claiming the help of the god himself, from whose altar the king of this land raised me so that I might come here, with warranty to speak and hear and go my way unharmed. I will crave, strangers, that these pledges with me be kept by you, and by my sisters here, and by my father. But now I wish to tell you, father, why I came.

I have been driven, an exile from my fatherland, because as eldest-born I claimed to sit in your sovereign seat. Therefore Eteocles, though the younger, thrust me from the land, when he had neither worsted me in argument nor come to trial of might and deed; no, but he won the city over. I deem it most likely that the cause of this is the curse on your house; so I hear from soothsayers also. When I came to Dorian Argos I took the daughter of Adrastus to wife; and I bound to me by oath all of the Apian land who are foremost in renown of war, that with them I might levy the sevenfold host of spearmen against Thebes, and die in my just cause or cast the doers of this wrong from the realm.

Well, and why have I come here now? With suppliant prayers to you, my own father, and the prayers of my allies who now have set their siege around the plain of Thebes with seven hosts behind their seven spears. Swift-speared Amphiaraus, matchless warrior and matchless augur, is one; then the son of Oeneus, Aetolian Tydeus; Eteoclus the third, of Argive birth; the fourth Hippomedon, sent by his sire Talaos; while Capaneus, the fifth, vaunts that he will burn Thebes to the ground with fire; and sixth, Arcadian Parthenopaeus rushes to the war, named from that virgin of other days whose marriage in aftertime gave him birth, trusty son of Atalanta. Last I your son—or if not yours but offspring of an evil fate, yet yours at least in name—lead the fearless host of Argos to Thebes.

By these your children and by your life, father, we all implore you, praying you to remit your stern wrath against me as I go forth to chastise my brother, who has thrust me out and robbed me of my fatherland. For if any truth is told by oracles, they said that victory should be with those whom you should join.

Then by our fountains and the gods of our race, I ask you to hearken and to yield. A beggar and an exile am I, an exile you; by court to others we have a home, you and I, sharers of one doom; while *he*, king in the house—woe is me!—mocks in his pride at you and me alike. But if you assist my purpose, with small toil or time I will scatter his strength to the winds; and so will bring you and establish you in your own house, and establish myself, when I have cast him out by force. Be your will with me, and that boast may be mine; without you I cannot even return alive.

CHORUS. For his sake who has sent him, Oedipus, speak as seems good to you before you send the man away.

OEDIPUS. Nay then, my friends, guardians of this land, were not Theseus the man who sent him here to me desiring that he should have my response, never should he have heard this voice. But now he shall be graced with it before he goes, yes, and hear from me such words as shall never gladden his life. Villain, when you had the scepter and the throne which your brother now has in Thebes you drove me, your own father, into exile, and made me citiless, and made me wear this garb which you now weep to see when you have come to the same stress of misery as I. The time for tears is past. No; *I* must bear this burden while I live, always thinking of you as of a murderer; for it is you who have brought my days to this anguish, it is you that have thrust me out, to you I owe it that I wander begging my daily bread from strangers. And had these daughters not been born to be my comfort I would surely have been dead for any help from you. Now these girls preserve me, these who are men, not women, in true service. But you are aliens and no sons of mine.

Therefore let the eyes of Fate look upon you—not yet as they will look presently, if indeed those hosts are moving against Thebes. Never can you overthrow that city, and your brother likewise. Such are the curses that my soul sent forth before against you two, and such do I now invoke to fight for me, so that you may deem it meet to revere parents and not scorn your father utterly because he is sightless who begot such sons; these maidens did not do so. So my curses have control of your "supplication" and your "throne," if indeed Justice, revealed from of old, sits with Zeus in the might of the eternal laws.

Begone, abhorred of me and unfathered, begone you vilest of the vile! With you take these my curses which I call down on you—never to vanquish the land of your race, no,

nor ever return to hill-girt Argos, but by a kindred hand to
die, and slay him by whom you have been driven out. Such
is my prayer; and I call the paternal darkness of dread
Tartarus to take you to another home, I call the spirits of this
place, I call the Destroying God who has set that dreadful
hatred in you two. Go, with these words in your ears, go and
publish it to the Cadmeans all, yes, and to your own staunch
allies, that Oedipus has divided such honors to his sons.

CHORUS. Polyneices, in your past goings I take no joy, and now
go your way with speed.

POLYNEICES. Alas for my journey and my baffled hope, alas
for my comrades! What an end for that march on which we
set forth from Argos, woe is me!—such an end that I may
not even utter it to any of my companions or turn them back,
but must go in silence to meet this doom.

You, his daughters and my sisters, you hear these hard
prayers of your father: if this father's curses be fulfilled and
some way of return to Thebes be found for you, oh, as you
fear the gods do not on your part dishonor me, but give me
burial and due funeral rites. The praise which you now win
from yonder man for your service shall be increased by another praise not less, by reason of the office wrought for me.

ANTIGONE. Polyneices, I entreat you, hear me in one thing!

POLYNEICES. What is it, dearest Antigone? Speak!

ANTIGONE. Turn your host back to Argos, yes, with all speed,
and do not destroy yourself and Thebes.

POLYNEICES. No, it cannot be; how could I lead the same host
again when once I had blenched?

ANTIGONE. But why, my brother, should your anger rise again?
What gain is promised you in destroying your native city?

POLYNEICES. It is shame to be an exile and, eldest born as I am,
to be thus mocked on my brother's part.

ANTIGONE. Do you see then to what sure fulfillment you are
bringing the prophecies of the man who bodes mutual slaying for you two?

POLYNEICES. Yes, he wishes it; but I must not yield.

ANTIGONE. Unhappy me! But who will dare to follow you
when he hears the prophecies that man has uttered?

POLYNEICES. I will not even report ill tidings; it is a good leader's part to tell the better news and not the worse.

ANTIGONE. Brother! Your resolve then is fixed?

POLYNEICES. Yes, and do not detain me. Mine it now shall be to tread yonder path, with evil doom and omen from this my sire and from his Furies. But for you two, may Zeus make your path bright, if you do my wishes when I am dead— since in my life you can do them no more. Now release me, and farewell; nevermore shall you behold me living.

ANTIGONE. Woe is me!

POLYNEICES. Do not mourn for me.

ANTIGONE. Who would not bewail you, brother, when you are hurrying to death foreseen?

POLYNEICES. If it is fate, I must die.

ANTIGONE. No, no; hear my pleading!

POLYNEICES. Do not plead amiss.

ANTIGONE. Then woe is me indeed if I must lose you!

POLYNEICES. But that rests with Fortune, that end or another. For you two, at least, I pray the gods that you never meet with ill, for in all men's eyes you are unworthy to suffer. (*Exit.*)

CHORUS. *Behold, new ills have newly come, in our hearing, from the sightless stranger, ills fraught with a heavy doom; unless, perchance, Fate is finding its goal. For it is not mine to say that a decree of Heaven is ever vain. Watchful, aye watchful of those decrees is Time, overthrowing some fortunes and on the morrow lifting others again to honor. (Thunder is heard.) Hark that sound in the sky! Zeus defend us!*

OEDIPUS. My children, my children! If there be any man to send, would that someone would fetch the peerless Theseus here!

ANTIGONE. What, father, is the aim of your summons?

OEDIPUS. This winged thunder of Zeus will lead me soon to Hades; but send, and do not tarry. (*A second peal is heard.*)

CHORUS. *Hark! With louder noise it crashes down, unutterable, hurled by Zeus! The hair of my head stands up for fear, my soul is sore dismayed; again the lightning flashes in the sky. Oh, to what event will it give birth? I am afraid, for never in vain does it rush forth or without grave issue. O dread sky! O Zeus!*

OEDIPUS. Daughters, his destined end has come upon your sire; he can turn his face from it no more.

ANTIGONE. How do you know? What sign has told you this?

OEDIPUS. I know it well. But let someone go, I pray you, with all speed, and bring the lord of this realm here. (*Another peal.*)

CHORUS. *Ha! Listen! Once again that piercing thunder-voice is around us! Be merciful, O thou god, be merciful if thou art bringing aught of gloom for the land of our mother! Gracious may I find thee, nor, because I have looked on a man accurst, have some meed not of blessing for my portion! O Zeus our lord, to thee I cry!*

OEDIPUS. Is the man near? Will he find me still alive, children, and master of my mind?

ANTIGONE. And what is the pledge that you would have fixed in your mind?

OEDIPUS. In return for his benefits I would duly give him the requital promised when I received them.

CHORUS. *What ho, my son, here, come here! Or if in the glade's inmost recess you are hallowing his altar with sacrifice in honor of the Sea-god Poseidon, come from there! Worthy are you in the stranger's sight, worthy are your city and your folk, that he should render a just recompense for benefits. Hasten, come quickly, O King!*

THESEUS (*enters*). Why does a summons ring forth from you all once again, from my people as clearly as from our guest? Can a thunderbolt from Zeus be the cause, or rushing hail in fierce onset? All forebodings may find place when the god sends such a storm.

OEDIPUS. King, welcome is your presence; it is some god that has made for you the good fortune of this coming.

THESEUS. What new thing has now befallen, son of Laius?

OEDIPUS. My life hangs in the scale; I wish to die guiltless of bad faith to you and to this city in respect of my pledges.

THESEUS. What sign of your fate holds you in suspense?

OEDIPUS. The gods, their own heralds, bring me the tidings, with no failure in the signs appointed of old.

THESEUS. What do you say are the signs of these things, old man?

OEDIPUS. The thunder, peal on peal, the lightning, flash on flash, hurled from the unconquered hand.

THESEUS. You win my belief, for in much I find you a prophet whose voice is not false; then speak what must be done.

OEDIPUS. Son of Aegeus, I will unfold that which shall be a treasure for this city such as age can never mar. Presently unaided and with no hand to guide me I will show the way to the place where I must die. Never reveal that place to mortal man, do not tell where it is hidden nor in what region it lies; so that it may always make for you a defense, better than many shields, better than the succoring spear of neighbors.

But for mysteries which speech may not profane, you shall mark them for yourself, when you come to that place alone; since neither to any of this people can I utter them, nor to my own children, dear though they are. No, do you guard them alone; and when you are coming to the end of life, disclose them to your heir alone, and so thenceforth.

Thus shall you hold this city unscathed from the side of the Dragon's brood; full many states lightly enter on offense, even though their neighbor live aright. For the gods are slow, though they are sure, in visitation, when men scorn godliness and turn to frenzy. Not such be your fate, son of Aegeus. But you know such things without my precepts.

But to that place—for the divine summons urges me— let us now set forth and hesitate no more.—My children, follow me, so, for I now have in strange wise been made your guide, as you were your father's. On, do not touch me, suffer me unaided to find out that sacred tomb where it is my portion to be buried in this land.

This way, here, this way, for this way doth guiding Hermes lead me, and the goddess of the dead!

O light, no light to me, mine once I allow, but now my body feels you for the last time! For now I go to hide the close of my life with Hades. Truest of friends, blessed be you, and this land, and your lieges; and when your days are blest, think on me, the dead, for your welfare evermore. (*Exeunt.*)

CHORUS. *If with prayer I may adore the Unseen Goddess, and thee, lord of the children of night, O hear me Aidoneus, Aidoneus! Not in pain, not by a doom that wakes sore lament, may the stranger pass to the fields of the dead below, the all-enshrouding, and to the Stygian house. Many were the sorrows that came to him without cause; but in requital a just god will lift him up.*

Goddess Infernal! And thou, dread form of the unconquered hound, thou who hast thy lair in those gates of many guests, thou untamable Watcher of Hell, snarling from the cavern's jaws, as rumor from the beginning tells of thee!

Hear me, O Death, son of Earth and Tartarus! May the Watcher leave a clear path for the stranger on his way to the nether fields of the dead! To thee I call, giver of the eternal sleep.

MESSENGER (*enters*). Countrymen, my tidings might most shortly be summed thus: Oedipus is gone. But the story of the event may not be told in brief words, as the deeds yonder were not briefly done.

CHORUS. He is gone, hapless one?

MESSENGER. Be sure that he has passed from life.

CHORUS. Ah, how? By a god-sent doom and painless?

MESSENGER. There you touch on what is indeed worthy of wonder. How he moved from here you yourself must know since you were here—with no friend to show the way but himself guide unto us all.

Now when he had come to the sheer Threshold bound by brazen steps to earth's deep roots, he paused in one of many branching paths, near the basin in the rock, where the inviolate covenant of Theseus and Peirithous has its memorial. He stood midway between the basin and the Thorician stone, the hollow pear tree and the marble tomb. Then he sat down and loosed his sordid raiment.

And then he called his daughters and bade them fetch water from some fount, so that he should wash and make a drink-offering. And they went to the hill which was in view, Demeter's hill who guards the tender plants, and in short space brought what their father enjoined; then they ministered to him with washing, and dressed him as use ordains.

But when he had had content of doing all and no part of his desire was now unheeded, there was thunder from the Zeus of the Shades. The maidens shuddered as they heard; they fell at their father's knees and wept, nor ceased from beating the breast and wailing very sore.

When he heard their sudden bitter cry he put his arms around them and said: "My children, this day ends your father's life. For now all has perished that was mine, and no more shall you bear the burden of tending me, no light one, well I know, my children. Yet one little word makes all those toils as nought; *love* you had from me as from none beside; and now you shall have me with you no more, through all your days to come."

On such wise, close-clinging to each other, sire and daughters sobbed and wept. But when they had made an end of wailing and the sound went up no more, there was a stillness; and suddenly a voice of one who cried aloud to him, so that the hair of all stood up on their heads for sudden fear, and they were afraid. For the god called him with many callings and manifold: "Oedipus, Oedipus, why delay we to go? You tarry too long."

But when he perceived that he was called of the god, he craved that the king Theseus should draw near, and when he came near said: "O my friend, give, I pray you, the solemn pledge of your right hand to my children, and you, daughters, to him. Promise never to forsake them of your free will, but to do all things for their good, as your friendship and the time may prompt." And he, like a man of noble spirit, without making lament, swore to keep that promise to his friend.

But when Theseus had so promised, Oedipus felt for his children with blind hands, and said: "O my children, you must be nobly brave of heart and depart from this place, nor ask to behold unlawful sights or to hear such speech as may not be heard. Go with all haste; only let Theseus be present, as is his right, a witness of those things which are to be."

So he spoke, and we all heard; with streaming tears and with lamentation we followed the maidens away. But when we had gone apart after no long time we looked back. Oedipus we saw nowhere any more, but the king alone, holding his hand before his face to screen his eyes, as if some dread sight had been seen, and such as none might endure to behold. And then after a short space we saw him salute the earth and the home of the gods above, both at once, in one prayer.

But by what doom Oedipus perished no man can tell, save Theseus alone. No fiery thunderbolt of the god removed him in that hour, nor any rising of storm from the sea; but either a messenger from the gods, or the world of the dead, that nether adamant, riven for him in love, without pain; for the passing of the man was not with lamentation or in sickness and suffering, but above mortals wonderful. And if to any I seem to speak folly, I would not woo their belief who count me foolish.

CHORUS. Where are the maidens and their escort?

MESSENGER. Not far from here, for the sounds of mourning tell plainly that they approach.

(*Enter* ANTIGONE *and* ISMENE.)

ANTIGONE. *Woe, woe! Now indeed is it for us, unhappy sisters, in all fullness to bewail the curse on the blood that is ours from our sire! For him, while he lived, we bore that long pain without pause; and at last a sight and a loss that baffle thought are ours to tell.*

CHORUS. *And how is it with you?*

ANTIGONE. *We can only conjecture, friends.*

CHORUS. *He is gone?*

ANTIGONE. *Even as you might wish; yes, surely, when death met him not in war or on the deep, but he was snatched to the viewless fields by some swift strange doom. Ah me! A night as of death has come on the eyes of us two; how shall we find our bitter livelihood, roaming to some far land, or on the waves of the sea?*

ISMENE. *I do not know. Oh that deadly Hades would join me in death to my aged father! Woe is me! I cannot live the life that must be mine.*

CHORUS. *Best of daughters, sisters both, Heaven's doom must be borne. Do not be fired with too much grief; you have so fared that you should not repine.*

ANTIGONE. *Ah, so care past can seem lost joy! For that which was no way sweet had sweetness, for then I held him in my embrace. Ah, father, dear one, ah you who have put on the darkness of the underworld forever, not even there shall you ever lack our love, her love and mine.*

CHORUS. *He has fared—*

ANTIGONE. *He has fared as he would.*

CHORUS. *In what wise?*

ANTIGONE. *On foreign ground, the ground of his choice, he has died; in the shadow of the grave he has his bed forever; and he has left mourning behind him not barren of tears. For with these streaming eyes, father, I bewail you; nor do I know, ah me, how to quell my sorrow for you, my sorrow that is so great. Ah me, it was your wish to die in a strange land; but now you have died without gifts at my hand.*

ISMENE. *Woe is me! What new fate, think you, awaits you and me, sister, thus orphaned of our sire?*

CHORUS. *Since he has found a blessed end, my children, cease from this lament. No mortal is hard for evil fortune to capture.*

ANTIGONE. *Sister, let us hasten back.*

ISMENE. *To do what?*

ANTIGONE. *A longing fills my soul.*

ISMENE. *For what?*

ANTIGONE. *To see the dark home—*

ISMENE. *Whose?*

ANTIGONE. *Ah me! Our sire's.*

ISMENE. *How can this thing be lawful? Have you no understanding?*

ANTIGONE. *Why this reproof?*

ISMENE. *And do you not know this also—*

ANTIGONE. *What would you tell me more?*

ISMENE. *That he was perishing without tomb, apart from all?*

ANTIGONE. *Lead me there and then slay me also.*

ISMENE. *Ah me unhappy! Friendless and helpless, where am I now to live my hapless life?*

CHORUS. *My children, do not fear.*

ANTIGONE. *But whither am I to flee?*

CHORUS. *Already refuge has been found—*

ANTIGONE. *How do you mean?*

CHORUS. *—of your fortunes, that no harm should touch them.*

ANTIGONE. *I know it well.*

CHORUS. *What then is your thought?*

ANTIGONE. *How we are to go home I cannot tell.*

CHORUS. *Do not seek to go.*

ANTIGONE. *Trouble besets us.*

CHORUS. *And erstwhile bore heavily on you.*

ANTIGONE. *Desperate then, and now more cruel than despair.*

CHORUS. *Great indeed is the sea of your troubles.*

ANTIGONE. *Alas, alas! O Zeus, where shall we turn? To what last hope does fate now urge us?*

THESEUS (*enters*). Weep no more, maidens. Where the kindness of the Dark Powers is an abiding grace to the quick and to the dead, there is no room for mourning; divine anger would follow.

ANTIGONE. Son of Aegeus, we supplicate you!

THESEUS. For obtaining what desire, my children?

ANTIGONE. We wish to look with our own eyes upon our father's tomb.

THESEUS. But it is not lawful.

ANTIGONE. How do you say, King, lord of Athens?

THESEUS. My children, he gave me charge that no one should draw nigh to that place, or greet with voice the sacred tomb where he sleeps. And he said that while I duly kept that word I should always hold the land unharmed. These pledges, therefore, were heard from my lips by the god, and by the all-seeing Watcher of oaths, the servant of Zeus.

ANTIGONE. Then if this is pleasing to the dead, with this we must content us. But send us to Thebes, the ancient, if haply we may hinder the bloodshed that is threatened to our brothers.

THESEUS. So will I do; and if in anything beside I can profit you and pleasure the dead who has lately gone from us, I am bound to spare no pains.

CHORUS. *Come, cease lamentation, lift it up no more; for verily these things stand fast.*

ABOUT THE EDITOR

The late MOSES HADAS was Jay Professor of Greek at Columbia University and author of the authoritative *History of Greek Literature,* the companion *History of Latin Literature,* and *Hellenistic Culture Fusion and Diffusion.* Bantam Books edited by Professor Hadas include *The Complete Plays of Aristophanes, Ten Plays by Euripides,* and *Greek Drama.*

ASK YOUR BOOKSELLER FOR THESE
BANTAM CLASSICS

THE SWISS FAMILY ROBINSON, Johann David Wyss, 0-553-21403-9
EARLY AFRICAN-AMERICAN CLASSICS, 0-553-21379-2
FIFTY GREAT SHORT STORIES, 0-553-27745-6
FIFTY GREAT AMERICAN SHORT STORIES, 0-553-27294-2
SHORT SHORTS, 0-553-27440-6
GREAT AMERICAN SHORT STORIES, 0-440-33060-2
SHORT STORY MASTERPIECES, 0-440-37864-8
THE VOICE THAT IS GREAT WITHIN US, 0-553-26263-7
THE BLACK POETS, 0-553-27563-1
THREE CENTURIES OF AMERICAN POETRY (Trade), 0-553-37518-0,
    (Hardcover), 0-553-10250-8